The Vocation of Writing

SUNY SERIES
LITERATURE...IN THEORY

SERIES EDITORS

David E. Johnson (Comparative Literature, University at Buffalo)
Scott Michaelsen (English, Michigan State University)

SERIES ADVISORY BOARD

Nahum D. Chandler, *African American Studies, University of California, Irvine*
Rebecca Comay, *Philosophy and Comparative Literature, University of Toronto*
Marc Crépon, *Philosophy, École Normale Supérieure, Paris*
Jonathan Culler, *Comparative Literature, Cornell University*
Johanna Drucker, *Design Media Arts and Information Studies, UCLA*
Christopher Fynsk, *Modern Thought, Aberdeen University*
Rodolphe Gasché, *Comparative Literature, University at Buffalo*
Martin Hägglund, *Comparative Literature, Yale University*
Carol Jacobs, *Comparative Literature and German, Yale University*
Peggy Kamuf, *French and Comparative Literature, University of Southern California*
David Marriott, *History of Consciousness, University of California, Santa Cruz*
Steven Miller, *English, University at Buffalo*
Alberto Moreiras, *Hispanic Studies, Texas A&M University*
Patrick O'Donnell, *English, Michigan State University*
Pablo Oyarzún, *Teoría del Arte, Universidad de Chile*
Scott Cutler Shershow, *English, University of California, Davis*
Henry Sussman, *German and Comparative Literature, Yale University*
Samuel Weber, *Comparative Literature, Northwestern University*
Ewa Ziarek, *Comparative Literature, University at Buffalo*

The Vocation of Writing

Literature, Philosophy, and the Test of Violence

Marc Crépon

Translated by D. J. S. Cross and Tyler M. Williams

Originally published as *La Vocation de l'écriture. La littérature et la philosophie à l'épreuve de la violence*

© Odile Jacob, 2014

Translation copyright © 2018 by the State University of New York

Cet ouvrage, publié dans le cadre d'un programme d'aide à la publication, bénéficie du soutien de la Mission Culturelle et Universitaire Française aux Etats-Unis, service de l'ambassade de France aux EU.

This work, published as part of a program of aid for publication, received support from the Mission Culturelle et Universitaire Française aux Etats-Unis, a department of the French Embassy in the United States.

Published by State University of New York Press, Albany

All rights reserved

No part of this book may be used or reproduced in any manner whatsoever without written permission. No part of this book may be stored in a retrieval system or transmitted in any form or by any means including electronic, electrostatic, magnetic tape, mechanical, photocopying, recording, or otherwise without the prior permission in writing of the publisher.

For information, contact State University of New York Press, Albany, NY www.sunypress.edu

Library of Congress Cataloging-in-Publication Data

Names: Crépon, M. (Marc), 1962- author. | Cross, Donald J. S., translator. | Williams, Tyler M., translator.
Title: The vocation of writing : literature, philosophy, and the test of violence / Marc Crépon ; translated by Donald. J. S. Cross and Tyler M. Williams.
Other titles: La vocation de l'écriture. English
Description: Albany, NY : State University of New York, [2018] | Series: Suny series, literature . . . in theory | Originally published: La vocation de l'écriture. Paris : Odile Jacob, 2014. | Includes bibliographical references and index. | Description based on print version record and CIP data provided by publisher; resource not viewed.
Identifiers: LCCN 2017027467 (print) | LCCN 2018002577 (ebook) | ISBN 9781438469621 (e-book) | ISBN 9781438469614 (hardcover   ) | ISBN 9781438469607 (paperback   )
Subjects: LCSH: Violence—Philosophy. | Violence in literature. | Literature, Modern—20th century—Themes, motives. | Language and languages—Philosophy.
Classification: LCC B105.V5 (ebook) | LCC B105.V5 C7513 2018 (print) | DDC 303.6—dc23
LC record available at https://lccn.loc.gov/2017027467

10 9 8 7 6 5 4 3 2 1

Contents

Translators' Note	vii
Acknowledgments	ix
Introduction: Practices of Language and Experience of Violence	1
1. Self-Knowledge (A Reading of Kafka's *Diaries*)	17
2. Impossible Anamnesis (Kafka and Derrida)	37
3. Shares of Singularity (Celan-Derrida)	51
4. On a Constellation (Levinas, Derrida, Blanchot, Readers of Celan)	65
5. "that tumor in the memory" (Levinas)	81
6. On Shame (Levinas)	91
7. A "balancing pole" over the Abyss (Victor Klemperer and the Language of the Third Reich)	101
8. Duped by Violence? (A Reading of Sartre)	113
9. "the spirit of storytelling" (A Reading of Kertész)	125
10. "Surviving": The Novel (A Reading of Kertész's *Galley Boat-Log*)	137
11. "a profound feeling of protest" (A Reading of Singer)	149
12. "And nobody here knows who I am" (Emigrant Voices: Arendt, Sebald, Perec)	157
13. On Fear of Dying (Three Russian Stories)	169
Notes	183
Bibliography	193
Index	197

Translators' Note

One of the most difficult decisions in translating *La Vocation de l'écriture. La littérature et la philosophie à l'épreuve de la violence* was, in fact, one of the first. The term *épreuve* has no strict equivalent in English. In *La philosophie face à la violence* (*Philosophy in the Face of Violence*, co-authored with Frédéric Worms and published in 2015), Crépon explains the word's etymological and political legacy as follows:

> As literature in the Middle Ages attests, the term *épreuve* is from its first uses synonymous with suffering, misfortune, and adversity. In feudal law, the judicial *épreuve* signified the suffering—if not the torture—to which the accused were submitted, while God was called upon to intervene in order to designate the guilty. Only those who survived this *épreuve* could be declared innocent. But the term *épreuve* very quickly came to designate in addition that which allows judgment on the value of an individual or an idea. And from there a whole series of expressions arise: "to put the to test [*mettre à l'épreuve*]," "to be tested [*être à l'épreuve*]." All these locutions gesture in common toward a double signification: an evaluation and a resistance simultaneously. To be put to the test is to bend to the ritual of a judgment and the accompanying verdict, with the idea that this judgment and verdict are a function of resistance—as one says of material that resists cold, heat, and jolts that make it tremble. (18–19, translation ours)

Literature, Philosophy, and the Test of Violence. Though far from the only possibility, we have decided to translate *épreuve* as "test" because, while its academic sense might be stronger in English (although not absent in French, as in *une épreuve orale* or *une épreuve écrite*), the term's other connotations best capture the flexibility of the French. Insofar as something "put to the test" is assessed, judged on the basis of its limit, "test" retains the juridical implications, the affective connotations, and the defensive posture of *épreuve*. Other options—such as "challenge," "trial," "tribulation," "ordeal," "proof," etc.—might capture one sense of the term but always at the expense of eliminating or introducing others. "Challenge," for instance, seems too agonistic to reflect the affective connotations, and "trial" risks subordinating the whole semantic spread to juridical implications.

While we found "test" best suited for the book's title, however, *épreuve* remains syntactically flexible in ways inaccessible to it. Our decision to treat the "test" as a third term in a series—*Literature, Philosophy, and the Test of Violence*—is a case in point. Although our English version risks losing a clear indication of the relation between literature, philosophy, and the test, the cumbersomeness of a literal translation leaves little alternative: literature and philosophy put to the test of violence. Readers should thus remain cognizant that, although the English title does not directly indicate it as such, the French title makes clear that the titular test of violence constitutes—tests the limits of—the instances of literature and philosophy treated in the pages that follow.

Finally, for the same reason, we have chosen not to standardize the translation of *épreuve* throughout the book. Elsewhere, befitting the context, *épreuve* is indeed translated as "ordeal," "tribulation," etc. Wherever these alternative translations risk confusion or bear directly upon the title of the book, we have glossed the word in editorial brackets.

Acknowledgments

Reading and writing owe much to friendship's sharing. The majority of the chapters that comprise this book were written (and occasionally published), in much earlier versions, at the behest of invitations from dear friends. I thank them all, and this book is dedicated to them: Paul Audi, Christophe Bouton, Barbara Cassin, Danielle Cohen-Levinas, Catherine Coquio, Vincent Delecroix, Michel Espagne, Marc de Launay, Jean-Claude Monod, Florence Noiville, Perrine Simon-Nahum, Frédéric Worms.

Introduction
Practices of Language and Experience of Violence

I. Education

The storm rages between the kitchen walls. The child, accustomed to it, crossed the hall upon returning from school, climbed the stairs in silence, and locked himself in his room, which lets onto the courtyard shaded by the chestnut tree. He knows that the lightning-sharp phrases, thunderous reproaches, and hurtful recriminations will join him before long. He knows all about the flaring tempers, the mood swings, the unjustified anger that give language the strange power of becoming a weapon of intimate destruction. He is used to the cries, the outbursts, the irrevocable judgments, the definitive verdicts that transform affection into a tribunal and break what little confidence he might have kept in his ability to divert the furious lightning with everyday words. He has experienced it many times: everything that he might say in his defense is capable of being turned against him; there is no argument that holds when a loving word from which he would expect help and protection blows, on the contrary, a tempestuous wind. At that moment, his own words—hardly heard, hardly understood, immediately contradicted—are swept up like so many strands of straw, as if they did not deserve the attention for which all attachment calls. So far, he knows it only intuitively, but he will learn it endlessly: every affective relation is haunted by the possibility of sudden breaks, of brutal interruptions and reversals that lodge violence in the heart of the relation we maintain with language from our first steps in life, weakening all the relations that compose the fabric of existence.

But he also experiences it on school benches. All mastery, the mastery of language first of all, is indissociable from the constraints and sanctions imposed by exercises meant to assure that mastery and to control it. Year after year, it accumulates and retains the traces of these constraints and sanctions. This is the price of all the sentences, the phrasings, the ways of speaking and thinking, the expressive capacities he is made to appropriate: they are imposed upon him, mold him, only through the discipline that education demands, the discussion that it bridles, the commentary that it interrupts. As days go by, the child becomes the person he is required to be only by suspending, from morning to evening, any protest against the rules, by forbidding any untimely initiative, any invention, any fugitive word and, later on, any fugitive writing seeking to free itself. Over the course of interminable days, he learns how to keep quiet as much as how to speak, how to mimic attention, concentration, and interest even when everything in these repetitive operations cultivates distraction and evasion. Such is the law of all instruction, education, and training. It imprisons anyone that bends to its rules at the same time as it liberates them. Every morning, the child sets out on the road to elementary school, to junior high school, and then to high school. He descends the staircase, mounts his bicycle, and crosses the railroad tracks fully aware that, when he encounters a difficulty, the pacifying virtues of the word that teaches, the joy that results from it, the consolation, its calming effect, the encouragements that he would love to gather from his teachers' mouths, are never guaranteed to overcome their impatience, weariness, and irritation. If he leaves home with a sense of serenity, it is not out of the ordinary for him to return at night with a heavy heart, discouraged, because he remains so apprehensive, at his desk, of the words that punish his hesitations, his forgetfulness, or faults; he dreads the words that order him to be quiet, that cover him with shame, and the grades and evaluations that fall like guillotine blades when he does not meet the expectations imposed upon him. He is well aware that his teachers and family will accept no excuses then; he knows that his protests and denials, if not ruses, his declarations of intent, everything *singular* that he could say, everything important to him, will carry hardly any weight before the imperative and communal law that demands submission, discipline, and results—as if it were impossible for our experience of language to avoid being caught in the trap of evaluation and competitive performances from the beginning.

II. Inheritances

Violence thus essentially belongs to this experience, to the most familiar uses of language, and to the way we learn it. No one knows, however, the makeup of their first impression, what untimely cries and what melodious songs, what moments of tenderness and what sudden bursts of brutality left the first traces. Everyone has a singular way of using language, without knowing how it was inherited, without knowing the circumstances under which, in other words, one developed the timidity or volubility, the particular intonations, the rhythm, the slow or staccato delivery, the syntactic turns, and the idiomatic expressions that distinguish one in the eyes of others and give a unique timbre to one's voice. Each time we speak, we thus have only a partial and illusory mastery of what leaves our mouths. While we imagine that we alone are responsible for the sentences that we address to others, we depend upon more than one inheritance, and we bend to *more than one law* that we did not choose. Family and its system of education, school and its rites of passage, the social milieu and its linguistic codes (not to mention neighborhoods, towns, and regions) are so many factors that compromise and upset the comfortable idea of our own sovereignty, as if nothing and no one—none of these familial, educational, or social forces—played a part in what we believe we say and think on our own. The paradox, then, is the following: in a sense, nothing singularizes us more than our relation to language; at the same time, nothing testifies more to the risk that we constantly run of being *locked in* a language that is not ours. We must thus admit the resulting dependence as another form of "violence" inscribed at the heart of our relation to language. If the first manifestation of violence, understood as recrimination, blame, and judgment, was identified as the exterior but nevertheless familiar threat of the security of familial or educational circles—guaranteed, they say, by a mother tongue—turning into insecurity, the second manifestation, understood as the language of others inhabiting, invading, and haunting our own, possesses everyone from within. In the first case, we are assaulted by a language characterized, suddenly and unpredictably, by its power to destroy the confidence we need. In the second, we are exposed to a veritable "identity crisis." Who are we, whatever our certainty of our own existence, if there is nothing in our way of speaking that has not in one way or another been imposed, if everything that we are capable of saying does not really belong to us, if we are never the person that we believe ourselves to be, if we are deceived or betrayed by the language, more foreign than we imagined, that accompanies our thoughts?

III. Discriminations

But the violence does not end there. It is linked to our experience of language in a third and still more radical fashion. We have at least the diffuse impression or feeling that this third violence takes place upon every compromise concerning the possibility, not of communicating in general, but rather of addressing a word to the other *as such*, a word concerned with what constitutes his or her singularity, convinced that he or she cannot be confused with anyone else and that no judgment, no label, no category exhausts what makes up his or her uniqueness. This violence, more explicitly, names this compromise itself whenever ideological, political, or religious apparatuses erase the possibility of seeing in whoever or whatever stands before us a being to whom such a word is due. Its most common and recurrent manifestations are racism and anti-Semitism, but it is also every undue characterization that reduces the other to *his or her* social class, to *his or her* religious group, or to any other form of affiliation or collective or communal identity, as if the victim's very individuality were thus contained, constricted, and denied in advance. In such circumstances, words no longer designate or, when necessary, address a singular individual; they designate the category with which he or she is supposed to identify—"Jew," "Arab," "petit-bourgeois," "kulak," "black"—and are taken as an explanation and guarantee of everything that could be said to or about him or her.

In the schoolyard, an argument breaks out and escalates. When arguments run out, the students turn with an illusory spontaneity to the insults learned from those older than them, unaware of the violent past crystalizing in their mouths, all during a time for recreation. As he grows older, becoming more familiar with the darkest pages of twentieth-century history, the memory of deportations and all the plans for extermination that have bloodied it, at what point does the child discover that these judgments—which turn language into both a weapon of collective stigmatization and a verbal assault, into a singular wound and a justification for murder—belong to the world in which he lives? What injustice must one commit, suffer, or witness, what survival stories must one hear in order to become indelibly aware of it? What book or photo album must one have opened, what lesson learned, what film seen in order to become conscious once and for all of the mortifying power contained in every act of denominating and characterizing of this order? One thing is certain: one day the adolescent, freed from all tutelage, had to start distinguishing between, on the one hand, those among his contemporaries who will never find anything wrong with such judgments and will mechanically reproduce such prejudices their whole lives and, on the other hand, those for whom such judgments will always be unbearable, causing indignation, calling for protest, nourishing rebellion.

From the perspective of language, finally, life is made up of the orientation and the choices that, from the days of our first relations in the halls of elementary school, junior high, and high school, distinguish those for whom exchanging words is a token of confidence. Friendship exercises a power of discernment that is inseparable from a heightened attention to the "language of others," language to which the heart becomes sensitive. Children and adolescents learn very early that there are certain words, ways of speaking, judging, deciding, affirming, and dominating, ways of using language with absolute certainty that, because they are synonymous with violence, make friendship impossible. He knows from then on that there is no exchange between friends that does not secretly rest on the promise that things will be otherwise for them, the promise, in other words, that language will escape this instrumentalization that dupes everyone seduced by it with the same violence. But he also knows that this promise is difficult, if not impossible, to keep; it threatens to reverse into its opposite at every moment. One day, in the course of a friendly dinner, another truth of what they share becomes as clear as day. And if what revealed itself were nothing but a masked competition to get the upper hand on the other without acknowledging it! Does every use of language turn out to be a theatrical power play? And if it is impossible to escape this suspicion, is it still not best to keep quiet?

IV. Political Awakening

But it is above all political consciousness that takes shape in proportion to its attention to the instances of violence that language facilitates and to the multiple forces—families, political parties, small groups, organizations, and other forms of community—that manipulate language to bring about exclusion while winning others over. Political consciousness shows itself to be all the more vigilant insofar as it knows how to resist the ease and escalations of the discriminating characterizations emphasized a moment ago, as well as the destructive magic of names that simplify the world by locking it into a conveniently legible grid (the diversity of peoples, classes, races, religions, and civilizations crudely identified and characterized, constructed as a password for understanding, deciding, and acting). The years go by, indeed, bruised at the turn of the century by ethnic cleansings in the Balkans, the Rwandan genocide, bloody fratricides in the Near East, the unsettling resurgence of European nationalisms and fundamentalisms of every kind, the "War on Terror," all of which must be understood as testimonies to the fact that the murderous invocation of the name of the other still remains the horizon of our time. No system on its own, moreover, seems ready to renounce the convenient inscription of "reasons" for violence in the heart of political rhetoric, not even the democracies that are most capable, on the basis of their founding principles, of protecting themselves against it. The most solid institutions, treaties, international agreements and pacts, declarations, communal rules and principles henceforth appear to be fragile seawalls, and one wonders how long they will resist the tumultuous tide of deafening declarations, vindictive speeches, and heinous programs that make this spiteful invocation the foremost element in their seduction. Because political awakening is indissociable from becoming conscious of all the manipulations authorized by language, beginning with the most murderous, from lies to threats, nothing could replace the need to perceive the violence brought on by these manipulations. The rules of our sensibility (the very ones that govern our relation to the suffering and misfortune in the world) and, with them, the principles of our opposition and resistance to injustice and oppression are forged in this perception. It thus traces, in consciousness, the uncrossable red line of refusal. Yet, because the denunciation of ruses and deceit is never simple, because it can itself become an excuse and justification for other forms of violence, our political judgments threaten, at every moment, to get caught in the endless downward spiral of the murderous consents that frame history. If it turns out that they are put to use for crime, the most solicitous words—justice, freedom, equality—therefore run the risk of losing all their credit.

V. Preoccupation

A word addressed to the other that grants rights to the irreplaceable, unsubstitutable singularity of the one to whom it is addressed! If it is true that this address is never more compromised than when one gets carried away with denominating, with generalized identifications and characterizations that deny singularity by reducing the other to his or her affiliations, the violence of the negation is not limited to extreme cases. Indeed, in its most radical and most brutal form, this violence is a product of the effacement or eclipse of a dimension of language that the latter's daily uses or quotidian practices cause us to forget or, at least, prevent us from dwelling on: the "ethical" responsibility engaged in every situation that involves speaking and listening. Above all, the analysis of its failures or shortcomings, its pitfalls or deviations, proves that language use implies an ethical engagement of this order and, in this respect, constitutes the ethical element in every *encounter*, the ethical element that the encounter distributes at the same time that the ethical element makes the encounter possible. Two friends that have not seen each other for a long time rejoice upon meeting again for a long walk along the quays of the Seine; they have so much to tell each other, so much news to catch up on, and so many thoughts to share. But the hours pass, and something entirely different occurs. A strange unease takes hold of them both; disappointment overrides the joy of meeting again. Each one ends up leaving with the confused feeling of not having been heard and also, perhaps, of having been unable to listen—of having let himself be distracted, carried off, transported by his own sentences or by those of the other to another time (yesterday, tomorrow, the day after) and to another place (other bodies, other faces, and other landscapes) a thousand leagues away from the friend.

This distance, this division, these absences are yet another form of violence. It erupts every time the "benevolent" attention of the speaker and, reciprocally, that of the listener—the necessary conditions for every "encounter"—eclipse each other for the sake of a relation of an entirely different order. Several modalities of darkness result. Let us distinguish two of them. The first is *preoccupation*, understood as *distraction*. Night has fallen; the family gathers round the dinner table in the large dining room, whose plate-glass windows lead onto a shadowy balcony. As he often does, the child asks a question. He asks about the Watergate scandal, which he has been hearing about on the radio and which fills so much of the news on television, an issue that his aunts and uncles, in turn, take up in their conversations. He thinks he is old enough to understand, but he receives no answer. He insists, but they ask him to be quiet; he is bothering the adults and must learn to stay out of their conversations. The next time, they consent and say a few words to him, but they do so distractedly, without paying any more attention to him. It is not certain, moreover, that those seated around the table are any more concerned with each other. Everyone seems to play their role, blocked by their own selves and preoccupied with the impression that they produce on the rest of the family. If the child is brushed aside, as he quickly comes to understand, it is because he has no place in these language games and because he does not count, at least not yet, in the preoccupation that plays out between rival adults.

VI. Love and Friendship

This preoccupation makes language use a social game, a rehearsed distraction that withdraws words from the responsibility of addressing. However relative it might be, its "violence" is thus a product of the fact that everyone's words and sentences seem besieged by a whole theater of ulterior motives, of calculations and interests that always come down to the same: the barely masked staging of an ego essentially preoccupied with itself. In the end, nothing of any importance is said; the very distinction between truth and falsity is secondary because all that counts is the appearance that the word validates and the mirror effect to which it leads: the illusion of sovereignty. Does that mean, inversely, that every true, friendly, or amorous encounter must presuppose something like a breakout or an unblocking, a suspension, an effacement or a retreat of the ego far away from the bustle that restricts it to itself? Is this what we must hope for, if not demand, from every relation, at the risk of flying too close to the sun? Put back in his place, the child does not yet know, no more than the adolescent who is revolted by this theatricality, how often existence will offer him proof: such preoccupation is ordinary and undoubtedly inevitable; however, as long as nothing contradicts it, as long as nothing prevents the ego from finding in language the means to relate everything back to itself, it is also destructive. Because this preoccupation suspends attention, listening, and, with them, that which in an address testifies to a responsibility, it effectively leads every relation to disaster.

If it is true, indeed, that each of these (attention, listening, and responsibility) is present in the promise of what it awaits from language's help, namely, continuous maintenance of the attachment called love or friendship, the invading preoccupation, as we have described it, compromises the trust necessitated by this promise. This happens every time two beings that love each other have the feeling that no words they could exchange—the very words that were once at the heart of so many intimate rites, in the secret of collusion—will lead anywhere now and that, consequently, they have nothing more to say to each other. Then comes preoccupation's reverse: the renunciation produced by disappointment and waning desire. One no longer expects or hopes for anything from the other, who is in any case elsewhere, no longer in the world formerly shared, a stranger to its landmarks. In these final death throes, speech becomes empty, and it is no better than silence. The contract (of speaking) that linked (tacitly) two beings to each other is broken. These words, ruminated and brooded over in the void, pave the way for separations.

This risk is not proper to the amorous word or to the affective relations that link us emotionally to others, more or less close to us. Indeed, one must take this ordinary collapse, from distancing to rupture, as a more general symptom. It is the sign and the effect of a vulnerability inscribed in the heart of our relation to language, and it reminds us that, in the end, every word is perhaps in this sense a "search for friendship." Every time we speak, we depend upon listening and answering, upon signs of attention, upon the care and concern that are implicitly promised and that, consequently, threaten never to come. Every word is thus haunted not only by the risk of being misheard or misunderstood but also by the risk of no longer knowing how and no longer being able to address the person to whom the word is addressed. Whence the fragility that lodges the possibility of violence in the heart of our most ordinary and most common experience of language: it is intrinsically linked to a thousand and one detours taken by the *destruction,* whether by my own hand or another's—of the relations that it maintains and promises, that is, the rupture of the link that holds together the past, the present, and the future in shares [*partage*] of language.

VII. Aggression

Earlier, we recalled that there exist at least two ways for the ethical responsibility engaged by speech to be eclipsed. If the first is its effacement before the bustle that monopolizes the ego in search of self-affirmation, the second is the address that turns into aggression. When attempting to discern, as we are doing here, the link that associates, over the course of life, our experience of language with the test of violence as an inevitable dimension of its apportioning [*partage*] rather than something secondary or accidental, one first thinks of this second violence. Indeed, what is violence, the analysis of which constitutes the pivot of these reflections, if not first and foremost the experience of an aggression? What do being brutally reprimanded, belittled by a humiliating command, or insulted by an abusive word have in common if not the feeling of having one's psychical and physical integrity attacked and scathed by a rerouted use of language? Now, whether sudden or expected, this attack always produces the same thing: the rupture of the minimum trust required for sharing space and time to remain possible. This is the essence of lingual violence: it compromises the possibility of such belief. When nothing can prevent words from wounding or propositions from becoming murderous, speech unchained and freed of all ethical responsibility has no objective other than losing itself in the impossibility of this trust and, by that very fact, rendering illusory every promise of an address that grants rights to the singularity of the person to whom it is addressed—what I am here calling an *encounter.* Thus, for the violence inscribed at the heart of our experience of language to be, if not surpassed, at least *contradicted,* we *need to believe* that speech is not simply an instrument of exploitation and domination, that it brings peace and not war, that everything cannot be reduced to a fierce competition between egos, that the irreplaceable, unsubstitutable, and imperative singularity of the one to whom speech is addressed matters in and for itself and is, in itself, something other than a mere means at the mercy of whoever manipulates it with his or her own words.

VIII. The Shoah

A December afternoon. The adolescent rides his bicycle to the small, blooming city that serves as the sub-prefecture a few miles from his town. In the light of the municipal library, he finds the first book, full of illustrations, of a long series that he will read on the expansion of Nazism, the contagion of its ideology, the power of its murderous slogans, the conversion of entire populations to its racial politics, and the deportation and the extermination of European Jews during the Second World War. Upon returning to his room, he cannot tear his eyes away from the book for hours on end. He intuitively discovers, without having the words to say it, that the link between language and violence not only concerns isolated individuals; it changes the direction of history. He imagines the deadly slogans and the calls for murder spewed across storefronts, the crowds captivated by an inflammatory rhetoric whose only goal will have been the encouragement of hating others and the justification of their elimination. The malefic power of words is without limits once it can legitimate the worst. But who can date *his or her* consciousness of radical evil exactly without ceding to illusory reconstructions? Who can name the moment when the most murderous pages of history left their trace on a sensibility that they will never release?

These are not just any pages, not just any events. Indeed, the radical evil exemplified by the plans and methods of the extermination practices implemented by the totalitarian systems of the twentieth century signify both the complete subjugation of language in support of unchained forces of destruction and language's absolute collapse. On the one hand, the *sedimentation of the worst* contaminated entire societies in their most ordinary language practices; on the other hand, nothing of those societies' linguistic and cultural capital—the very capital that was identified, with a complacency assured of its right to dominate the world, with civilization itself—could oppose this contamination. The extraordinary character of the lie and the terror, which took shape as murders to which those same societies consented, became ordinary, usual, common; no force was able to oppose it. This is the most difficult paradox to accept: the abyssal *imbalance* between *language that destroys*, with an infinite power to seduce, and *language that saves*, between ideology's disastrous power, as well as all the forms of violence inscribed in our relation to language, and the weakness, if not the impotence, of any word still meant to oppose it.

Yet, can we simply give up our belief in the possibility of that other relation to language, however weak: a counterword that brings meaning back to its promises? Must one mourn the concepts of "justice," "freedom," "equality," and even "truth," resigning oneself to life under a variable but permanent regime of lies and terror, like those that fill the world in different ways? Supposing this to be case, our only way out would be consenting to this violence; we would have to remain suspicious of every word that we address to others as much as those that are addressed to us, suspecting that behind every word lies a self-affirmation, a will to domination, a calculation of self-interest, a more or less disguised aggression taken to be the only "truth" of language.

If we attempt to summarize the preceding pages, it appears that violence infects our relation to language in more than one way. First, from the perspective of education, violence is inseparable from our childhood experiences of language in the family circle, as Kafka's *Diaries* recall so well, and in the context of educational institutions and their restrictive programs. Next, between silence, cries and whispers, violence constitutes one of the most visible signs of what threatens every relation: the absolute loss of all trust in what those sharing it—husband and wife, parents and children, brothers and sisters—might have left to say to each other, as so many of Ingmar Bergman's films teach us (if we did not already know). Further, the responsibility that links us in speech also strays toward insults and abuses, effacing the singularity of the one that the words address. Finally, and above all, the violence of language culminates in its ideological instrumentalization for murderous propaganda. It is then a question of words collectively stuck in one's head like a chorus. These ideological choruses sediment the worst in the hearts and minds of the addressees, who end up seeing no obstacle for and no objection to the bloodthirsty logic that they implement. Victor Klemperer reminds us of this better than anyone else in his philological testimony, *Language of the Third Reich: LTI—Lingua Tertii Imperii*, which emphasizes the extent to which the Nazi's subjugation of language came down to impregnating "words and syntactical structures" with the "poison" of their ideology (16).

IX. Books

The child took refuge in his room, among books that he has already begun to collect, to accumulate, and with which he builds a rampart against the wave of words, formulations, assertions, and denials that assail him—most often without those who make such formulations even realizing it. This is most likely the origin of his passion for bookstores, second-hand bookshops, displays of random books at second-hand markets and other improbable trading centers, like the one that takes places at the gates of Paris every weekend under the large windows of old abattoirs, an irresistible attraction to printed piles that will make him cross entire neighborhoods of Jerusalem and Tokyo with bright eyes, even when he does not understand the language (Hebrew and Japanese) in which the worn books, presented and abandoned to displays, are printed. He has always known that these places consecrated to books are vectors of freedom everywhere in the world, no matter the political, "ethnic," or religious affiliation of those that venture there. And the collusion that the passion for books creates in all circumstances remains a bridge that reconnects languages and cultures and that overcomes all differences; it is the possibility of a line of resistance—as was, in the 1930s, the whisper of a poem that got Osip Mandelstam deported, vanishing in the plains of Kolyma. The most authoritarian powers have no illusions when they take on the task of keeping books under their control and fear more than anything else the diffusion and circulation of books that they have not authorized. But it is in vain because, whatever they do, whatever constraining measures and restrictions they impose, whatever persecutions they organize, the air that we breathe next to books freely chosen is always less oppressive, freed of those constraints that the child, discovering them, does not yet know how to name.

Yet, even there, retrospectively, this enigma seizes him belatedly through the absence of an answer. How is all of this decided? From where does this passion come, a passion that is first a continuous invasion of time and space? Year after year, the walls of his office, of his bedroom, of his dining and living rooms are covered with books; volumes pile up so high under his desk that it has become impossible for him to slide his feet under it. For decades, there has not been a single day or night, neither in his private space nor in hotels or guest rooms, without books lying close to him on the nightstand like an indispensible crutch. For a long time, one of his principal preoccupations before every departure has been deciding which of these invasive paper companions will be chosen for the trip. He is well aware, despite everything, of the place occupied and the alternative offered by these novels, books of poetry, and plays that he brings back from expeditions to bookstores and used-book markets with the feeling that he holds the most precious treasure in his hands: neither a withdrawal into himself nor a flight from the world into a hypothetical refuge. A fortress, perhaps, but above all the whole chance or promise of a reconciliation with language's words—an other address, an other sharing out [*partage*], an other breath.

X. Literature and Philosophy

Literature and philosophy find their place in the grey zone that separates the language that destroys from the language that saves. The grey zone and not the interval. For nothing is less fixed than their border, and writers (poets, playwrights, novelists) and philosophers alike get lost on occasion when they in turn begin to serve violence. Both literature and philosophy, then, take place at the edge of the abyss, where it is never certain that the border between destruction and redemption definitively holds. No doubt, it would be vain to hold that the vocation of writing takes root, in each case, exclusively in the experience of violence. Philosophy itself ceaselessly invents initial impulses (wonder, doubt, enthusiasm) that refer to emotions entirely different from those incited by the spectacle, recognition, or test of violence. Literature, for its part, presupposes a play with language, an obsession of language, as well as a "possession" and a "dispossession" of names and syntax, of imperative voices, none of which necessarily implies a kernel of violence as the original experience.

Why does one write? To tell the truth, one could not respond to the question univocally or reductively by confining literature and philosophy to their confrontation with all the forms of destruction that comprise the framework for the fates of individuals and historical collectivities alike; nor could one respond by confining literature and philosophy to any other form of motivation or initial momentum. One could not, moreover, overload writing with the (ethical or political) responsibility of confronting the proliferation of murderous consents that marks our epoch. The vocation of literature and philosophy, which is always singular (and perhaps even one of the most irreducible forms of the invention of singularity), does not lend itself to or comply with any general injunction. Every reduction of this order would come down to postulating a vocation transparent to itself and, therefore, to denying or minimizing that which is precisely in question, namely, the infinite complexity of our relation to language and the unfathomable mystery of its history (the debts, inheritances, laws, transgressions, traumatisms, and madness that constitute it)—a history that is nothing more or less than the history of our own subjectivity.

Nevertheless, we cannot ignore that our confrontation with violence is an inevitable dimension of our experience of language and that its traces have a stake in our intimate history, where the latter cannot be separated from collective history. The way literature and philosophy face the test of violence is thus not insignificant, accidental, or secondary. For neither of them does violence constitute an object, a subject for reflection, or one theme among others. For both deal with language in a given epoch and take responsibility, not without risk, for the possibility that, crushed under the weight of conventions and clichés and submitted to communication's imperatives for utmost efficiency and performance, words do not say (no longer say) anything of the singular, the possibility that they are thus cut off from their history and lose their meaning, if the sudden jolts and vicissitudes of politics do not reactivate them and reroute them for murderous ends first. The risk that they measure and that they cannot ignore is the risk of captivity (repeating others' language) and appropriation (dissolving into a community) in the illusion of a sovereign mastery of language and of the rights that it grants. The error is to believe that freedom is granted and that justice is assured at the very moment when the desire to grant rights, with and in language, to that which should make every word the invention of a singularity is eclipsed. This is what confronts literature and philosophy: the undeniable and irreducible fact that we are, in more than one way, *possessed* by languages that are not really ours and *threatened* by what this possession is capable of ordering. Family, school, the social milieu, community authorities, and powers of every order (religion, politics, the media) that frame existence impose *their* language. This is their ideological force—and no language (just as no culture) escapes it. Everywhere that there is *language*, the temptation of uniformity exists, a homogenization [*uniformisation*] that the educational and communication sciences henceforth take it upon themselves to control and to spread, in the very place where they claim to substitute for the practice of literary texts. The fantasy of a single language and thought is not only one of the most frequently recurring nightmares among those called forth by totalitarian fables such as those of Orwell, Zamyatin, or Bradbury; it is the specter that haunts every experience of language, as soon as it allows its law to be dictated.

Yet, that remains at the level of fantasy and fable. Even the most restrictive and compromising powers—those that will have rallied a majority of writers and philosophers to the various causes of their (political, social, religious, racial) violence—will never manage to bar completely and definitively the detoured path of a counterword, the perilous road of a resistant and alternative experience of language that some will have continued taking. Whatever literature and philosophy are, in different ways and by the very fact of their existence, they both challenge, against power's seductions and ruses, the passivity that would constitute accepting that language is inevitably doomed to serve violence without attempting to invent a few lines of flight or opposition. At stake primarily in philosophy is its "critical" vocation. Because there is no exercise of violence that does not sooner or later draw upon lies, manipulated opinions, and hasty approximations, because there is no exercise of violence that does not play with words in order to turn them into a destructive weapon, care and "courage of truth"—which belong to the essence of critique—naturally trace critical lines of opposition, if only they escape the vertigo of force.

Literature, for its part, at least knows what could ruin it; it is threatened on all sides by an always possible submission to a foreign order and law that it suffers, even if willingly: the law of an authoritarian power, a Church, a party, a murderous cause, or even the market and its audience. The essence of the relation to language that literature puts to work is therefore the *power* to be subjected, perverted, and thereby destroyed. At times, this power occurs for the sake of the most murderous instances of violence, as so many compromised writers and misguided works exemplify throughout the twentieth century. Each time, the possibility of what I will call—through readings of Kafka, Celan, Kertész, and others in the chapters that follow—the "idiomatic" invention of singularity is irrevocably ruined. Every literary work worthy of the name comes from such an invention, and it implicitly or explicitly affirms, from the simple fact of its being, that such an invention is possible with and in language. This is the way violence concerns literature. Literature finds itself necessarily exposed to all the forces (which vary according to era, to regime and society, to family and tribe) that could or would compromise the lingual expression of this vital singularity and the no less vital sharing of it.

But neither philosophy nor literature is exclusive. And I will not maintain, in the pages that follow, the dreadful idea that writing (including images) would be our only way of confronting the constitutive violence of our experience of language, of becoming conscious of it, and of responding to it with a singular creation. For the demand to which philosophy and literature respond, through an address that does not know its addressees, in reality inhabits each relation that links us to others—all the links and attachments that carry in themselves the secret hope of escaping violence for as long as possible. Their promise inscribes them in a common history: ethics itself.

XI. Corpus

The chapters that follow all seek to grant rights to some of the singular inventions distinguished, throughout last century's history, by their confrontation with the test of violence. They sketch out a trajectory and a constellation. The majority of the voices retained here—in particular those of Kafka, Celan, Derrida, Levinas, Mandelstam, Klemperer, Singer, and Kertész—cross and (sometimes) respond to each other in a time and place punctuated by the lies, terror, and crimes of totalitarian systems. No doubt, they cannot be put on the same plane. Their different confrontations with violence (their ways of living and thinking it, of remembering it and bearing witness to it, the part it plays in "the vocation of their writing") prevent one from putting them on the same plane. But they therefore join together—and this forms their constellation—to let us know that we are not alone when facing the test of violence (the experience and memory of it) as long as the *help* and the *consolation* of books, the gift of their writings, persist. Such is the part that each of them plays in the shared invention of writing's own singularity, comparable to the poems that Celan describes as a bottle thrown out to sea and heading "[t]oward something open, inhabitable, an approachable you, perhaps, an approachable reality" ("Speech," 35).

1
Self-Knowledge
(A Reading of Kafka's Diaries)

June 19, 1916. Forget everything. Open the windows. Clear the room. The wind blows through it. You see only its emptiness, you search in every corner and don't find yourself.

—Franz Kafka

Let us imagine that one day someone comes to remind us that there will have been, among the multiple beginnings that philosophy has invented for itself, this injunction: "Know thyself." Let us imagine next that centuries and centuries later, in reality more than two millennia later, we are told that this knowledge is divided into three questions: "What can I know? What ought I to do? What may I hope?" Let us imagine further that we are thus invited to remember all the forms not only of wonder (beginning with Socratic wonder) and enthusiasm (like that of the Romantics) but also of doubt (Cartesian doubt), anxiety, or despair that these questions nourish: "Who am I? What ought I—what ought we—to do? What awaits us? What awaits me? In the name of what promise, with what plans, can I give meaning to my existence, whatever identity that I assign it?" A life of study, reading, and education spent in classrooms and dusty libraries will not be enough to explore the infinite variety of answers brought to these questions. But, above all, such a life could not in the end guarantee our aptitude for making these answers *ours*—that is, for *living* them fully. The answers could just as well remain strange and exterior—one object of knowledge among so many possible others, without coming from an imperative necessity.

We are familiar with at least a few of the conditions that make this threatening "exteriority" weigh upon existence. This "exteriority" is inevitable each time any authority imposes answers, each time families, schools, religions, customs and the institutions that incarnate them claim to possess the answers and to recognize a universal scope for them. For no matter the laws decreed, the rules or precepts, the obligations or restrictions, no matter the constraints of communal life, it is up to each individual to answer these three questions *for him- or herself, by him- or herself,* and *in his or her own name*: "What can I know? What ought I to do? What may I hope?" At stake in the Socratic maxim—"Know thyself!"—is an injunction that addresses each individual in his or her own uniqueness, independently of the nature of the answer—singular, particular, or universal—that might be brought to it. "Self-knowledge" therefore could not be delivered to us ready-made by those that would like to determine its framework. There is a reason that the maxim pronounces itself as an imperative—and the sense of the command that each one addresses to him- or herself is the following:

> You are not who your family, your father and mother, your brothers and sisters, your uncles, your circle of friends, your coworkers, your hierarchical superiors, but also the woman (or women) that you love, with whom you at once dream, desire, and dread to build your life, imagine and claim you to be! Nothing of what you are in a position to know about yourself, nothing of what you should do, nothing of what you have the right to expect from yourself can be identified with what everyone wants to make you believe. There are many reasons to feel such a distance, but the first is that the words they use are not your own; when they claim to know you, to know from your perspective and better than you who you are, what you should do, and what you are in a position to expect, the language they speak remains profoundly foreign to you. And, so, it is not you that they know with those words!

"Know thyself!" One will have understood that at stake in this imperative is, if not an opposition, at least a resistance. One does not know oneself without resisting the knowledge of others—that is to say, without resisting the knowledge that others claim to have not only of the self but also, by extension, of the totality of the world; one does not know oneself without resisting their laws, their verdicts, and, in the same stroke, without appearing in their court. One does not know oneself without trying to valorize, against these judgments, a singularity that cannot be reduced to the generalities of all orders that claim to contain it—without trying, in other words, to make this singularity exist in a proper language, a singular language, an idiom that does not make self-knowledge relapse or fall back into the marshes or quagmires of platitudes, prejudices, received opinions, or definitive judgments. But this valorization is never produced without a struggle, and the price to pay for this knowledge is at times the hostility and coldness of the world, a sentiment of estrangement and exile such that, far from translating into a gain of clarity or transparency, the demands of self-relation [*rapport à soi*] implies the obscuration of relationships [*relations*],[1] solitude, and the paralysis of language. The battle is never won in advance. And no one can be assured of eventually finishing with the illusions that so many opposing forces, internal and external, incite and force him or her to maintain concerning his or her own life.

I. Impossible Self-Knowledge

Nobody in twentieth-century literature waged this battle in such great disarray and with such firm steadfastness, to the point of exhausting the resources of literature, as Franz Kafka. Self-knowledge and the obstacles it comes up against, the tribunals to which it is exposed, the verdicts whose obscure and implacable violence it suffers, not only constitute the common thematic of his three novels (*Amerika*, *The Trial*, and *The Castle*) and the guiding thread of his numerous stories; they are also the raison d'être and the primary motive of the *Diaries* that Kafka kept sporadically between 1909 and 1923, as well as one of the recurrent leitmotifs in his correspondence with those close to him: family, friends, fiancées. Above all, however, the vocation of literature that he ceaselessly recalls, as if tormented by it, is from the beginning inseparable from the complex, if not impossible, trial of self-knowledge. One of the very first entries in the *Diaries* (January 12, 1911) thus testifies to this inseparability:

> I haven't written down a great deal about myself during these days, partly because of laziness (I now sleep so much and so soundly during the day, I have greater weight while I sleep) but also partly because of the fear of betraying my self-consciousness [*Selbsterkenntnis*]. This fear is justified, for one should permit a self-knowledge to be established definitively in writing only when it can be done with the greatest integrity [*Vollständigkeit*], with all the incidental consequences, as well as with entire truthfulness. For if this does not happen—and in any event I am not capable of it—then what is written down will, in accordance with its own purpose and with the superior power of the established, replace what has been felt only vaguely in such a way that the real feeling will disappear while the worthlessness of what has been noted down will be recognized too late. (35, translation modified)

"[O]ne should permit a self-knowledge to be established definitively in writing only when it can be done with the *greatest integrity*, with all the incidental consequences, as well as with *entire truthfulness*" (emphasis added). At stake is what Kafka calls "incidental consequences,"[2] a self-knowledge that is at the same time an opening to the rest of the world. One, he says, cannot be separated from the other. Further still, the integrity and truthfulness of the first make possible the second. This immediately dispels a misunderstanding: it would be a mistake, indeed, to identify the impossible "self-knowledge," for which this entry in the *Diaries* nevertheless yearns, with some withdrawal into oneself, for on no account does it come from a complacent introspection closed off from all exterior relationship. On the contrary, this self-knowledge's only destination is to make possible another relation to the world where the latter has become unbearable, obscured by suffocating relationships. Is this the "vocation of literature"? Are these relationships the first form of violence that it confronts? And must one thus conclude that the vital necessity of such a knowledge makes literature a fate, in the sense that Kafka, as he ceaselessly recalls in his *Diaries* and in his correspondence with Felice and Milena, does not conceive life outside it and detests anything that might in the least compromise it? But this vocation does not concern only the rule that binds writing in the *Diaries*. It refers just as much to the demand that pushes one to start and restart, in solitude and suffering, writing new stories without always finishing them. The nature of this vocation that mixes self-knowledge, relation to the world, and literature is thus from the beginning more complex than it seems. The first sign is constituted by the simple fact that, although we are confronted with texts of very different natures in reading this largely posthumous oeuvre—three novels (at least two of which remain unfinished), fragments and stories (often interrupted), copious letters and *Diaries*—it is nevertheless impossible to separate them completely because they are all carried by the same concern, if not obsession, with literature. How, then, to untie the knot? The hypothesis that I would like to test in this first chapter is that, if this vocation is so imperative and perhaps even, according to Kafka, vital, it is because the vocation is from the beginning engaged in the triple relation, strained and each time aporetic, of an impossible syllogism. First, the world would not be livable or bearable without this other self-knowledge, as if the Socratic maxim bore a codicil: "Know thyself, if you want the world to come to you!" Yet, this knowledge is itself dependent upon a relation to language that is impossible outside of literature. This is why there is no life possible outside of literature. The relationship to the world—not only, then, knowledge of the world but also being-in-the-world itself—is impossible without literature; or, rather, the world without literature is no longer anything but coldness and hostility—strange and inhospitable.

A whole series of questions immediately results. If it is true that an "integral" and "true" self-relation and relationship to the world are at stake, what are "integrity" and "truth" in literature? Outside of integrity and truth, what makes those relations illusory, false, deceitful, or strange? Is it ordinary language? Words that steal away? How can one imagine that, confronted with the majority of relationships that constitute the fabric of existence (familial relationships, coworkers, and perhaps even romantic encounters), the poetic work that imposes this "integrity" and "truth" is *alone* prone to offer what Kafka calls, on October 3 of that same year, "a heavenly enlightenment and a real coming-alive" (62)? How is one to understand the idea that so many sacrifices must be made for the apparently *vital* call of this "integrity" and "truth," as if they alone could save us from the abstraction and generality of concepts, categories, and judgments?

What can I know? What ought I to do? What may I hope? Who am *I* as a singular being at the crossroads of these three questions, where a few of the marked traits of this singularity should be able to take shape precisely? It is significant that, in the *Diaries*, the opposition between, on the one hand, the generality of the law, what it permits and forbids, what it regulates and orders, the judgments that it authorizes, and, on the other hand, singularity as the unique object of self-relation and self-knowledge manifests itself with respect to reading. Nothing is more ambivalent, indeed, than the practice and passion of reading. In a sense, its apprenticeship and exercise come from constraints that submit the relation to language to their law. The constraints allot rules, time, place, and object. They are also, in most societies, one of the first and minimal requirements for social integration. One must learn to read and to count to make a place for oneself in society. And, at the same time, no other acquisition carries to this degree, in itself, the germs of its own transgression, offering to everyone the means to invent his or her own singularity—as if reading were virtually always also an invitation to read elsewhere, otherwise, something other, differently. Once it becomes a source of infinite pleasure, once it devours time and overrides every other activity, once it prevents one from going out, making the idle chatter of living-room conversations and café discussions unbearable, reading turns against this "integration." Nothing, then, remains intact concerning the relationship to others and the relationship to the world on which reading imposes new demands. So, does the relation to language once again imply it? Does language no longer let itself be spoken ordinarily without secretly revealing itself to be an illusion, a lack, a fault, as if, having opened the world otherwise through reading, it no longer lent itself to the false opening of its ordinary usage in familiar circles, at home, at the office? We will soon see the extent to which the *Diaries* ceaselessly return to such experiences.

We are, for the moment, in 1916. It will be another three years before Kafka writes the famous "Letter to His Father" (1919), but he already recalls the bundle of rules and laws that, as he admits, were preventing him from being himself. He already makes the obstacles that compromised this "self-invention" and the traces that they left both the object and the condition of impossible and nevertheless necessary "self-knowledge," the quest for which pushes him to write. A concept then appears in his work—sometimes in the singular, sometimes in the plural—on which it is worth lingering: "singularity" or "singularities" [« *singularité(s)* »].

> Every human being is singular [*eigentümlich*], and by virtue of his singularity [*Eigentümlichkeit*], called to play his part in the world, but he must have a taste for his own singularity [*Eigentümlichkeit*]. So far as my experience went, both in school and at home the aim was to erase all trace of singularity [*Eigentümlichkeit*]. In this way they made the work of education easier, but also made life easier for the child, although, it is true, he first had to go through the pain caused him by discipline. (Kafka, "Fragments," 221-22, translation modified).³

And he continues a bit further on:

> Although being forbidden to read is only an example, it is a characteristic one, for this prohibition went deep. My singularity [*Eigentümlichkeit*] was not accorded any recognition; but since I felt it, I could not fail—being very sensitive on this score and always suspicious—to recognise a definitive judgment [*Aburteilen*] in this attitude to me. (223, translation modified)

Finally, these notes conclude with the following injunction, which perhaps constitutes a reformulation of the Socratic maxim: "Emphasis of singularity [*Eigentümlichkeit*]—desperation. / I have never discovered what the rule is" (226, translation modified).

A "definitive judgment": this is where the shadow of the tribunal enters the scene of writing! As everyone knows about Kafka's work, especially with respect to his three novels, there is always an indictment at the heart of the story. This is true of *Amerika*, in which, on at least two occasions, Karl Rossmann is subject to a judgment and suffers the weight of a definitive verdict: first by his uncle, who shuts the door on him and sends him wandering about, and then by the doorman and the boss of the bellboys at Hotel Occidental, who judge him guilty of negligence and, after an expedited trial, also run him off like a criminal. Tribunals, irrevocable verdicts, shutting doors: here we are already at the heart of Kafka's universe. But, as everyone knows, an indictment as mysterious as implacable also constitutes the narrative frame of *The Trial*. There again, one loses count of the doors that remain closed or impossible to enter, the dark anterooms that hold an endless wait for those that run aground in them. From beginning to end in *The Castle*, finally, the surveyor seems to suffer the weight of a verdict already rendered by an invisible tribunal. Now, in each of the stories, the proper *singularity* of the hero, his right to exist singularly, is put into question and indicted. They all see their right to live how they wish and where they want, to continue their own activities, contested without anything that seems capable of justifying the interdiction other than an inaccessible law translated by "a definitive judgment."

"Know thyself!" Yet, how to imagine that such a knowledge could be of any weight or that it could even have some chance of being acquired, opening the world otherwise, if it runs into such a judgment from the beginning? And, above all, how to understand the singularity that is simultaneously denied by and resistant to such judgment? Both tormented and revolted by the memory of the restriction weighing on reading, Kafka offers a few specifications in a long journal entry from July and August of 1916. If he was not allowed to read beyond a "reasonable" hour, it was in order to avoid damaging his eyes, because it was time to sleep and because the book that he was reading, he was told, was not worth it. From then on, singularity could manifest itself only unreasonably. Reading, from the beginning, contested this order of reasons. It asserted against this order the experience of an irreducible desire and pleasure, opening onto an endless time. Kafka writes that, concerning his parents' reasoning, "it all did not even come anywhere near beginning to be worth thinking about. For everything was endless, or streamed away into vagueness in such a way that it could be equated with what was endless" ("Fragments," 222).

But Kafka does not limit himself to this undoubtedly central analysis. He completes it by making use this time of the concept of "singularity" in the plural [« *singularité(s)* » *au pluriel*], dividing it into "displayed singularity" and "concealed singularity." The interest of such a distinction is immediate. It pertains to the fact that everything that is described under the heading of singularity is identified with the concrete manifestation, visible or secret, of a transgression of the law. The "displayed singularities," indeed, are overt provocations that defy authority, as it happens, essentially the authority of the father, while "concealed singularities" are those that are protected from all avowal. A self-knowledge results that is guilty twice over. Two counts of indictment unite: on the one hand, transgressing the interdiction; on the other, lacking courage by hiding part of these transgressions. Consequently, no manifestation of "singularity" could be sufficient. The weight of conventions and the compromises they demand, the concessions made to the rules they impose (marriage, for example), and the trite arrangements made with the language spoken by authorities all remain too powerful for this manifestation ever to be sufficient. One therefore always falls short of the narratives that would need to be produced for self-knowledge to be freed definitively from the gravity of tribunals, for the shadow of definitive judgments and implacable verdicts to cease its doubtful clouding of every singular enterprise:

> The singularities I displayed [*Eigentümlichkeiten vorgezeigten*] increased more and more the nearer I came to the life to which I had access. Yet this brought me no liberation, it did not cause the quantity of what was concealed [*Geheimgehaltenen*] to diminish, and on more refined inspection it appeared that it would never be possible to confess everything. Even the seemingly complete admissions made in the earlier period later turned out to have their root in my inner being. But even if that had not been so—with the loosening up of the entire psychic organisation that I had undergone, without decisive interruptions, even *one* concealed singularity [eine *verborgene Eigentümlichkeit*] was enough to upset me so much that, however much I adapted myself in other respects, I still could not hold on anywhere at all. But there was still worse. Even if I had not kept any secret [*Geheimnis*] to myself, but had flung everything so far away from me that I would have stood there in complete purity, in the next instant I would again have been choked with the old muddle and confusion, for in my opinion the secret would not have been completely recognised and assessed, and in consequence would have been restored to me by the generality and imposed upon me anew. (224–25, translation modified)

But "self-knowledge," the self-relation that is supposed to open another relationship to the world, has another pitfall: a destructive narcissism. Indeed, to respond to the call of this knowledge and to the call of writing does not turn introspection into salvation, no more than introspection saves one from the hostility of the world; in other words, it is not in this way that one must "talk to oneself," if it is true, as Kafka recalls in one of the very first entries in the *Diaries*, that writing takes place entirely in the concern with such an address.[4] What, indeed, does it mean "to talk to oneself"? Nothing more or less than the *mediation* of self to self that alone allows one to escape the traps of introspection. One must thus understand what introspection consists in, especially if the vocation of writing should ultimately prove to reside in the endless search for such mediation, as endless as the pleasure of reading, and if one should discover that, in the final analysis, it constitutes the secret spring that leads the author of *The Metamorphosis* from story to story.

What, then, is the nature of this mediation? As soon as it implies a gap between self and self or, put otherwise, an irreducible difference between self and self, it first presupposes the test [*épreuve*] of an estrangement not only from the person that a given familial, bureaucratic, or communitary authority would like us to pretend to be but also, and more radically still, from all self-identification. This estrangement first of all comes from time. It is therefore no surprise when, in one of the rare passages of the *Diaries* in which Kafka reflects on the merits of keeping a diary, he lingers on the temporality of this estrangement. This is, no doubt, a capital point: the self-knowledge that takes the form of a narrative, even if discontinuous like the writings of the *Diaries*, participates in becoming. It sanctions transformations and metamorphoses that nullify every idea of atemporal self-identity. The slow maturation of time, revealed in the regular intervals at which Kafka resumes the narrative, invalidates any withdrawal of self-knowledge into a permanently established character and any *definitive judgment* that an *authoritative tribunal* would render in that sense, once and for all.[5] Moreover, the writing of the *Diaries*, under conditions that we will later see, itself participates in these changes. It is not limited to recording the changes; it provokes them over time, following the demands to which it submits.

This estrangement, next, results from the "terrible uncertainty of . . . inner existence" (220) provoked by the hostility of the world. It is true that the latter is reciprocated. While Kafka never misses an opportunity to emphasize the incomprehension that his literary vocation arouses in those close to him, the hatred he confesses when confronted with anything that distracts him from literature exposes the human relations that make up the fabric of his existence to a secret law whose eventual effect is to make them all strangers. The testimonies that move in this direction occur throughout the writings of the *Diaries*, as much in the creative periods as in the periods of doubt and impotence. Thus, in the log that balances the pros and cons for his marriage, Kafka writes on July 21, 1913: "I hate everything that does not relate to literature, conversations bore me (even if they relate to literature), to visit people bores me, the sorrows and joys of my relatives bore me to my soul. Conversations take the importance, the seriousness, the truth of everything I think" (225). And he continues a few days later as the prospect of marriage gnaws at him with doubts and worries: "I'll shut myself off from everyone to the point of insensibility. Make an enemy of everyone, speak to no one" (229). Or again, on August 21, 1913, he notes in the letter that he plans to address to Felice's father:

> My job [*Posten*] is unbearable to me because it conflicts with my only desire and my only vocation [*Beruf*], which is literature. Since I am nothing

but literature and can and want to be nothing else, my job will never take possession of me, it may, however, shatter me completely, and this is by no means a remote possibility. Nervous states of the worst sort control me without pause, and this year of worry and torment about my and your daughter's future has revealed to the full my inability to resist. (230, translation modified)

In a sense, this passage says it all. The letter that Kafka addresses to Felice Bauer's father, in the form of an auto-indictment, as if it were important for him to be the judge for once in the tribunal before which one must appear, makes literature the only justification of the relation to the world and of the relation to others that constitute what the author of *The Trial* calls "[s]ome secret law of human relationship" (*Diaries*, 228)—the law by which he is judged. But the *Diaries* only relay all the tribunals that Kafka imagines [*fantasme*] in each human relationship. For pages on end, they describe a circle: because there is no relation with others that is not stamped by lies, with all the violence that results, literature is the only way out. It alone opens the door of a true entrance into life. It alone is liberating. Yet, this succor and recourse [*ce secours et ce recours*] do not make relationships more livable. No familiarity, no harmony, no greater comprehension emerges. The path of literature is not a false harmony; it does not appease any of the preexisting tensions; it does not abolish violence or erase it by waving a magic wand. And this is not, moreover, its vocation. On the contrary, it increases the distance and gaps; it moves quotidian exchanges further away. As soon as it imposes the demand for another relation to language, it makes every relationship that falls short problematic.

These gaps, this distance, this remove—the price paid for "the vocation of writing"—make each relationship a potential tribunal. Whoever takes responsibility for it is exposed to a radical indictment and, once again, to "definitive judgments." The sentence is never far off. Between 1912 and 1916, Kafka's life is monopolized by his affair with Felice Bauer and their marriage plans, which the author of *The Trial* ceaselessly shirks. At the risk of a widespread misunderstanding, Kafka opposes the solitude and silence required by literature to the many commitments and preoccupations that life as a couple would impose. At this point, the letters and the *Diaries* resemble an inextricable labyrinth of infinite explications and justifications, like K.'s procedures in *The Trial* or the meanderings of the surveyor at the foot of the castle. Among the thousand and one passages that one could extract from hundreds of pages, let us retain the following two. The first, once again, is extracted from the letter that Kafka, while he was preparing himself to make the engagement official, planned to write to Felice Bauer's father to convince him that he, Kafka, would not make a good husband for his daughter, as if in so doing he wanted to avert the fate of the engagement that he would indeed end up breaking off.

> Conclusions can at least be drawn from the sort of life I lead at home. Well, I live in my family, among the best and most lovable people, more strange than a stranger. I have not spoken an average of twenty words a day to my mother these last years, hardly ever said more than hello to my father. I do not speak at all to my married sisters and my brothers-in-law, and not because I have anything against them. The reason for it is simply this, that I have not the slightest thing to talk to them about. Everything that is not literature bores me and I hate it, for it disturbs me or delays me, if only because I think it does. I lack all aptitude for family life except, at best, as an observer. I have no family feeling and visitors make me almost feel as though I were maliciously being attacked. (231)[6]

A week later, on August 30, 1913, Kafka draws the following conclusions:

> Where am I to find salvation? How many untruths I no longer even knew about will be brought to the surface. If they are going to pervade our marriage as they pervaded the good-bye, then I have certainly done the right thing. In me, by myself, without human relationship, there are no visible lines. The limited circle is pure. (231)

Does this mean that one must oppose the lies of human relationships to a form of truth that one would reach only in and through the relation to language that literature institutes? Would the proper of "human relationships" be that they are always, if not false, at least deceitful, that they harbor, engender, or rest on deception? But what, then, of this "alternative" relation toward which all the analyses converge? It is time to describe more fully, not the struggle that Kafka leads against the hostility of the world with his own estrangement, but rather the struggle that summons him day after day before the tribunal of writing, which is implacable otherwise. It is time to understand why, for reasons pertaining to the nature of language, what Kafka himself calls his "talent for portraying [his] dreamlike inner life," emphasizing the oneiric character of that inner life and recognizing his "fate" in it, pushes "all other matters into the background" (302).[7] It is time, finally, to grasp the way in which there is no self-knowledge that holds up without this reverie and struggle mixed with the words of the language comprising the singularity of not only Kafka's *Diaries* but also, even more so, his stories.

II. The Tribunal of Writing

In the few words uttered in his cavernous voice as an exergue at the beginning of his film adaptation of *The Trial*, Orson Welles suggested that he saw in Kafka's novel nothing more or less than a nightmare and perhaps also the anxious prophecy of the judiciary and policing terrors that would shake the world some twenty years after the novel was written. But the nightmare, if there is one, has still other roots. From the moment it lingers in the folds of inner life, its source lies in what the perilous exercise of self-knowledge always runs the risk of digging up. At the beginning, then, everything is obscure, uncertain, nebulous, indecisive. Nothing is grasped with the force of evidence. No clear and distinct idea that could serve as an Archimedian point stands out. No method assured of its principles and rules could guide the exercise. On the contrary, on many occasions in the *Diaries* the image returns from a world of drifting thoughts, from a cloud of diffuse impressions and sensations that resist all analysis. If it is so difficult for him to speak to others, Kafka explains, it is because, while "conversation with people demands pointedness, solidity, and sustained coherence," the content of his consciousness remains "entirely nebulous" (*Diaries*, 329). The hostility thus comes not only from the exterior world; it also comes from the fact that obscure ideas, dissimulations, a knot of desires and interests, which Kafka does not hesitate to compare to a veritable "rat's nest," gnaws on inner life:

> At a certain point in self-knowledge, when other circumstances favouring self-security are present, it will invariably follow that you find yourself execrable. Every moral standard—however opinions may differ on it—will seem too high. You will see that you are nothing but a rat's nest of miserable dissimulations. The most trifling of your acts will not be untainted by these dissimulations. These dissimulated intentions are so squalid that in the course of your self-scrutiny you will not want to ponder them closely but will instead be content to gaze at them from afar. These intentions aren't all compounded merely of selfishness, selfishness seems in comparison an ideal of the good and beautiful. The filth you will find exists for its own sake; you will recognize that you came dripping into the world with this burden and will depart unrecognizable again—or only too recognizable—because of it. This filth is the nethermost depth you will find; at the nethermost depth there will be not lava, no, but filth. It is the nethermost and the uppermost, and even the doubts self-scrutiny begets will soon grow weak and self-complacent as the wallowing of a pig in muck. (*Diaries*, 330)

How should this alarming darkness, this unsettling nebulosity, this world of doubtful thoughts be understood? They go hand in hand with a litany of writing's impotence and paralysis—all the pages in the *Diaries* where Kafka contents himself with counting the days and the weeks during which he wrote nothing, although nothing stopped him because he was, for once, free from all constraints. They go hand in hand with all the pages in which he is alarmed by his distraction, his loss of memory, and even, on September 13, 1915, his "stupidity" (341). For nothing haunts self-knowledge more than the silence to which writing is exposed from the moment it refuses to make concessions to the sentences of others, without any assurance, however, that it will find in writing the force and the necessary resources for getting rid of those sentences. This regularly worries Kafka; there is nothing that he dreads more than those long periods of sterility. If it is true, in other words, that literature is "help [*Hilfe*]" (314, translation modified)—as he writes a year earlier on September 13, 1914—which he vows never to let anyone take from him, it remains intermittent, fragile, and uncertain. That is to say, nothing is more foreign [*étranger*] to the author of *The Metamorphosis* than the certitude of possessing and mastering his language, of being the herald, defender, and promoter of a literary heritage. Literary passion is not the passion of an inheritance but, rather, a struggle with writing.

"Know thyself!" It is now clear that this maxim never left Kafka's thoughts. But what is probably the most decisive question still remains: what does this knowledge owe to the particularity of a language and, even more so, to the singularity of an idiom? How does it free itself from the language of "judgments" and the tribunals that have summoned him to appear? To what *other* tribunal, in other words, does self-knowledge choose to submit from then on? A tribunal: it is certainly no accident that, from the first pages of the *Diaries*, when he finds no excuse for the fact that he his written nothing, these are the terms in which Kafka evokes the call of writing on December 20, 1910: "I have continually an invocation [*Anrufung*] in my ear: 'Were you to come, invisible tribunal [*Gericht*]!'" (31, translation modified). Everything happens, in reality, as if the demands of an "integral" and "true" self-knowledge, freed from all authoritarian tutelages (of the father, uncles, and the rest of the family, of school and the workplace), had no way out other than the substitution of one tribunal for another, the tribunal of writing for that of tutelage, as if it had to give itself its own law, its own judges, and its own sentences—as if, in the end, this were the price of judging the silences, the moments of fatigue or laziness, the lethargy, the distractions to be guilty.

Now, to what are these tribunals, laws, judges, and sentences due? First and foremost to the language that is at the origin of a double judgment.

At stake, first, is an attention to the words that condemn the ordinary usage of language. If Kafka continually repeats that he has nothing to say to people, that conversation bores him because it diverts him from his vocation, it is because he gets nothing from the language they speak. But this is not the only condemnation. As soon as this usage is recused, another relation to language is called forth, and other demands weigh upon language. Language is invested from the beginning with a promise that is not foreign to what Kafka calls the "help of . . . writing" (314, translation modified).[8] And even if it is first a question of the help that reading brings, reading is itself only a springboard for writing. As long as they are "good works," as he writes in one of the frequent descriptions of his readings in the *Diaries*, he "merge[s] with them" (164), and the language of the work becomes a sort of second language in Kafka's union with what he reads.[9] But this promise imposes its law above all as soon as it is a question of writing. Among the many passages that one would need to cite in their entirety, I isolate only three. First, an entry from 1910 that figures among the very first in the *Diaries*:

> Almost every word I write jars against the next, I hear the consonants rub leadenly against each other and the vowels sing an accompaniment like Negroes in a minstrel show. My doubts stand in a circle around every word, I see them before I see the word, but what then! I do not see the word at all, I invent it. Of course, that wouldn't be the greatest misfortune, only I ought to be able to invent words capable of blowing the odor of corpses in a direction other than straight into mine and the reader's face. (29)

And then two entries written three days apart in 1911, December 13 and 16:

> When I begin to write after a rather long interval, I draw the words as if out of the empty air. If I capture one, then I have just this one alone and all the toil must begin anew. (137)

> Such fear of writing always expresses itself by my occasionally making up, away from my desk, initial sentences for what I am to write, which immediately prove unusable, dry, broken off long before their end, and pointing with their towering fragments to a sad future. (138)

More generally, however, the entirety of the *Diaries* takes on the task of keeping this promise, not only in all the passages that, like those just cited, testify directly to the anxiety over the right word and sentence but also in the simple narrations of events and descriptions of the people that were met throughout the day—beginning with the actors and the actresses of the Jewish theater, their gestures, their diction. If it is true that responsibility for the Socratic maxim "Know thyself!" implies the invention of an unprecedented language, a language for oneself to say the world [*une langue à soi pour dire le monde*], the *Diaries* recount the painful genesis and the imperious necessity of the confrontation with the reticence, if not the hostility, of the world just as much as they constitute the laboratory for the invention of that language.

And yet, this laboratory could not suffice by itself. At stake, in reality, are a double passage and a double gap in language, as well as a double distancing and a double metamorphosis. The first, clearly, is the passage from speech to writing. "When I say something," Kafka writes on July 3, 1913, "it immediately and finally loses its importance, when I write it down it loses it too, but sometimes gains a new one" (223). "Self-knowledge" thus presupposes a first mediation: it substitutes the solitary rigor of writing for the speech of the father and uncles, for all oral commentaries, for idle chatter, for run-of-the-mill explications, indictments, and reproaches, as well as for the accompanying fits of anger, for the spontaneous manifestations of mood always aggravated by the thoughtless immediacy of speech, bodily movements, certain looks, and relaxed language. One cannot be acquitted of one's relationship to the world by speaking. The relationship could find its truth only in writing. This is the first credo.

But this is not all, for this first mediation would be nothing, or almost nothing, if it did not call for a second that, alone, constitutes the metamorphosis of language required by an "integral and true self-knowledge." This second mediation moves from a "narrative account of the self," such as the *Diaries* stage, to other narratives that, while many remain unfinished, are still in a certain sense a "writing of the self" and, as such, participate in self-knowledge, perhaps as its most accurate manifestation, the only manifestation that liberates from all tutelage, even though it does not take the form of a narrative account of the self. This is, ultimately, the paradox at work in writing: a self-knowledge that no longer owes anything to autobiography. It is at this point that the tribunal of writing proves to be the most impartial and the most implacable. Kafka means nothing else when he writes that he is and wants to be nothing but literature. To everyone who thinks they know him, to everyone who would want him to be other than he is, to fathers, uncles, fiancées, colleagues, Kafka responds: I am not what I say in all the circles that detain me; I am not he that addresses you in the thousand and one exchanges of daily life, not he that violently forces himself to remain among you; I am my stories and narratives; I am fully myself only in the torturous mediation of their writing. Thus, on June 21, 1913, he notes: "The tremendous world I have in my head. But how to free myself and free it without being torn to pieces. And a thousand times rather be torn to pieces than retain it in me or bury it. That, indeed, is why I am here, that is quite clear to me" (222).

At stake, we said, were three questions: "What can I know? What ought I to do? What may I hope?" It is time to see how, in the final analysis, the *Diaries* respond to each of them. No doubt, one will say, the answer to the first question cannot be identified with the problem posed by self-knowledge. To know the world is not necessarily or exclusively "to know oneself." Except, perhaps, when "self-knowledge" no longer has anything to do with psychology and is conditioned by the vocation of literature. From the moment knowing oneself no longer means observing oneself or describing the inner states of the soul but, rather, granting rights to inner life, however oneiric, in narratives—letting it, in other words, live its life in literature—nothing prevents self-knowledge from imposing itself at the same time, and even before every other consideration, as a finally freed knowledge of the world. This is, at bottom, the great lesson of the *Diaries*, which is also a great liberation: as soon as they are jointly concentrated in the narratives produced by writing, knowledge of self and knowledge of world come down to the same. They liberate simultaneously from representations of the world imposed from the outside and from the psychological characterization always distinguished by the precipitation and the impatience of the judgments it produces. Thus, on October 20, 1917, Kafka can note: "From the outside, one will always triumphantly impress theories upon the world and then fall straight into the ditch one has dug, but only from inside will one keep oneself and the world quiet and true" (*Octavo Notebooks*, 74).

"What should I do?" Nothing attests to the fact that this question comes entirely from self-knowledge as much as the recurrence of the injunctions that the author of the *Diaries* addresses to himself.[10] From the moment this knowledge submits to the tribunal of writing, the question naturally finds some responses: one must not concede to exterior pressures; one must resist the weight of conventions, laziness, temptations of comfort, impatience; one must keep to writing's course. But, further still, the nature of self-knowledge, transformed by writing, imposes its response. For writing consists less in the acquisition of knowledge than in a "doing." To "know oneself" is not to acquire a self-representation that would come to substitute another representation projected by one's close friends and relatives; it is not only, as Kafka attempts in the *Diaries*, to take measure of its creative forces but also, at least as much, to put them to work. The substitution of the tribunal of writing for that of the family, education, or the office thus declines in the imperative mode. It enjoins one to free oneself of all the false identifications and false appropriations of the self by the self, even to disencumber oneself of the ego [*moi*] that is not the self. And to melt into reading and writing is the only way to do so. This is the law: to unite, to become one with what one reads and writes—because this is where integrity and truth lie. In this respect, there is nothing ambiguous in the entry recorded on October 23, 1917:

> "Know thyself" does not mean "Observe thyself." "Observe thyself" is what the Serpent says. It means: "Make yourself master of your actions." But you are so already, you are the master of your actions. So that saying means: "Misjudge yourself! Destroy yourself!" which is something evil—and only if one bends down very far indeed does one also hear the good in it, which is: "In order to make of yourself what you are." ("Octavo Notebooks," 79–80)

Finally, the third question remains: "What may I hope?" In a sense, all of the preceding considerations are related to this question. If there is, indeed, a sentence to be expected from the tribunal of writing, it could not consist in a condemnation or call for any punishment—for there was in reality only one verdict possible: *help, or nothing at all*. Literature knows no half measures. Through language, it reaches a knowledge of self and a knowledge of world freed from the categories and judgments that immure it in lies—or it is nothing at all. For only then, at the price of an arduously desired, defended and forbidden [*defendue*] solitude, does it become possible to invent one's own singularity. "Make of yourself what you are!" Kafka writes. The injunction carries the distant echo of Pindar's maxim, which a youthful Nietzsche made his slogan: "Become who you are!" But it also emphasizes that such a change, such a becoming, such access to oneself is not self-evident. Indeed, there is probably nothing less certain, nothing so ceaselessly put into question, nothing that calls so much for reinvention at every instant. Thus, a suspicion becomes clear: what if it were this metamorphosis that, in its very repetition, called for help?

It is time to say a few words about the famous letter that Kafka wrote, but never sent, to his father in 1919. What is it about? First and foremost, a crushing sovereignty—the strong, imposing, majestic body of the father opposed to the skinny, lanky body of the son. It is also about imperial and magisterial judgments that command and sanction, suffering no objection, no retort; it is about clear-cut, decisive, and definitive opinions—an implacable tribunal—that condemn in advance all other opinions and ideas, beginning with those of the son. This sovereignty is a confiscation: it recognizes no knowledge, no right to knowledge, traditions, or languages, much less to literature, of which it is not the origin; it recognizes no obligation, no proper responsibility that escapes its control. If we keep to the first two questions ("What can I know?" and "What ought I to do?"), the sovereignty leaves the dominated son no chance of inventing a *singular* way of responding to them; it does not even leave any hope that, one day, things might be otherwise. Anchored in the son's memory, the father's sentences resound from then on like so many verdicts condemning in advance everything that might permit the son to be himself and not merely or definitively the person that the father, from the heights of his sovereign authority, can only regret that he is not, the person the father would have liked him to be: "'Is that all you're so worked up about?' . . . or 'Where is that going to get you?' or 'What a song and dance about nothing!'" (*Sons*, 122). Such is, in other words, the situation concerning the father figure: nothing escaped him; if he himself did not order it, no decision, pleasure, or joy found grace in his eyes.

> In keeping, furthermore, was your intellectual *sovereignty* [*Oberherrschaft*]. You had worked your way so far up by your own energies alone, and as a result you had unbounded confidence in your opinion. That was not yet so dazzling for me as a child as later for the boy growing up. From your armchair you ruled the world. Your opinion was correct, every other was mad, wild, *meshugge*, not normal. Your self-confidence indeed was so great that you had no need to be consistent at all and yet never ceased to be in the right. It did sometimes happen that you had no opinions whatsoever about a matter and as a result every conceivable opinion with respect to the matter was necessarily wrong, without exception. [. . . I]n all my thinking I was, after all, under the heavy pressure of your personality, even in that part of it—and particularly in that—which was not in accord with yours. All these thoughts, seemingly independent of you, were from the beginning burdened with your belittling judgments; it was almost impossible to endure this and still work out a thought with any measure of completeness and permanence. (*Sons*, 121–22, emphasis added, translation modified)

According to Kafka, this sovereign monopolization of the right to judge and sentence everything, experienced as violence, was both an agony and a shame. Above all, however, it was translated by the loss of all self-confidence with words. It made all spontaneous relation with "the usual fluency of human language" impossible (126). No doubt, one must mistrust the temptation to read the stories through the torments in Kafka's life, even though every page of the *Diaries* would invoke such a reading. Each of the preceding analyses takes place on the border of this pitfall. But they say nothing about interpreting the stories. They make no prejudgments concerning them. If they play with words that inevitably invoke the stories—"verdict," "trial," "tribunal," "metamorphosis"—the play halts at the threshold beyond which the stories would be reduced to a transposition of life. Literature has other demands. Beyond what they signify in themselves, however, the multiple texts that Kafka dedicates to literature and, even more so, the right to dedicate his life to it legitimate asking what he expected from literature in a context that, however universal in scope, loses none of its singular significance. What is the invention of singularity? What does this desire to change into who one is signify? Nothing more or less than a struggle for an other form of sovereignty. This is what Kafka expected from literature: nothing other than an unheard-of freedom—the freedom that results from literature when the words and the sentences willingly agree. At the moment of concluding this first perspective on the most common and ordinary form of violence, the violence that prevents someone from inventing his or her own singularity, one recalls what Kafka wrote on September 1, 1914, only a few weeks after the beginning of the First World War:

> In complete helplessness barely wrote two pages. I fell back a great deal today, though I slept well. Yet if I wish to transcend the initial pangs of writing (as well as the inhibiting effect of my way of life) and rise up into the freedom that perhaps awaits me, I know that I must not yield. My old apathy hasn't completely deserted me yet, as I can see, and my coldness of heart perhaps never. That I recoil from no ignominy can as well indicate hopelessness as give hope. (*Diaries*, 313–14)

2

Impossible Anamnesis

(Kafka and Derrida)

Does literature have something to teach us about what lodges violence at the heart of our relation to the law [*la loi*]? And, if this is the case, what does it teach us? Does it teach us how to adapt to it? To live with it? To surmount it? To resist it? Supposing that these questions interrogate the relation between law [*droit*] and literature, they immediately call to mind a third term, and we cannot know in advance what status to accord what the term designates: a discipline, a knowledge, or a discursive order—namely, philosophy. Philosophy has long taken both law and literature as its object: a "philosophy *of* literature" exists, just as a "philosophy *of* law" exists. Above all, however, philosophy makes the origin of the law one of its recurrent questions and ceaselessly calls upon "fictions" in order to respond to the enigma of the law and to understand both the potential violence of the institution of law and the violence it is charged with restraining. To cite only two examples, this is the case of, first, the narrative that Rousseau proposes about leaving the state of nature in the *Discourse on the Origin of Inequality* and, second, the way Freud in *Totem and Taboo* accounts for the origin of guilt, prohibitions, and law—hence, all our moral and juridical institutions—with *his* story of the primal horde and patricide. How, then, to determine the status of these stories? Can they be considered "literary"? And who could judge? To what tribunal should they be submitted for a verdict? A tribunal of jurors, literary theorists, philosophers, or psychoanalysts?

There are, no doubt, at least two ways to think the relation between law and literature. The first, *extrinsic*, concerns novellas, novels, or dramas that take as their object the strictness of the law, the judiciary apparatus or machine, in other words, literature whose "subject" is law offices, courtrooms, tribunals, and trials with their procession of interrogations, testimonies, depositions, and verdicts. As is known, the description implied by such a relation can then be realist, almost a sociological inquiry, or fantastic, nightmarish, or hallucinatory. In this second scenario, it is no longer only the judiciary apparatus that is in question but the imaginary of justice as it determines our relation to the law and the different affects that complicate or contaminate it. If it is true, indeed, that this relation is never purely rational but at least equally affective and sometimes even "over-affected," anxious, anguished, if not anxiogenic, it is obviously in the space of these affects, precisely where they lead to the desire or the madness of the law, that literature finds law as its object. The contribution, then, is not negligible. From the moment the relation to the law is a constitutive element of the genesis of all subjectivity or, in other words, from the moment the irreplaceable and unsubstitutable singularity of every one is at stake in this relation, literature makes this singularity known and reminds law of it.

But a second relation exists that is complex in another way, a relation closer to the one evoked above when recalling the names of Freud and Rousseau, among others. It is constructed around a double uncertainty: the uncertainty of the origin of the law and that of the literarity of the literary text. Or it articulates two essential questions: the question of the accessibility (or the inaccessibility) of the origin and the question of the possibility (or impossibility) of the narrative that claims to give access to it. Now, as soon as one enters the order of such negative prefixes (*in*accessibility of the law, *im*possibility of the narrative), Kafka's works again demand attention, devoted as they are to a double incompletion and a double search left unfinished: the Kafkaesque heroes that never manage to know *whence* come the laws, the decrees, and the reasons for the judgment that, not without violence, apply to them and the many stories that never come to an end.

Nevertheless, Kafka's stories are not unrelated to the first descriptive relation that we evoked above. If it is true that they give rise, as everyone knows, to numerous commentaries, these commentaries are distributed, at the very least, between two receptive constellations that align with these two general orientations. From the 1930s and 1940s, an era marked by the rise of fascism in Europe, discriminatory politics, exile, and the deportation and extermination of European Jews, the first constellation groups the first readings by Hannah Arendt, Walter Benjamin, and Günther Anders. The singular trait of the constellation outlined by these first readers consists in the fact that they all read, comment, and preface Kafka's stories after being forced to flee their own countries, sharing with K., the "hero" of *The Castle*, the status of "foreigner" or "exile," which exposes one to a life of waiting for a manifest decision that recognizes his or her right to exist where he or she has arrived. In Kafka's universe, they discover, each in turn, the description or the prophecy of the nightmare that was shaking Europe, when every new decree and every new law was identified as a threat to freedom and basic rights. The second constellation, forty years later in the 1970s and 1980s, gathers another generation of philosophers: Gilles Deleuze and Félix Guattari, Jean-François Lyotard and Jacques Derrida, not to mention Maurice Blanchot, who ceaselessly turned to Kafka from the 1940s to the 1980s. There again, their different approaches are not unrelated: in different ways, they all have in common the interrogation of the political function of these stories as a "politics of literature." In an even more general way, they draw support from Kafka's stories in order to think the "essence" or the "function" of literature, in the place where literature is inseparable from a reflection on law.

Are these two general orientations—one seeking in literature a description of our relation, real or imagined, to the law and the judiciary apparatus, and the other interrogating the possibility of a story that gives access to the law, to its origin or foundation—rigorously separable? Do Kafka's stories not, on the contrary, allow us to experience and to think their interlacing, their knot? Supposing that we retain this hypothesis, at least one text would let it be thought: the short story entitled "Before the Law"—especially if we remember that it was part of *The Trial* before being detached to comprise a separately published story. Indeed, a priest recounts it to K. at the very moment K. suspects that anyone taking an interest in his case has a prejudice against him. In the novel, this story already lends itself to something of a veritable Talmudic exegesis, which has since been globalized to the point that one loses count not only of the interpretations but also of the adaptations and rewritings that it has occasioned in many different languages. In the pages that follow, one interpretation in particular will retain our attention: the reading that Derrida offers in a text entitled "Before the Law."[1] More than any other, it is indeed Derrida who, in his reading of Kafka's story, has again posed the double question that retains us: the question of the accessibility of the origin of the law and the question of the possibility of a "literary" story that gives access to it, where the paradoxical tension between, on the one hand, the generality or universality of the law and, on the other hand, the absolute singularity of the one suffering its yoke plays out in all its violence.

I.

We all know the story: arriving at the door of the law, a "man from the country" (Kafka, "Before the Law," 3) is blocked from entering by a doorkeeper and must wait. He waits patiently for years on end, coming up against the same refusal every time he renews his request. Worn out, grown old, in the end he wonders why he was the only person to have demanded access to the law in all these years, and he receives the following response: "No one else could ever be admitted here, since this gate was made only for you. I am now going to shut it" (4). At stake is thus the accessibility of the law or, rather, its inaccessibility, the mystery or opacity of its origin, as Derrida does not fail to recall. Yet, from the beginning, Derrida also poses the question that associates the questioning of the origin with an interrogation of "the definition or the circumscription of literature," as if the two themes were in reality indissociable: "The double question, then, would be as follows: 'Who decides, who judges, and according to what criteria, that this relation belongs to literature?'" (Derrida, "Before the Law," 187).

It is no coincidence that I have begun here by citing the end of the text: "No one else could ever be admitted here." From the first reading, it indeed appears that, if the story can be taken as emblematic of the relations between law and literature, it is insofar as the story puts into perspective the paradoxical relation between the generality of the law and the absolute singularity of the one to whom the law applies. Few texts, indeed, have shown as much as Kafka's the extent to which one's relation to the law is singularly inscribed in one's body, voice, gestures, and postures, the way one stands straight or leans, like the silhouettes drawn by the author of *The Trial*. Far from being abstract, the law is not foreign to life but belongs to its most intimate story. No one knows, finally, when it all began or how he or she first incorporated the law. In varying ways, we keep only the memory of some violence in the form of disciplinary constraint, imposed exercise, transgression, and punishment. This incorporation thus remains, with the consciousness of our finitude, the most secret part of what is imposed upon us without our awareness. Nevertheless, no one can ignore that one must *live with* it one's whole life. For, if the origin of the relation to the law remains indeterminate, its end is at least known. This long duration is the first theme of "Before the Law"; we do not know how old the man from the country is when he presents himself at the door to gain admittance to the law, but we know when the story ends: on the threshold of death. The story, although very short, is thus punctuated with notations that evoke the inexorable passage of time spent waiting for a response and a way out:

> The doorkeeper gives him a stool and lets him sit down at one side of the door. [. . .] During these many years the man fixes his attention almost continuously on the doorkeeper. [. . .L]ater, as he grows old, he only grumbles to himself. He becomes childish [. . .] Now he has not very long to

live. Before he dies, all his experiences in these long years gather themselves in his head to one point, a question he has not yet asked the doorkeeper. He waves him nearer, since he can no longer raise his stiffening body. (Kafka, "Before the Law," 3–4)

For the law cannot be known, and access remains closed. We do not know, finally, the type of law in question: natural law, moral law, juridical law, fundamental law. Which is to say, the law's generality is redoubled. There is indeed a "law," real or imagined, indicated by the singularity of the relation that the man from the country has with it, but we know nothing about it. Above all, the story fails to teach us any more about it. It does not make the law any more comprehensible. The only thing capable of such a task is saying and reproducing, redoubling the inaccessibility of the law in its very writing. This is the hiatus: on the one hand, the law says the general. It seeks universality. It is supposed to have nothing to do with particular cases. It does not have to take into account the subjective vagaries of its incorporation or the enigma that, for those to whom it applies, its origin constitutes. On the other hand, the story implements the singularity of waiting, of a request, worry, and anxiety. One might expect the story to bring a corrective to this generality by relating it to the individual who, for his or her part, reckons that he or she has the right to know. Just as one could expect that Joseph K. will discover the reason behind the charges in *The Trial*, or the surveyor the source and logic of the decrees governing his compromised arrival in *The Castle*, or, yet again, Gregor Samsa the effective cause of his sudden and unforeseeable transformation into a giant insect in *The Metamorphosis*. Nothing of the sort. To account for all these "extraordinary" events, there should indeed be a law—whatever its nature: natural, moral, or juridical—that explains and justifies them. But the more these events seem usual, trivialized, and finally admitted as ordinary, the more they give the feeling of either becoming or having always been a part of everyday life, the less this law can be known. The further one advances in the story, the more the prospect of access to that law is lost in infinite detours.

This is why Derrida, reading "Before the Law," from the outset underlines as the story's central theme the failure of the encounter between the singularity of the relation to the law and the general or universal essence of that same law:

> There is a singularity about relationship to the law, a law of singularity which must come into contact with the general or universal essence of the law without every being able to do so. Now this text, this singular text, as

you will already have noted, names or relates in its way this conflict without encounter between law and singularity, this *paradox* or *enigma* of being-before-the-law.... (Derrida, "Before the Law" 187)

And he continues a bit further on:

What remains concealed and invisible in each law is thus presumably the law itself, that which makes laws of these laws, the being-law of these laws. The question and the quest are ineluctable, rendering irresistible the journey toward the place and the origin of law. The law yields by withholding itself, without imparting its provenance and its site. This silence and discontinuity constitute the phenomenon of the law. (192)

If we recall the two questions that we raised at the beginning of this chapter, what should hold our attention here is the way in which the question of the accessibility (or inaccessibility) of the law in effect shows itself to be indissociable from the question of the possibility (or impossibility) of the story and, in any case, its completion. In the 1980s, this inaccessibility is one of the major questions on which Derrida's work focuses. If it is true that, since the publication of the three great books of 1967 (*Of Grammatology, Writing and Difference,* and *Voice and Phenomenon*), his thought consists in the deconstruction of an allegedly sovereign subject or, in other words, self-assured identity, in the 1980s this deconstruction takes a more openly political dimension by bringing to the fore what he calls in "Force of Law," following Montaigne, "the mystical foundation of authority." One must therefore read the commentary on "Before the Law" from this perspective. Indeed, nothing prevents understanding the impossible access to the law in Kafka's stories as another figure or, more precisely, the always-singular effect of this "mystical foundation." The "foundation" that always escapes us is precisely what, in the final analysis, makes laws of laws and what makes us submit to them, whatever the reasons that one gives for this submission. No matter what the representatives of the law say, nothing in this regard will be changed by attachment to one's homeland, citizenship, sense of duty, or any of the questions that the doorkeeper of the law puts to the man from the country "indifferently, as great lords put them" (Kafka, "Before the Law," 3). Whatever the answers offered—for example, by a philosophy of law or right, a moral philosophy, or a treatise on the education of citizens—they do not resolve the enigma of our relation to the law. Above all, they do not at all exhaust the desire to rediscover or reconstruct its origin: how is it that the law thus determines the course of our existence, that it circumscribes, frames, and constrains our existence within limits that exceed us, and yet nothing of what we do, of what we think or feel, nothing of what makes up our proper singularity escapes it? From whom shall we demand an explication? Who will give us an account?

II.

Three facts thus call for articulation. The first is the resistance of the law that conserves its categorical authority only by guarding the secret of its foundation. To respect the law, indeed, no one needs to know its history [*histoire*]. On the contrary, in itself and by itself, the law calls for no story [*récit*] to come and condition this respect. It must even protect itself from all historical tergiversation that might contest and question this authority. Nor is there any need to turn to oneself or to interrogate one's past in some vain introspection. No one knows, finally, the good or bad reasons for which the man from the country appears at the door of the law in Kafka's story. Is it in search of an additional reason for submitting to it? Or to learn to know himself better? Are we certain only that to want "admittance to the Law" (Kafka, "Before the Law," 3), as the story says, is a legitimate wish? And yet, the desire to penetrate the mystery or the secret of the law is undeniable, perhaps even ineluctable. And it lasts, the story tells us, an entire life.

Hence, the second fact that demands to be taken into account and articulated with this resistance is the resulting "genealogical impulse." This is what it comes to: on the one hand, there is the sovereignty of the law that cannot be approached, that requires no justification, that has nothing to do with particular cases kept at a distance (we do not know how many doorkeepers protect the law), and that is accountable to no one. Then, on the other hand, there is at the same time the fact that no one in the world lives his or her relation to the law in that way; everyone even maintains in his or her flesh an absolutely singular relation with the law translated in one's gestures and voice, speech and silences. So, the man from the country, for his part, wants to know. There is nothing he wants to know more. He wants to be admitted to the law, to see it and to touch it. His impulse is irresistible—and it disappears only with death, because life is at stake, because knowing the secret of the law appears as the only knowledge that could finally make life more livable. Is it an illusion? madness? hyperbole? In any case, it is always in this way that the relation to the law is at stake: *in life and in death* [*il y va du rapport à la loi*: à la vie à la mort].

The third fact, then, is the very possibility of literature and of the language invented there. If it is true that the origin of the law is inaccessible, that the law is itself authoritarian and that, at the same time, everyone is constituted in their most intimate recesses by an absolutely singular relation to the law, a relation irreducible to all social, "ethnic," political, and even religious categories, to any predetermined membership, a relation in this way irreplaceable, then a language is called for, searched for, desired in order to fill this hiatus—that is to say, *to grant rights* [rendre droit] to the desire to bring one's singularity and the law's generality into agreement. But how to grant rights to the singular? What makes the "singularity of the singular"? First and foremost, its story [*histoire*]. The singular exists, as such, in being recounted. This is why one must begin with a narrative, in the hope that it will end up reaching the place from which the law comes— the law that nevertheless remains general toward and against everything, that is to say, the law that continues to resist. Such is the truth that Kafka's story carries: it is the statement of this difficult paradox—a statement itself paradoxical from the moment the story remains impossible. For it to take shape, for it to respond to the expectations it excites, at least two things, indeed, are necessary. First, the law must become accessible; second, the singularity of the one demanding access to the law must be articulated. Yet, singularity fails the test on both sides. The law continues to guard the secret of its foundation, and the singularity of the one dedicating him- or herself to the search for its origin stumbles on the generality of language. In other words, the guardian of the law might be nothing other than language itself, which says only the general, at the same time that it bears in itself the impossible promise of granting rights to the singular.

Derrida has often emphasized this relation between language and law. He comes back to it above all in *Monolingualism of the Other*, a text written some ten years after "Before the Law" and whose subtitle is worth recalling here: *or, the Prosthesis of the Origin*. Among the multiple themes that make up the fabric of this book, there is one, indeed, that should retain our attention. There is, Derrida tells us, always something lost [*perdu*] and even desperate [*éperdu*] in our relation to language, inhabited as it is by a nostalgia for an undiscoverable origin: each of us has only one language, and we bend to its law; at the same time, because this law is imposed upon us by family, school, society, and all the institutions that regulate, with a relative and variable violence, the way that language is learned and used, it is never our own. It does not belong to us; it comes from elsewhere. All its codes, the rules of good diction and writing, of grammar, orthography, and rhetoric are, on the one hand, a constitutive element of the relation that we maintain with ourselves and, on the other, a yoke that we suffer. This is the reason why there is no transparent self-relation that could assure the ego of its identity. In language we are uprooted, exiled, strangers to ourselves, like the man from the country before the door of the law and like Kafka, according to his *Diaries*, so often felt in society. Nothing, in other words, guarantees us or proves to us that we will find ourselves in what we say, in what we think, in what we believe we can be convinced of thinking and expressing on our own.

This is why the question of our relation to language, perhaps like the question of our relation to law, is indissociable from the question of madness. As Derrida explains in *Monolingualism*, the impossible identification of the ego is on the brink of three forms of madness, not before the law, but *in* and *with* language.

The first form of madness is the complete "disintegration" of identity, a relation to self and to language so fractured, so de-structured, that the very possibility of any singular invention in language, the very invention to which Derrida gives the name "idiom" (*Monolingualism*, 59–60), finds itself destroyed: a quasi-aphasia, then, like the one into which Friedrich Hölderlin sank, in his tower and abandoned to the care of the carpenter Ernst Zimmer, or that of Friedrich Nietzsche, who was *guarded* by his sister for years on end.

The second form of madness, for its part, is never admitted as such. Far from being thought in these terms, it is convinced, on the contrary, of its "normality"—and there is no doubt nothing as mad or threatening as this conviction. This madness inhabits all normative identification, including its potential exclusions and discriminations. It represses the work of *différance* in the illusion of a self-identity that is, at the same time and entirely, the illusion of the collectivity with which it identifies. We are once again undoubtedly best prepared for this madness by family, school, and any of the forces that dictate their law to us. But it is no stranger to Kafka's novels and stories either, which after all, in *The Trial*, *The Castle*, or *The Metamorphosis*, perhaps recount nothing other than the disjunction of a social or familial integration overdetermined by relationships—filial, professional, or otherwise—in a horrifying short circuit of the law, the body, and language. K., Joseph K., and Gregor Samsa, like Kafka himself, are also distinguished by mixed and irreconcilable refusals and desires to find explications, justifications, or exonerations that, through language, the relation to others, to authorities, is supposed to make possible. "Normality," integration, and conformity remain beyond their reach.

Finally, there is the third form of madness that perhaps defines one of the privileged vocations of writing, exposed to the search for undiscoverable origins, which Derrida describes in the following terms:

> the madness of a hypermnesia, a supplement of loyalty, a surfeit, or even excrescence of memory, to commit oneself, at the limit of the two other

possibilities, to traces—traces of writing, language, experience—which carry anamnesis beyond the mere reconstruction of a given heritage, beyond an available past. Beyond any cartography, and beyond any knowledge that can be taught. At stake there is an entirely other anamnesis, and, if one may say so, even an anamnesis of the entirely other.... (*Monolingualism*, 60)

An "anamnesis of the entirely other": if only we manage to understand what is in question, we could retrospectively grasp what is at stake in Kafka's story "Before the Law." Supposing, then, that we begin again from the point that was just established: the absence of "a stable model of identification for an *ego*" (60) by and in language, that is, by and in the mastery, possession, or disposal of a language that would be ours, perfectly ours, with which it would always be possible for us to find ourselves [*nous trouver*] and to meet each other [*nous retrouver*]; supposing, furthermore, that we cannot rest on (*one's*) language to answer the question, "Who am I?"; it would nevertheless be necessary to admit that everyone speaks. It would be necessary to admit that there is indeed, for everyone, a language: the language he or she speaks. It would even be necessary to admit that there is, in reality, more than one language. We try, indeed, to translate every singular event, every perception, every emotion, and every sensation into a language that would be appropriate for them, that is to say, a language that grants rights to what makes their arrival, irruption, astonishment, or surprise in the secret of their encounter a singular event. Each time, in other words, we must experience or experiment with [*expérimenter*] a lingual singularity in and with language—not to grant rights to *our* proper singularity but, rather, to grant rights to the singularity of what happens [*arrive*] and makes an event.

This is why Derrida can write, paradoxically, that there are only "target languages [*langues d'arrivée*]" (*Monolingualism*, 70) in this monolingualism that is ours. This is why there is plurality upon arrival [*à l'arrivée*]. If there were no plurality, if we posited in advance that there should be no plurality, that it is an illusion to think that there should be, we would from the outset be on the brink of that other madness of integration evoked a moment ago: the madness of sovereign mastery and possession of a source language [*langue de départ*] that no experience or experiment could overturn. Our language would never bend to what happens [*arrive*] to it, as if everything had always already been said, as if everything were indefinitely programmable and predictable. As for the violence that would result, we are familiar with language's hyper-normative imaginary: it haunts the most implacable totalitarian fables, such as Yevgeny Zamyatin's *We* or George Orwell's *1984*.

But if one admits or recognizes that there is no unique source language [*langue de départ*] established once and for all, then only target languages [*langues d'arrivée*] remain, but a target or arrival [*arrivée*] that remains indefinite, that never comes to term, languages that "cannot manage to reach themselves [*qui n'arrive pas à s'arriver*]," as Derrida says (*Monoligualism*, 61). Why? This is, to be sure, the most decisive point, which reminds us that the term, the end, and completion are impossible. If this were not the case, there would be no madness of language but, rather, programs that it would fulfill and that would amount to the same thing each time: reduction to the same. What makes, on the contrary, the madness of language is the irreducible transcendence of what happens [*arrive*] to it, of what comes to it. Every time we speak or write, we are tested by this transcendence; we experience the irreducible alterity of what happens [*arrive*]. And there is no ipseity, no self-relation, outside this test. There is no ipseity constituted beyond the desire to grant rights to this alterity, where in fact it is nevertheless impossible to succeed. Everything occurs as if the interminable constitution of ipseity were always in suspension, suspended from the desire to invent a language, bent on the promise of a language to come.

The invention of one's proper singularity in language thus imposes itself on everyone. Now, what about the relation to law? What about the "man from the country"? If his position before the door is related to a form of madness, which madness is in question? Kafka's story, we said, combines two inaccessibilities of the law: the inaccessibility of the man that stays at its door and to whom the doorkeeper forbids access and the inaccessibility of the narrative itself, which gains no more access to the law than the man from the country. The story is therefore both possible and impossible, legible and illegible, necessary and forbidden, or rather, like most of Kafka's texts, its possibility and legibility are not self-evident. They resist, like the law resists the one wanting to see and touch it, to enter it directly and immediately, without detour. The doorkeeper knows what the man from the country does not know: it is never like that for anyone. The doorkeeper knows that the law, like every text, demands to be deciphered by everyone, *in absolutely singular fashion*. The law, like every narrative, calls for the impossible invention of a language to decipher it. Derrida forcefully emphasizes this:

> Reading a text might indeed reveal that it is untouchable, literally intangible, *precisely because it is readable*, and for the same reason unreadable to the extent to which the presence within it of a clear and graspable sense remains as hidden as its origin. Unreadability thus no longer opposes itself

to readability. Perhaps man is the man from the country as long as he cannot read; or, if knowing how to read, he is still bound up in unreadability within that very thing which appears to yield itself to be read. He wants to see or touch the law, he wants to approach and "enter" it, because perhaps he does not know that the law is not to be seen or touched but deciphered. This is perhaps the first sign of the law's inaccessibility, or of the delay it imposes upon the man from the country. ("Before the Law," 197)

In this invention alone—the invention of a language that deciphers—the hiatus between the generality of the law and the singularity of the relation that everyone maintains with it becomes livable again. Nevertheless, it will not be fulfilled—and for this reason the narrative, although possible and necessary, ultimately remains impossible and forbidden. But one will at least be determined [*se sera-t-on promis*] to make the impossible possible, being certain that any other approach at the doors of the law leads even more surely to the edge of collapse. If we recall the three forms of madness that *Monolingualism of the Other* allowed us to identify retrospectively, it seems, indeed, that neither of the first two are absent from Kafka's story.

The first, the complete destructuration of subjectivity that progressively leads to silence or precipitates more brutally in aphasia, describes quite precisely what happens to the man from the country, and we have perhaps not sufficiently emphasized the way his relation to language evolves as the years pass at the doors of the law. First, he "wearies the doorkeeper by his importunity" ("Before the Law," 3); then, he "curses his bad luck, in his early years boldly and loudly" (3–4). Later, "as he grows old, he only grumbles to himself. He becomes childish" (4). He then remains prostrate, silent. Only a final surge gives him the words to pose his last question: "Everyone strives to reach the Law . . . , so how does it happen that for all these many years no one but myself has ever begged for admittance?" (4). Exhausted, broken, he joins the long line of those that the law, inaccessible and authoritarian, will have broken from within.

Yet, the second form of madness that Derrida describes is no less present in "Before the Law." It is translated by the submission, resignation, acceptance of the codes and the rules, their passive incorporation, which are various ways of wanting, at all cost, to enter the law in order to be one—*(no) more than one* [*plus qu'un*]—with it. It resonates with K.'s madness in *The Trial* and the surveyor's madness in *The Castle*, to which the first readers of Kafka were so sensitive and for which certain among them, such as Günther Anders, went as far as to reproach him. In reality, this form of madness lies in wait for all veneration and all sacralization of the law.

There remains, then, the "excrescence of memory." More closely than the other two forms of madness, their proximity and threat to which the fates of Hölderlin, Nietzsche, and Artaud bear witness, this third form of madness engages, Derrida tells us, "traces of writing, language, experience, which carry anamnesis"—that is to say, the question of the origin and, in particular, the origin of the law, "beyond the mere reconstruction of a given heritage, beyond an available past. Beyond any cartography, and beyond any knowledge that can be taught." This madness comes from an injunction that could have accompanied the doorkeeper's final answer, if it were not too late and if he did not have to shut the door: "[t]his gate was made only for you." Why? Because it demanded a deciphering, a singular invention, a trace of writing—perhaps a story—from he who knocks at the doors of the law. Thus, the injunction is also addressed to the story itself, as an "impossible story of the impossible" (Derrida, "Before the Law," 200). There, where the man from the country demands an immediate reentry into the law, the story attempts in vain to find access through detours, to do the impossible—to make the impossible possible. Derrida recalls:

> In a certain way, *Vor dem Gesetz* is the story [*récit*] of this inaccessibility, of this inaccessibility to the story, the history [*histoire*] of this impossible history, the map of this forbidden path: no itinerary, no method, no path to accede to the law, to what would happen there, to the *topos* of its occurrence [*événement*]. (196)

What are these paths? First, one must recall the role of laughter. One would be wrong, indeed, to neglect the comic thrust and the marks of humor in Kafka's story, which are, no doubt, one way among others *to live with* the law's interdiction. There is first, one recalls, the caricatured description of the doorkeeper that makes one think of the portraits of Ivan the Terrible "in his fur coat, with his big sharp nose and long, thin, black Tartar beard" (Kafka, "Before the Law," 3). Next, there is the petition to the fleas: "[s]ince in his yearlong contemplation of the doorkeeper he has come to know even the fleas in his fur collar, he begs the fleas as well to help him and to change the doorkeeper's mind" (4). Finally, there is perhaps the size difference reversed at the end of the story. To laugh at the inaccessibility of the law, to laugh at and make fun of it through narration in a story where one cannot keep a straight face before this same law—however sovereign, majestic, authoritarian, or mysterious—is already to escape the two forms of madness that were outlined a moment ago: the alienating paralysis and the blind incorporation or its fantasy.

Above all, however, the first path, the path that Kafka's entire oeuvre perhaps exemplifies (not only the stories but also the diaries and the correspondences), is writing itself: writing as postponement [*ajournement*]. No doubt, it comes down to the doorkeeper to notify the man from the country about the ordeal of indefinitely differed access to the law, but this inaccessibility is first the story that gives it form. Indeed, like Scheherazade's tales in *A Thousand and One Nights*, it does nothing other than put *différance* to work or into language—as if, at bottom, the reason for all writing were there, as if the impossible anamnesis of the origin destined us to defer its encounter indefinitely in and through the invention of a language and the resumption of a story, which are so many suspensions of the relation to the law or at least of any relation to the law that would be direct, immediate, frontal. Yes, in the final analysis, it could very well be that our relation to the law and our relation to language join together in this improbable place that we call literature and make the melting pot for all singularity: "For the law is prohibition/prohibited [*interdit*]. [. . . O]ne cannot reach the law, and in order to have a *rapport* of respect with it, *one must not* have a rapport with the law, *one must interrupt the relation*"— like the story does. Derrida continues: "One must *enter into relation* only with the law's representatives, its examples, its guardians. And these are interrupters as well as messengers. We must remain ignorant of who or what or where the law is, we must not know who it is or what it is, where and how it presents itself, whence it comes and whence it speaks" ("Before the Law," 203–4).

It is therefore not surprising that, in the end, Derrida attributes this *différance* of the law to a madness—a laughter, a madness, but perhaps also a subversive desire. For the story opposes to the language of the law, first of all, the singularity of its idiom, shared out to everyone who hears it; it is even, to put it more precisely and without playing on words, the law of this singularity. This is where the subversion lies! Literature "imposes" its law that, before the law, puts it outside the law. It resists the law's resistance in and through the repeated invention of its idiom. There is no other way. This is what the man from the country does not know, the man for whom—final violence—it remains closed.

3
Shares of Singularity[1]
(Celan-Derrida)

In *Ce qui alarma Paul Celan* [*What Alarmed Paul Celan*], a short essay that attempts to understand what, in his last years, disturbed the poet Paul Celan and drove him to take his own life, Yves Bonnefoy recalls that what devastated Celan was not so much the accusation of plagiarism as the misunderstanding and the denial with respect to poetry itself that the accusation supposed. It implied, indeed, that writing a poem can be considered a rhetorical exercise that could be imitated, if not copied or stolen. It denied poetic work the relation to self and to others that challenges all such practices and gives each poem its irreducible singularity, folding that singularity back onto a "conceptual formulation" that can always be reproduced. The alarm, if there was one, came from the fact that such a misrecognition indicated the coming of a strange, if not lost, time for poetry, a time therefore open once again to the most murderous ideological ventures—as if the vocation of poetry were to declare resistance to the violence of those ventures and as if, inversely, the scorn of this destructive accusation constituted the early warning signs of their return.

> Poetry is remarking that most meaning in ordinary speech is lain with traps by conceptual formulations, which implies forgetting the lived time and the character of chance situations that every person has to live. Poetry thus seeks from the beginning to transgress this sort of meaning, opening itself for that purpose to notations that raise the person's depths: which is to live writing as a continuous and irresistible drive from within and which assures in turn that it grasps something irreducibly singular in the poem, although, in being singular, it will only be richer in universal. (Bonnefoy, *Ce qui alarma Paul Celan*, 21)

We return neither to what such a reconstitution, however just, presupposes concerning the relation between conceptual thought and ideology, as if no conceptual work could free itself of ideology, nor to what such a reconstitution seems to decide, without hesitating or trembling, concerning the border separating philosophy and poetry. Rather, we will retain the vigilant attention that it brings to the *singularity* of poetic writing that is at the same time the key or the path of its *universality*. Indeed, it signals toward an enigma, *perhaps a secret*, that no hermeneutical, critical, or philosophical reading of Celan's poetic work has confronted with as much rigor as Derrida's reading: the enigma of a poetic and improbable, if not impossible, link or liaison between singular experience, whatever the trauma, and its universal vocation. In fact, the concept of singularity recurs, as we will see, throughout the first essay that Derrida consecrates to Celan in 1984, "Shibboleth: For Paul Celan." But it can also serve as a guiding thread in the interpretation that Derrida proposes in his last seminar, *The Beast and the Sovereign*, of *The Meridian*, Celan's acceptance speech on the occasion of receiving the Georg Büchner Prize. In the end, during the almost twenty years that separate Derrida's two texts on Celan, few oeuvres will have imposed themselves on Derrida's thought more transversely and more demandingly than Celan's, so true it is that questions of responsibility awaited and called for him, questions on which part of Derrida's work focused as an ethics that radical demands, impossible to uphold, rendered "hyperbolic" and thus, in this way, always aporetic—beginning with those of the secret, of witnessing, or of mourning, but also of hospitality.[2]

I. The Singularity of Dates

What singularity and what universality, what *impossible* tension between the two is in question? First and foremost, the singularity and the universality of each of the dates to which the entirety of the trajectory proposed by "Shibboleth" is dedicated, a trajectory that, unlike the seminar, lingers less on the speech of *The Meridian* and the "Letter to Hans Bender," as Levinas does in "Paul Celan: From Being to the Other," than on other *singular* poems, following the example of Maurice Blanchot, who also dedicates to the poet an essay entitled "The Last to Speak."[3] To read Celan, Derrida recalls, is necessarily to experience such dates. It is to expose oneself to their enigmatic and recurrent presence whose meaning escapes us most of the time, resisting all attempts to interpret, all commentary, however legitimate and "informed" it might be. This resistance is not secondary. Indeed, one must begin by saying that every date is singular. Its inscription in the poem refers each time to an event whose memory and secret that inscription keeps. Even when the date seems familiar to us and we believe we recognize in it the trace of a fact that is not strange or unknown to us, like July 14 or January 20, we cannot be sure about what it commemorates. In claiming the contrary, indeed, nothing guarantees that we do not substitute a common fact for what, on the contrary, has an irreplaceable character, which all singular poetry recalls. Such will always be for Derrida the limits of hermeneutics, and it is no coincidence if, in his homage to Hans-Georg Gadamer in "Rams," he retains from his readings of Celan the moments in which Gadamer admits his indecision. The mention of more or less precise and explicit dates shares the implication of this suspension of univocal deciphering and explication with the insertion of more or less known proper names. Thus, as they appear in the poem, both offer themselves, each time in an exemplary fashion, as the renewed sign of that which links each poem to what Bonnefoy calls "something irreducibly singular." Commenting on the passage of *The Meridian* in which Celan formulates his hypothesis that "each poem has its own '20th of January' inscribed in it" (*The Meridian*, 30a),[4] Derrida can thus write:

> Here is a generality: to the keeping of each poem, of every poem, the inscription of a date, of this date—for example, a "20th of January"—is entrusted. But despite the generality of the law, the example remains irreplaceable. And what must remain, committed to the keeping, in other words, to the truth of each poem, is this irreplaceable itself: the example offers its example only if it is valid for no other. But precisely in that it offers its example, and the only example possible, the one which it alone offers: the only one. ("Shibboleth," 6)

In Celan's language, each poem, he says, singularly keeps the memory of *its* 20th of January. Yet, when Derrida transcribes the phrase in "Shibboleth," the possessive pronoun is replaced with an indefinite article—"*a* '20th of January'"—as if the poem now conserved not only its own proper date, a propriety accessible to no other and not a date in general, but also the constellation of anniversaries that each date carries within it. This substitution is neither random nor accidental. It is anticipation. It outstrips that to which our attention must necessarily turn, namely, singularity's exit outside itself. In Celan's text, this exit resounds in the cry: "But the poem does speak! It stays mindful of its dates, but—it speaks. For sure, it speaks always only on its own, its very own behalf [*in seiner eigenen, allereigensten Sache*]" (*The Meridian*, 31a).

Each time one speaks of singularity, indeed, there is a misinterpretation that must be avoided: confusing invention with the desire for an "encrypted singularization," the bias of a hermeneut that, in the present case, would close poetry off to all readers or, in the words of the poet Osip Mandelstam, every "providential interlocutor" ("About an Interlocutor," 62). As soon as it is inscribed in the poem, the date no doubt keeps its secret, but it also escapes. Addressing anyone that will listen, it undoes anything that could give place to an exclusive or private appropriation, even by the poet. Poetry makes the recollection of dates a collective memory, or at least a memory capable of being shared [*partagée*]. However, in doing so, none of the dividing lines or shares [*lignes de ce partage*] can be decided in advance; that is to say, no predetermined destination can capture or confiscate the memory from the beginning. With respect to his or her poems, the poet does not circumscribe the circle of addressees in advance. He or she does not decide who can or who should hear them, which "people" or community based on language, belief, or culture the poems address. When one supposes or demands the inverse, poetry is never far from bending to the rhetorico-political imperatives of this or that ideology, as Mandelstam painfully experienced when, contrary to the majority of his contemporaries, he refused to submit to the pressures of the political and literary authorities of his time.[5] As Celan knew better than anybody, the history of the last century is, finally, made of these thousand and one anniversary dates, the celebration and commemoration of which were imposed, even violently, *on everyone*.

At stake is an other sharing out [*partage*], an unprecedented, unheard-of and, one might say, poetic sharing out of singularity. Reading Celan, Derrida ceaselessly explored its aporetic paths. When he wrote "Shibboleth" in 1984, his reflections had not yet centered on the concept of responsibility or, with it, the new thought of the possible and the impossible, that is, the vocation of making possible the impossible that, some years later, would define responsibility in the course of his work on hospitality, the secret, testimony, or forgiveness. He does not yet broach, as he will in *The Beast and the Sovereign*, the phrase that somewhat concludes the speech of *The Meridian* in which Celan defines the route that poetry traces as an "impossible route," the "route of the impossible" (50a). And yet, it is already a question of such a challenge of the impossible with this tension between, on the one hand, the singularity of every date and, on the other, the demands of sharing out implied by its poetic inscription. In a time weighed down by so many commemorations—individual and collective, intimate and public—there is no poetic work *today*, Celan writes, that can avoid the burden of remembering dates, which is the mark of singularity. But this task makes sense, as such, only if their inscription signals towards all those that such a "providential interlocutor" could understand. Their singularity thus *must*—this is its law—open onto the singularity of other dates. Better, it is itself singular only in the secret of this opening—what

Celan calls "the secret of the encounter."[6] It is thus divided between a secret and a call, between what it encrypts and what it offers. The whole question, then, consists in knowing how such an aporetic division is possible.

In any case, it is *necessary*. What poetry maintains, as certainly as it keeps the memory of *these* dates, what it confirms in the second half of a century haunted by the memory of the most terrible dates—above all January 20, the date, among other things, of the Wannsee Conference where a decision was made to exterminate European Jews in death camps—what poetry restates to all that can hear is that every singular existence is a fabric of dates and anniversaries that links us to the living and the dead. We do not live otherwise. As Celan recalls: "But don't we all write ourselves from such dates? And toward what dates do we write ourselves?" (*Meridian*, 30b).

Living with others is necessarily relating to *their* dates that require attention and sometimes even help, like the help Celan wanted to give Nelly Sachs with his poems. That is why, among the multiple forms of violence, insult, and outrage that can victimize everyone and deny them in their singularity, one must count those that can be done to *one's* dates: organizing forgetfulness, denying anniversaries, erasing traces. And we know, through numerous testimonies and his correspondences, that such forms of violence were not foreign to "what alarmed Celan." Supposing this to be the path of responsibility in the Derridean sense of the term, responsibility consequently displaces the weight of the date. The singular in a poem is not so much *its* proper dates as the way it encounters on their basis, like a miraculous inscription, other dates, *the dates of others*. But why speak of aporia? Derrida emphasizes the difficulty in a whole series of questions:

> [h]ow can such an *other* date, irreplaceable and singular, the date of the other, the date for the other, be deciphered, transcribed, or translated? How can I appropriate it for myself? Or, better, how can I transcribe myself into it? And how can the memory of such a date still dispose of a to-come [*avenir*]? What dates to come [*à venir*] do we prepare in such a transcription? (84)

To say "the poem does speak" is to grant rights to the encounter that is incalculable in the sense that it cannot be programmed—referring, as we saw, to no circle or community, to no determined people. It cannot be immured in a language that would be invoked and convoked as the property of a "we" circumscribed in advance. We understand better, then, how the articulation of singularity and universality can be thought. On the basis of a singular date's inscription, concerning which there is no reason and no need to imagine in advance that the *undetermined* interlocutor should have or even acquire knowledge, the poem *opens itself* to other dates that it does not know either. It hangs by a thread between two abysses: "pure singularity" ("Shibboleth," 9) that speaks to no one and generality that does violence to all singularity. Every date thus bears within itself *more than one* event, and we do not read it otherwise. These events form the date's utopic constellation, its proper time and space: the unpredictable and always promised to-come [*avenir*] of its repetition as the providential character of interlocution. Between these two abysses, the poem searches and traces its path, a median route, the shares of singularities [*partage des singularités*] that Celan names a meridian and to which Derrida, for his part, gives another name borrowed from the poet: the name, precisely, "Shibboleth."

II. The Time of the Other

Almost twenty years after writing "Shibboleth," Derrida will have returned to "the secret of the encounter" in *The Beast and the Sovereign*, the last of the seminars that the philosopher will have consecrated to questions of responsibility at the École des hautes études en sciences sociales. The route that he takes then is a more methodical reading of Celan's speech, *The Meridian*. And because, over the course of his seminars, the thought of responsibility that imposes itself defines responsibility, each time it is engaged, as the unconditional and, in this way, hyperbolic demand of making the impossible possible, because one could not speak of justice without taking care of such a demand, Derrida begins his reading at the end of the speech:

> Ladies and gentlemen, I find something that consoles me a little for having in your presence taken this impossible route, this route of the impossible.
>
> I find what connects and leads, like the poem, to an encounter.
>
> I find something—like language—immaterial, yet terrestrial, something circular that returns to itself across both poles while—cheerfully—even crossing the tropics: I find . . . a *meridian*. (*The Meridian*, 50a-c)

So, this "impossible path," which is that of poetry and perhaps more generally of all literature insofar as it is exposed to violence, is at the same time a "route of the impossible." It is both at once. In other words, it traces the path that, always in a singular way, makes the impossible possible. But what possibility and what impossibility are in question here? Nothing less that what we are trying to think here in the name of "shares of singularity." Yet, there again, a misunderstanding must be dispelled. Indeed, such a sharing out does not mean the movement by which a sovereign singularity would "express itself" in the poem, by consigning its dates to it, for example, before generously offering itself to others. If an impossibility is at stake, it is precisely because such a path does not in the least satisfy the ethical *and* poetic ("po-ethic," one might say) demand that we recalled a moment ago. It perhaps prevails in a certain conception of art, which motivates "puppeteer" artists that want at all costs to exhibit themselves in their art—but it is not the path of poetry in the sense that Celan understands it. And it is no coincidence if the reading that Derrida proposes of it is inscribed, finally, within the frame of a deconstruction of sovereignty: the singularity that has been in question from the beginning is not and, indeed, cannot be that of a sovereign artist whose "genius" would come to awaken or reawaken, to clarify or to guide, a given "people" or "community."

What, then, is it about? And how does it concern the test of violence that serves as our guiding thread through these various chapters? The three "returns" that Derrida subsequently undertakes in his reading of Celan's speech are a way of recalling this relation while advancing on the path of this *possibilization of the impossible*;[7] they are, in other words, three ways of understanding how the encounter with the time of the other, the sharing out of his or her dates, opens *its impossible path*. At stake first is an *other* sovereignty. Further on, the author of *The Beast and the Sovereign* comes back to the attention Celan pays to the cry that Georg Büchner, in his play *Danton's Death*, expresses through Lucile, the wife of Camille Desmoulins; at the foot of the scaffold where the executioner awaits her husband, she cries: "Long live the King!" Celan describes this cry, indeed, as homage to "the majesty of the absurd as witness for the presence of the human [*die Gegenwart des Menschlichen zeugenden Majestät des Absurden*]" (*The Meridian*, 8c).

To understand how this "homage," in which the author of *The Meridian* recognizes poetry, specifies what we are attempting to think here in the name of "poetic sharing out of singularity," we must imagine the scene at the Place de Grève: the crowd's excitation at the spectacle of the execution, the hollow words and grandiloquent commentaries, all those gestures and words that, in one way or another, remain inappropriate, maladapted, like the majority of things that we do and say, individually or collectively, when we are confronted with violence, carried off by its manifestations or powerless to counter them. And we must, then, weigh not only every word that, in opposition, refuses to succumb to the facilities of language, those verbal furies that excite the taste for murder, vengeance, and the fascination with death, but also every gesture, attitude, and posture that counters it. For, in reality, we are saying three things about this homage. First, it means that there is no signature of a poem that is not an "idiomatic" invention of singularity—that does not, in other words, take on the risk, in and with language, of unfolding against grandiose judgments and their collective tribunals. If the notion of the idiom imposes itself here, it is because it refers to the necessity of a gap, a difference, a sidestep that defies the facility, cowardice, or stupidity [*bêtise*] of speaking or crying *in unison*, the temptation of barking with the dogs and howling with the wolves. Without the invention of idioms, there is room only for repetition, the conventional reproduction of mechanical cries and ready-made words like those of the "'bystanders'" (*The Meridian*, 7b) that gather at the foot of the scaffold and cannot speak grandly or humbly enough of history, politics, and death. Hence, this approach of poetry first tells us that it is a "counterword" (7b). Next, it reminds us that this signature engages a responsibility of both a secret and a testimony: the poet's word is a witness to a presence of the human that is stronger than terror, death, and the fascination they incite. This is its wager, its challenge, its fortune or misfortune, as a certain constellation of brothers and sisters in poetry knew so well: Osip Mandelstam, Marina Tsvetaieva, Ingeborg Bachmann, and Nelly Sachs. Finally, the last thing specified in this relation between Lucile's cry and a poem is that the attestation of the majesty of a present is always at stake in both—a present to which one can attest only through displacement and, as Derrida emphasizes, "upping the ante" with respect to sovereignty:

> Celan's gesture... is a gesture that consists in placing one majesty above another, and thus upping the ante [*s'engager dans une surenchère*] with respect to sovereignty. An upping that attempts to change the meaning of majesty or sovereignty, to make its meaning mutate, while keeping the old word or while claiming to give it back its most dignified meaning. (*The Beast and the Sovereign*, 230)

Now, we already know that this upping the ante does not, cannot, and must not come from excesses of singularity, that it has nothing to do with the vertigo of hermetic introspection closed on itself or, more generally, with all the mythologies surrounding the artist that, like the cult of the "genius," will have nourished the fantasy; rather, it comes entirely from singularity's sharing out. If there is an upping the ante, it can come only *from the other*, from the time and the dates of the other. This is why poetry participates in the deconstruction of sovereignty, where the latter is always a source of violence. And this is also no doubt the reason for that secret affinity that Derrida ceaselessly felt between Celan's poetic approach and his thought of responsibility. This is what indicates the second "return" in his reading of *The Meridian*. There, the reading lingers on another definition of poetry: "Then the poem is—even more clearly than previously—one person's language-become-shape, and, according to its essence, presentness and presence" (*The Meridian*, 33d; cited by Derrida in *The Beast and the Sovereign*, 231).

That the poem is "one person's language" should be understood first in a political sense that recalls what connects poetic writing to the demand of a "radical individuation" (*The Meridian*, 33b). This individuation, indeed, signals toward [*vers*] that form of sovereignty that is the verso [*envers*] of all allegiance. Contrary to any "speculation" on the historical and fateful mission of a poet—contrary, in particular, to every interpretation of poetry that Martin Heidegger deploys in his commentary on the hymns of Friedrich Hölderlin[8]—a poem attests first and foremost to the presence of a joint solitude and singularity. It resists every renewal in a given affiliation, all immurement in or withdrawal into a community, all targeted connivance that would come to breach or compromise its universal and undetermined scope. Nevertheless, this solitude and singularity do not go without saying. The poet does not maintain the word that *takes form* there by himself, by his talent or his imagination, by his genius or interiority, for they do not explain much and, in any case, do not suffice to account for this "present" and "presence" that Celan emphasizes. So, whence the poem's "becoming-form"? To whom or to what is it due? This is where Derrida's third return intervenes. In *The Meridian*, the sentence upon which Derrida comments follows shortly after the one on which he had previously focused:

> The poem wants to head toward some other, it needs this other, it needs an opposite. It seeks it out, it bespeaks itself to it.
>
> Each thing, each human is, for the poem heading toward this other, a figure of this. (35a–b)

Poetry is a privileged path for facing the test of violence because the radical individuation that it supposes and that gives the poem's "here and now" its content can "become shape" only by letting itself be called, solicited, traversed, and shaken by *the time of the other* in a dialogue, which Celan says often causes him despair. If a majesty of the present is at stake in poetry, poetry is necessarily and constitutively decentered, excentered, disappropriated by the time of the other. This is why it is a witness to human presence. That which is human cannot be reduced to a monologue, to the speech of one alone, of a sovereign subject, artist or otherwise. And yet, poetry is most often confused with such monologue, not without violence, as one way among others to stage the self, a variant of self-presentations, self-valorizations, and egotistical promotions that make this same speech a source of satisfaction and an instrument of domination. It therefore testifies not to gods in retreat or the disappearance of the sacred but, rather, to *that other loss*, essential otherwise, a failure to witness the human, which probably alarmed Paul Celan more than anyone else. It attests, at risk of despair, to the imperative necessity of a counterword that evades the thousand and one traps that transform the use of language into a "self-affirmation": the illusion of a sovereignty assured of and closed on itself. Every time we speak, as a consequence, the risk is not sinking into idle chatter but, rather, into the forgetfulness and the brutal denial of all attention to the time of the other, that is, of the *gathering, being-together*, and the shares of singularity that is a witness to human presence.

> Even in this here and now of the poem—for the poem itself, we know, has always only this one, unique, momentary present—even in this immediacy and nearness it lets the most essential aspect of the other speak: its time. (*The Meridian*, 36b)

Derrida comments upon this passage in the following terms:

> What the poem allows to speak . . . is the time of the other, *its* time in what is most proper to it: the most proper and therefore the most untranslatably other of the time of the other. (*The Beast and the Sovereign*, 233)

Nothing is simple, however, because nothing less than two terms of an antimony are outlined here. In a sense, indeed, Celan's previous injunction refers to a responsibility inseparable from its poetics: that of hospitality. The time of the other is a time that poetry lets come, that it welcomes and takes in [*accueille et recueille*], *who or what comes* [*son arrivant*]. The very term "collection [*recueil*]," as in a "collection of poetry," finds here a triple dimension: two times that of a gathering (the gathering of poems and that of the time of the other) and once that of concentration and attention (the very ones connoted by the reflexive form of the verb "to collect one*self* [*se recueillir*])," in other words, the collecting that this *other time* demands every time, in every poem, and for everyone. At the same time, however, what is most proper to this time also proves to be irreducibly untranslatable. As soon as one attempts to summarize, interpret, judge, and, finally, translate it with one's own words in a language that is not its own, one does violence to it. The following question thus imposes itself: can one welcome the time of the other as other, without deforming it, "translate" it into one's own idiom without betraying it? If it is true that we come up against an aporia here, the aporia is what makes the encounter an "impossible route" or, again, "the route of the impossible." The ethics of poetry is thus *its* test of translation. What is impossible and what poetry *strives* asymptotically to make possible without ever totally succeeding is the translation of the untranslatable: "the most proper and therefore the most untranslatably other of the time of the other," its irreducible and, by that very fact, inaccessible singularity. This is why Celan writes that the poem "stands fast at the edge of itself" (*The Meridian*, 32b) and, continuing a little further on, "[t]he absolute poem—no, that certainly does not exist, cannot exist!" (38c).

Yet, this impossible path is a necessary path because, if sharing out singularity names both the gift of time and the partition of the same time between a "proper" present and the present of the other,9 it means that there is no singularity, as such, that is not divided, engaged in and by its own *différance*. Singularity is such only in and through what separates it, divides it, differentiates it from itself. And because this movement always requires another language, an "idiomatic invention," this question of the untranslatable, of an untranslatable time *that must nevertheless be translated*, is also, as we will have understood, the question of the idiom.

III. Circumcision of the Word

With Lucile's cry, we have seen that poetry can already be defined as a "counterword" distinguished by its "rupture," but this is not enough. It "cuts the 'string,'" and it is thus an "act of freedom"; it marks "a step" (*The Meridian*, 7b). This string, as all readers of Celan know, is first the string of the German language that, at the very moment when the rest was lost, was *the only thing left* of Germany—as the author of *No One's Rose* recalls in his "Speech on the Occasion of Receiving the Literature Prize of the Free Hanseatic City of Bremen":

> Only one thing remained reachable, close and secure amid all losses: language. Yes, language. In spite of everything, it remained secure against loss. But it had to go through its own lack of answers, through terrifying silence, through the thousand darknesses of murderous speech. It went

through. It gave me no words for what was happening, but went through it. Went through and could resurface, "enriched" by it all. (34)

Language was not lost, but it could not remain intact because it had been obscured by so many murderous injunctions. As a consequence, it was indeed necessary for the heritage of language to inscribe a sort of clearing or caesura, suspensions, interruptions, or discontinuity in its very body, semantically as much as syntactically. Derrida did not fail to recall this point in an interview entitled, "Language Is Never Owned." Echoing Lucile's "counterword," he interprets Celan's relation to the German language as a "counter-signature," according to which Celan—author of "Todesfuge" ("Death Fugue"), "Chymisch" ("Alchemical"), "Aschenglorie" ("Ashglory"), and so many other poems inscribed since then in a "poetic inheritance of German culture"—ceaselessly imposed on language a scar, a mark, a wound, so many forceful blows that each poem would launch not only against forgetfulness, of course, but also against the denial of what had happened to it and compromised it forever. The "enrichment" of language in the most murderous and desperate way possible had no other meaning. It consisted in making incisions in German with another language, imposing upon it, for example (but much more than an example is at stake), the memory, trace, charge, and responsibility of other idioms and other cultures—beginning with those that the Nazis had doomed to destruction. Derrida thus takes care to emphasize the crossing and intermediaries:

> there is in his writing quite an extraordinary crossing—almost in the genetic sense of the term—of cultures, references, literary memories, always in the mode of extreme condensation, caesura, ellipsis, and interruption. ("Language Is Never Owned," 100)

"Shibboleth" already measured the extent of this multiplicity and migration of languages and cultures. Both undo borders; they inscribe directly in the poem the refusal to subscribe to the partition of affiliations with which the name Babel is identified. Language, a given language, belongs to no determined community. The poem solicits its own alliance against this partition, an alliance foreign to every appropriation: the very one created by sharing out singularity, the unpredictable and "providential" universality of dates and names. *Monolingualism of the Other* would suffice to prove that Derrida is attentive to such "dis-appropriation," that is to say, the perilous inscription of a multiplicity of languages in poetic writing or, further, the *idiomatic heterogenization of language* that this writing implies.

While he was writing "Shibboleth" in 1984, the question of the idiom was not yet at the heart of his reflections. Another ten years or so would be necessary for the question of the idiom to come untie and displace, as an unheard-of thought of *the language of the other* and the *arrival of the other in language*, the threads that mix and confuse maternal language, so-called "national" language, proper language, and linguistic, cultural, and political affiliations.¹⁰ And yet, everything already signals toward what will give his reflections on language their most decisive impetus in the important book from 1995: there is no being-in-language that does not imply the singular invention of an idiom, but the idiom is never the fact of a sovereign subject assured of mastery or the possession of his or her language. If one only ever speaks one language, it nevertheless always comes *from the other*. The idiom exists only in its exposure to the arrival of who or what comes [*l'arrivée de l'arrivant*]—Celan would say "encounter."

To speak of "the other's language," as we here managed to speak of "the other's dates," comes down to radically displacing the stakes of the reflection on "poetry's language." It is a question not so much of thinking what happens to language *in general* as of understanding what becomes of it singularly in each poem. This is why, although lacking the later thought of the idiom, the question is not absent from the analyses of "Shibboleth," which use singularity as a guiding thread. It is even conclusive, in the sense that it occupies the seventh and final movement of the essay. There, it concerns what Derrida attempts to understand and to analyze under the enigmatic title of "circumcision of a word."

Circumcise: the word, as is known, comes here from Celan, who makes this circumcision an injunction. More precisely, it comes from the poem "To one who stood outside the door [*Einem der vor der Tür stand*]": "to him / circumcised the word [*Diesem, / beschneide das Wort*]" (Celan, *Glottal Stop*, 9, translation modified). What does it mean "to circumcise the word"? Is it to open it, to promise it to an other, for the other, at the risk of murdering it, to open it as one opens the door to who or what comes [*l'arrivant*]? Is it a condition of the "becoming-poetic of the word"? And is it what the "breathturn" in the speech of *The Meridian* (29b) designates? All these questions precipitate in the final pages of "Shibboleth" to give the book's eponymous title, in the very place where it guards its part of the enigma, its ultimate meaning.

> This word of opening permits one to pass through the doorway. It is yet another *shibboleth*, the *shibboleth* at the origin of all the others, yet still one among others, *in a given language*.

> The shibboleth is given or promised by *me* (*mein Wort*) to the singular other, "this one," that he may partake [*partage*] of it and enter, or leave, that he may pass through the doorway, across the line, the border, the threshold.
>
> But this word, given or promised, in any case, opened, offered to the other, also asks. ("Shibboleth," 61)

In this chapter, guided by a reading that crosses Celan's poetics and Derrida's commentary, it has been a question of understanding how poetry opposes and resists violence. And the hypothesis advanced from the beginning is that each poem does so by *openly sharing* singularity [ouvrant *un partage de la singularité*] such that, far from presupposing a given form of partition, exclusion, or withdrawal based on some identification with a community, it on the contrary *calls* for unpredictable alliances, inseparably demanding and bringing help. This care of the other is its prayer and blessing. And if it is true that the poems bear direct witness to this prayer and blessing, Celan's letters to Nelly Sachs, to Iliana Schmuëli, and to Ingeborg Bachmann confirm, for their part, that they are the truth of what, for Celan, must be given and received in poetry at the very moment when the memory of the most extreme violence, the madness of its nightmare and the haunting of its return, remained a wound. Celan addressed his poems to them as a response to their torment and as a sign of listening, of the attention and concentration that the ordinary and hurried use of language most often scorns: the renewed witnessing of the presence and present of the human. This prayer and blessing are a helping hand—and the "Shibboleth" is concentrated in them. The circumcision of the word named by Derrida, then, is nothing other than what assures its inscription in language. It recalls four things: (1) it makes an incision in the body of language as an opening to the time of the other, to the call of wounds and their dates; (2) this opening is the condition of legibility; (3) this opening's apportioning [*partage*] is thus the alliance of attention, care, and help; (4) finally, unlike every other word, this being-together in poetry comes from never presupposing, ordering, or decreeing any exclusion—this is its ethics.

4

On a Constellation
(Levinas, Derrida, Blanchot, Readers of Celan)

The movement of thought, at a moment in its history, is a sharing of singularities [*un partage de singularités*]. The trajectories composing the movement of thought trace their path, visible or invisible, through the constellation of singular works that these singularities encounter and interpellate, that they cite and upon which they comment, to which they choose to *respond*, in order to move forward. Each of the proper names comprising these trajectories outlines its singularity, whether it keeps it secret by erasing the debts or turns its disclosure into *the step* that must be taken. At times, from one work to another, these singularities intersect. In a common time and place, *more than one* singular approach then finds itself in the shared study of a third work. They submit, *together*, to the injunction of a reading that becomes constitutive of their mutual inclusion in the same epoch. In France, in the course of the twentieth century, the reception of the works of Hegel, Nietzsche, Husserl, and Heidegger no doubt imposed itself in this way on one such generation. Much later, the reception of Wittgenstein, Arendt, Benjamin, and Rosenzweig. Almost always, these shared readings demand crossing borders and passing through linguistic barriers, thanks to translation, in defiance of all geographical partitions and any indexing of thought according to determined cultural, linguistic, or national spheres.

Few singular oeuvres have testified to and reaffirmed the demand for such a movement between books and languages as Derrida's oeuvre. With every new step in thinking, Derrida's work restates its attachment to the living memory of texts that, *in the present and in the future,* every constellation outlines. And this is the way everyone reads it, following its trace in the confrontation with, among so many others, Plato, Kant, Hegel, Nietzsche, Husserl, Freud, or Benjamin, but also Mallarmé, Artaud, or Valéry. Reading some of these thinkers and poets is a unique and always decisive moment of the trajectory. Others will be taken up again and again.

Among the latter, certain names impose themselves: Heidegger, with whom Derrida ceaselessly debates [s'expliquer], and Celan, Levinas, and Blanchot, whom he discusses and comments upon, but also invokes and calls to for help more and more insistently in the last twenty years of his work. Celan, Levinas, and Blanchot: three stars in Derrida's constellation with a common trait, namely, that the author of *Being and Time*, with his shadows and flashes of light, resides at the heart of the confrontation proper to each.

Vertigo of intersections and reciprocal calls, from one trajectory to another. For if Heidegger's thought ceaselessly calls out to Levinas and Blanchot, they, too, have crossed the voice of Celan, each one singularly, on the path of this dialogue. Like a critical corner wedged into the reception of the Heideggerian texts dedicated to language and poetry, and in particular to Hölderlin's hymns, there will have been since the late 1970s a growing place occupied by readings of Celan's poems, as well as his "Conversations in the Mountains," his speech in *The Meridian*, his "Speech" at Bremen, and his "Letter to Hans Bender." Not everything in the encounter of these texts was destined to disrupt what Heidegger's thinking and René Char's hearing managed to impose upon both philosophers and poets as the "essence" or the "truth" of poetry; it is even certain that what is essential does not lie there. Yet, beyond what poetry might have signified for each one singularly, it will have had this effect, tracing the path of a distance with no return.

I.

Now, the first thing that must be said concerning this distance is that it is not without relation to the memory of the extreme violence of the Second World War, beginning first of all with the extermination of European Jews for which Heidegger, reader of Hölderlin, Rilke, and Trakl, never found the words. And this also likely explains why the deliberate distance from the poetics deployed in these approaches ineluctably carries the shadow of the war. In the very place where everything remains painfully fragile, one understands, finally, why no one dedicated him- or herself directly to this intersecting and conflicting attentiveness [écoute] and to the paths that it helps clear with as much attention as Levinas. In fact, in a short text entitled *Paul Celan: From Being to the Other*, the author of *Otherwise than Being: Or Beyond Essence* does not miss the opportunity to recall, not without irony, everything that divides the approach to poetry that one finds in *The Meridian* from Heidegger's thought. To understand the divide, one need only take stock of Celan's famous affirmation, so often discussed, that he sees no "difference"—because there is none—"between a handshake and a poem" ("Letter," in *Collected Prose*, 26). Reading the "advice" in the "Letter to Hans Bender" where this analogy is found, one is likely driven to retain everything that such a comparison *positively* signifies, and Levinas will not fail to do so. But one must also recall the negative determination that it entails. First of all, indeed, it tells us that the way the poem *makes* sense exceeds what it *says* and *does* with language. Far from having as its "truth" or for its primary function the revelation of the essence of language or, further, the call of mortals back to its sacrality, the poem suspends its precedence; it takes a *step*[1] beyond this supposed "sacrality" and its "elevation." It knocks it from its pedestal, putting it back in its place, which is not first:

> There is the poem, the height of language [*langage achevé*], reduced to the level of an interjection, a form of expression as undifferentiated as a wink, a sign to one's neighbor! A sign of what? Of life, of goodwill? Of complicity? Or a sign of nothing, or of complicity for no reason: a saying without a said. Or is it a sign that is its own signified: the subject signals that sign-giving to the point of becoming a sign through and through. (Levinas, "Paul Celan," 40)

In other words, Levinas emphasizes the paradox of the equation that Celan proposes. On the one hand, the height of language is nowhere more manifest than in a poem or, even more precisely, in each poem read singularly, in the economy of its rhythm, its syntax and semantics, its ruptures and silences. No practice, perhaps, requires more craft, greater precision or therefore a greater formal completion or achievement [*achèvement*], an accomplishment such that no sign could be added or taken away without breaking the balance. Celan himself does not deny it. If, however, he concedes to Hans Bender in the same letter in that there is indeed "craft" (*Handwerk*) in a writer's work, he immediately displaces this craftwork on language (or *poiein*) to a "matter of hands" (*Sache der Hände*), playing on the etymology of the word *Handwerk* (Celan, "Letter" in *Collected Prose*, 25–26). On the one hand, then, there is no greater "height" of language. Yet, on the other hand, the latter is nowhere more dethroned and desacralized than in a poem. Nowhere are the signs clearer that it does not have its end in itself.

And yet, as we saw, the poem is not a means for a poetic, sovereign subject, assured of his or her gift and powers. It is not in the service of some genius or mysterious interiority, the depths and contradictions of which could be explored through the poem, no more than it is in the service of an intercessor between gods and the men singularly chosen to fulfill a universal mission. Nothing, however, is more anchored in our most enduring and common representations of poetry. Everything leads us, everything pushes us, to redirect the poems that we read to the exceptional singularity of their author. Almost without realizing it, we bend to the play of this appropriation and identification without resistance. In the poem's language, we search and think we find traces of the poet, of *his* or *her* voice, *his* or *her* face, *his* or *her* vision, *his* or *her* singular outlook. Moreover, we normally do the same thing with respect to every other word received, and we expect as much from *others*; indeed, we count on it, anticipate and beg for it every time we speak: to be recognized for what we are, what we believe ourselves *to be*, or what we would like *to appear* to be.

Is this law of language that carries violence to the heart of speech ineluctable? Are we doomed, every time we speak, to want to dominate or to submit to the domination of others? Are we still exposed to the mask of force? Have the words that we exchange ever allowed us to move beyond ourselves and the fiction, fantasy, or culture of a sovereign self or ego, for whom words would be the weapons of existence? In whose eyes? The eyes of *others*? And if, to finish with these questions, we are to this extent entangled and locked in, burdened and weighed down by, what we ceaselessly want to say *about ourselves to others*, does poetry speak in unison? Unless one must say that, on the contrary, what distinguishes poetry is the *tension* that turns it around, orients and directs it in the opposite direction. This is its only, its most essential rigor and its first demand: to extend a hand, to give it against all expectations and even before seeking to make oneself known. This extended hand is the "breathturn" (Celan, *The Meridian*, 29b). We would thus have to recognize in each poem the fact that, far from favoring a given sovereign affirmation of any order on which one might think it (ingenious, inspired, or divine), it would accomplish each time a *step back*, a reversal of every position of the order of sovereignty. This is no doubt what Celan recalls to Hans Bender: "I remember telling you that once the poem is really *there*, the poet is dismissed, is no longer privy" ("Letter," 25).

II.

Yet, in *The Meridian*, as we saw in the previous chapter, Celan also locates the significance of attention in Lucile's cry, "Long live the King!," heard as the "counterword" (6c–7b) of one who knows it is useless to *hear oneself speak* or to stage an "ego-statement" in grand speeches harmonizing with the expectations of history or the audience. We then recalled another voice, before Levinas's but already in the same constellation: the voice of Derrida, who interrogated this passage, one will remember, in a session of his last seminar, *The Beast and the Sovereign*. As Derrida explains, presenting Lucile's cry simultaneously as an "[h]omage . . . to the majesty of the absurd" and as a "witness for the presence of the human" (*The Meridian*, 8c), Celan accomplished a gesture that radically displaces the meaning of whatever "sovereignty" there might be in the poetic act. It was already significant that poetry should be identified with a cry and not with a long speech, even less with an exercise in rhetorical oratory, with the cry, moreover, of the one who speaks the least, that is, the one who listens more than she speaks and who seems to be a stranger to all the grand and decisive things being said. It signaled, once again and against all expectations, that the alleged mastery of language or any mastery whatsoever—of language, tropes, or figures—does not constitute poetry's sovereignty. And one recalls that the question then became discerning the order of this *other* sovereignty. Where does it come from? It does not reside in self-affirmation, and yet all poetry is "absolutely" singular. It does not pertain to linguistic mastery, and yet nothing of what it does to and in language is incidental for countering violence. If it is true that a poem amounts to a witness for the human, human presence thus can be identified with neither the subject nor language. This is, at least, what it bears witness to. And it does so insofar as its signature is at stake, that is to say, insofar as it takes on a responsibility. In Büchner's play, finally, nothing distinguishes Lucile's cry from the speeches on the condemned, speeches that Celan calls "many artful words" (*The Meridian*, 6b), more than that for which or those for whom the speeches are held responsible. In distinction from the heroic words that, like "going-together-into-death" (*The Meridian*, 6b), commit to nothing other than the admiration that they attempt to incite, Lucile's "Long live the King!" gives its word [*est une parole qui engage*]. But for whom and for what, to whom and why, is it responsible?

This question leads us back into the steps of Levinas. For it is already in the name of a responsibility, the responsibility to one's neighbor, that he reads the "Letter to Hans Bender" and *The Meridian* as the witness of a poetic language that knows, as assuredly as one can, that its meaning is not, not primarily or essentially, in the truth of being. If one only follows his analysis, such is the significance, in the end, of the analogy that would have the poem do nothing more essential than extend or give a hand:

> A language of proximity for proximity's sake, older than that of "the truth of being"—which it probably carries and sustains—the first of the languages, response preceding the question, responsibility for the neighbor, by its *for the other*, the whole marvel of giving. (Levinas, "Paul Celan," 41)

Will Levinas and Derrida have heard and understood each other, will they have gotten along [*se seront-ils entendus*], when they read and comment upon *The Meridian*? Will they have spoken about it with each other or, separately, with Blanchot? Blanchot, the first to devote a text to the author of *No One's Rose* in a 1972 issue of *La Revue de Belles-Lettres* devoted to Celan: "The Last to Speak."² What were the singular paths, visible and subterranean, of such likely sharing? No doubt they existed, because there is no constellation without friendship. Life in books gathers people around a few oeuvres, people that know that these oeuvres build invisible bridges between them. On their library shelves, for each reader, a given title calls to the name of friends that preceded, accompanied, or joined in the reading. The history of thought is made from these exchanges. This gives the congresses, colloquia, conferences, and other seminars, like those that brought Derrida and Levinas together on occasion or those that gather other philosophers around their oeuvres, the little bit of meaning that they have left, reprieving their vanity. The passages leading to the site of the encounter are also at times more secret. But between Levinas and Derrida, who read and commented upon each other frequently, one thing is certain: *the thought of responsibility* is the bridge that unites their respective readings of Celan. This thought reverses, for Levinas, the meaning or direction [*sens*] of the analogy between a poem and a handshake, which we have not left behind. For, if it is true that the analogy implies, not without irony, the "fall" of poetry, henceforth desacralized, into what is most ordinary, common and "quotidian" but also perhaps most *otherwise* "authentic" in being together, this "plummet" does not exhaust its significance. It turns into the opposite, provided that we understand, precisely, that *nothing* is less evident and more imperative than a "sign to one's neighbor" (Levinas, "Paul Celan," 40). *Nothing* demands more tension, the very tension that characterizes Celan's writing with its blanks, silences, ellipses, and interruptions, than this "sign of nothing" or "complicity for no reason" (40) signified by, among other things, a handshake. In other words, in the very words of "Tübingen, Jänner" from *No One's Rose*, which evokes the memory of Hölderlin, it is less common to babble than to speak.³

III.

For responsibility resides in babbling this "sign of nothing." The entire force of Levinas's reading thus consists in clarifying this babbling with a few words from what constitutes one of the central themes of *Otherwise than Being*: "A sign of what? Of life, of goodwill? Of complicity? Or a sign of nothing, or of complicity for no reason: a saying without a said" ("Paul Celan," 40). Levinas will say hardly anything else on this point, suspending the explication with the fleeting insertion of a "saying without a said," as if he wanted only to indicate in passing, with the utmost reserve, the path that a reader could take in order to understand how Celan's poetry will have been inscribed, next to a few others, in his own constellation.4 There will be other signs that, just as brief and discrete as this one, will similarly efface themselves behind what Levinas calls "*The Meridian*'s vibrant formulas" ("Paul Celan," 40)—beginning with the following, which it is up to each reader to read, if she or he so desires, while recalling the analyses of saying and subjectivity in *Otherwise than Being*:

> The poem moves in one bound out in front of that other whom it presumes reachable, able to be set free, vacant perhaps . . . (*The Meridian*, 31f; quoted in Levinas, "Paul Celan," 41)

> The poem becomes dialogue, is often an impassioned dialogue, . . . meetings, paths of a voice toward a vigilant Thou. (*The Meridian*, 36a–b; quoted in Levinas, "Paul Celan," 42)

> . . . the poem speaks! Of the date that is its own . . . of the unique circumstances that properly concerns it. (*The Meridian*, 31a; quoted in Levinas, "Paul Celan," 42)5

The poem, "a saying without a said": vertigo of reading. For we can follow Levinas in attempting to understand, in light of the thought of such "saying without a said," how the poem moves out in front of the other, or we can traverse the inverse path and exemplify, on the basis of poetry, the responsibility of this saying. Whether we cross the bridge in one direction or another, indeed, we find Heidegger's "word that speaks" at the crossroads, that word whose poem as Celan understands or hears [*entend*] it in *The Meridian* and whose "saying without a said" as Levinas thinks it in *Otherwise than Being* should then be understood as the "counterstatement" like Lucile's cry. We recall that Celan makes this cry a witness for "human presence"—and because it is a question of such witnessing, according to Derrida, every poetic signature takes on a responsibility. But the "saying without a said" also refers to a testimony of this order, as it redirects every word to the responsibility of an address, before any determined content of signification and, therefore, before any constituted knowledge of or about the other, which is always prone to becoming a judgment and to bearing by that very fact the shadow of a potential violence. Levinas recalls this in a decisive passage from *Otherwise than Being* that strangely resonates with his reading of *The Meridian* speech, as if it were in this resonance that the secret of his encounter with the poems of *No One's Rose* and the inscription of Celan's name at the heart of his constellation resided.

> Signification to the other [*Signification à l'autre*] in the proximity that trumps every other relationship and has to be conceived as a responsibility for the other; it might be called humanity, or subjectivity, or *self*. [. . .] This saying has to be reached in its existence antecedent to the said, or else the said has to be reduced to it. We must fix the meaning of this antecedence. What does saying signify before signifying a said? (46, translation modified)

The result, in reverse, is a strange and double experience of reading that consists, on the one hand, in reading the difficult analyses of *Otherwise than Being* in light of these poems and, on the other hand, in measuring the scope of each poem, understood as a handshake, in light of the thought of the "saying without a said." Where philosophical writing and the poetic word bear in common the trace of the memory of the most extreme violence, each responds to the other—as if philosophical writing found in the poetic word *a posteriori* what "ethics" describes and prescribes, and as if the poetic word did so without needing to be told. Straight from poetic language, in this "breathturn" about which *The Meridian* speaks, it is not impossible from this perspective to find *a posteriori* something like the "without" of a saying *without* a said that is traced, that cuts its mark, to remind the German language of what was so terribly murderous with and by it. Poetry is from then on exemplary in that it must make the "without" of the "saying without a said" spring forth and, from it alone, this human witnessing that opposes the violence of mortiferous and poisonous discourses that make up the framework of history: a counterstatement. In this way, from the depth of the night, when everything is ash, poetry springs forth hope for help.

In the constellation on which we are focusing here, another voice then makes itself heard in support of Derrida's and Levinas's: the voice of Blanchot, who is never far off. One must emphasize, indeed, that this "without" of the "saying without a said," called forth by the nothing of a "sign of nothing," signals in turn towards that "other" *Nothing* that is in reality the same: first, the nothing of the "for nothing" that Celan invokes at the end of *The Meridian*, when poetry becomes "this infinity-speaking full of mortality and to no purpose" (44); next, the *Nothing* recalled at the heart of the poems as *that* without which no being-together is possible and around which Blanchot's entire reading in "The Last to Speak" unfolds:

> So even if we utter the uppercase word Nothing, in the abrupt hardness it has in the original language, it is possible to add: nothing is lost, so

that nothing is perhaps articulated with loss. Whereas the Hebraic cry of jubilation is divided to begin with a groan. (77–79)

With an extreme radicality as its condition, the nothing here is opposed to excess, to the too-full, overload of meaning, to all the fits of rage and vertigos of communication and judgment, and thus to the ready-made, hasty, precipitated sentences that no longer know to whom they speak, sentences that in reality no longer address anyone, the common regime of ordinary language and an inexhaustible source of brutality and violence. A little later, commenting upon a stanza of Celan's poem entitled, "REST (remainder) SINGABLE" (*Singbarer Rest*) in the collection *Breathturn*:

> *Forbidden lip,*
> *announce*
> *that something is still arriving*
> *not far from you*

Commenting on this poem, then, Blanchot writes:

> Phrase written with a terrible simplicity, fated to remain in us in the uncertainty where it remains, bearing, interlaced, the movement of hope and the immobility of distress, the demand of the impossible, for it is from the forbidden, from the forbidden alone, that what there is to say can come: *this bread to chew with the teeth of writing.*
>
> Yes, even there where Nothing reigns, even when separation does its work, the relationship is not broken, even if it is interrupted. ("The Last to Speak," 79–81)

Poetry, which knows whence violence comes, is born from a prohibition. It overlooks nothing of what words make us say and do when nothing interrupts the continuous flow of words that never escape violence: the violence of lessons, recriminations, trials, commandments, the calculations involved in all politics—everything that so easily leaves our lips. This is the course of the flow that poetry reverses, the breath that it turns, and this is the origin of the "nothing": if the poetic word is to go forth and encounter the other, that is to say, let the other come to it, if despite everything something is to remain and to survive the deeply murderous relations, in spite of all the world's destitution, then nothing of what turns language murderous should subsist. In Blanchot's reading, there then follows a citation of the poem (*PSALM*) that gives *No One's Rose* its title:

> We were
> a Nothing, we are, we
> will remain, blooming:
> the Nothing-, the
> No one's-rose. (*No One's Rose*, 47)[6]

From the *without* of the "saying *without* a said" to the *nothing* that happens or comes [*arrive*] to language so that it can host the infinite, at stake is a happening or an arriving [*arrivance*]. Neither the *without* nor the *nothing* make sense outside this receptiveness to an arrival [*arrivée*], which is, as Celan recalls on numerous occasions in *The Meridian*, always the arrival of an other. A coming is prepared, put forth [*se devance*]. This is the path of poetry. All the "vibrant formulas" that Levinas invokes, saying that they "require interpretation" ("Paul Celan," 40), formulas that Derrida cites and that Blanchot recalls, ultimately converge in this direction. "The poem," Celan writes, "wants to head toward some other, it needs this other, it needs an opposite. It seeks it out, it bespeaks itself to it" (*The Meridian*, 35a).[7] That is its responsibility. It is the guarantor of a *promise of language* that it *keeps* more than any other, because it stays on the course of this "saying without a said," of this withdrawal into the nothing, without which the other would never come—without which, as Martin Buber and Franz Rosenzweig already knew, no dialogue is possible.

IV.

As one will have understood, at stake is a transcendence to which Levinas, Derrida, and Blanchot will have been no strangers; at stake, in other words, is that which resists all judgment, monopolization, appropriation, assimilation, and all other reductions. It perhaps designates—but it will take time to see—the shibboleth that opens the door to the constellation that gathers all three around Celan's poems. But what arrival, what coming is in question? How does the other come to the poem? It comes with its time and dates. "*Time of the Other*," a word away from *Time and the Other*, could have been one of Levinas's titles. It is the guiding thread that ties together, across almost twenty years, Derrida's first text on Celan—"Shibboleth"—and his last seminar.[8] The first text emphasizes that, if every poem is entrusted with the inscription of a singular date that is, as *The Meridian* says, the irreplaceable sign of its "radical individuation" (33b), this inscription makes sense only to the extent that it concentrates in itself the date of others; it is on this condition that "the poem does speak." Reading and commenting upon Celan, Derrida focused on what, in the speech given at Darmstadt, recalls the poem's primary and constitutive exposure to the

You that it addresses—and, therefore, to "the most essential aspect" of this *You*, this *Other,* namely "its time" (*The Meridian,* 36b).

In *The Beast and the Sovereign,* led by questions of responsibility that he had been following for more than ten years, Derrida is inclined to push his interpretation even further. The poem becomes, in essence, *hospitality* offered to the time of who or what comes [*l'arrivant*]. Just as Levinas's reading of Celan joined, in the secret of the encounter, some of the most salient analyses of *Otherwise than Being,* Derrida's reading of *The Meridian* thus signals toward *Monolingualism of the Other.* Once again, a decisive book enriches the constellation of thinking that orbits around Celan's poetics. The "time of the other" calls for the language of the other. The one is welcomed [*s'acceuille*], taken in [*se recueille*], gathered in the other. In other words, it could not be promised to this time and to these dates without making language itself "the coming of the other," which Derrida names the messianic opening of the word:[9] the impossible and necessary translation of the time of the other and, therefore, of the language of the other in its own *idiom, its responsibility.* Thus the poem is shared out [*se partage*]. It is, Derrida says in the tenth session of *The Beast and the Sovereign* seminar,

> the division in the point, the pinpoint, the very punctuality of the now, as the very presence of the present, in the very majesty of the poetic present, in the poem as encounter—the dissociation, then, the partition that is also a parting [*partage*], between my present, the present itself, the very presence of the present, of the same present, in the present of the same [*le présent même, la présence même du présent, du même present, le présent du même*], and, on the other hand [*d'autre part*]—and this is the other part of the partition and the parting—the other present, the present of the other to whom the poem makes a present of its time, thus, in a *Mitsprechen,* letting the time of the other, its own time, speak. . . . (259–60)

To designate this "time of the other," Derrida does not use the word "transcendence." This is Levinas's word. Yet, when Levinas uses the word, it pertains not to time but to place or, rather, to the poem's non-place, that is, its utopia. There again, the words of his own books come to mind. We saw above the extent to which different definitions that Celan gives of the poem demands the desacralization, the dedivinization, or the demystification of the poet him- or herself. With a radicality that resonates with that of *Otherwise than Being,* Levinas draws the most decisive consequences in listening closely to *The Meridian.* With formulations as lapidary and elliptic as those of Celan, Levinas in turn advances on the poem's path, as close as possible to a thought of sacrifice. He tells us, indeed, that the coming of the other, the opening to the infinite through which the poet exceeds his or her own mortality—and transcendence, finally, means nothing else—would not be possible if the poet did not find this place of nowhere in which, letting go of him- or herself, the poet is loosened from what ordinarily encumbers existence attached to an *ego*. This is the antimony of poetry. In a sense—and this is one of the most definitive propositions of Celan's speech—the poet speaks "from the angle of orientation of his existence" (*The Meridian*, 33c).[10] Nevertheless, he does lean towards himself, towards *his selfish ego*; he is not inclined to self-knowledge. The angle, Celan writes, is the one from which "the creature declares itself" (33c). And it demands separation, cutting and caesura, "breathturn." This is why it is not found *outside the place* where the poet must *die by himself* in order to be opened to the transcendence of the infinite. The relation to self that the possessive pronoun presupposes (*his* existence) is thus deferred, suspended upon the coming of the other. *Différance* and *sovereignty* are Derrida's *words*, but they come from Levinas's pen the moment he gives the antimony its widest scope. They are thus, as always, two voices that closely interlace. The author of *Otherwise than Being*, who must be cited here at length, does not advance otherwise than by speaking the language of *The Meridian*:

> Is it not necessary to die, in order to transcend against nature and even against being? Or both to leap and not leap? Or does the poem perhaps allow the "I" to separate from itself? In Celan's terms: discover "a place in which the person, in grasping himself as a stranger to himself, emerges."[11] And does the poem that goes toward the other, "*turning, facing* him," postpone its ecstasy, "become more intense" in the interim, and in Celan's so ambiguous language, "persist at the limit of itself"? And does the poem, in order to last, adjourn its acumen, or in Celan's terms, "revoke itself . . . carry itself over continually in order to last from its 'already-no-longer' to its 'still-here'?"[12] But for this still-here the poet does not retain, in his passage to the other, his proud sovereignty of creator. (Levinas, "Paul Celan," 43)

The repetition of "or" traces the path of poetry's antimonies, which is also that of its utopia. It is neither ruptured nor torn apart. It is just exposed, with gravity, to the rectitude of a responsibility that, "before any appearance of forms, images, or things" (43), wants to make the impossible possible: attestation to the human faced with violence. Because it exceeds all sovereignty, because it implies "a stepping beyond what is human" (*The Meridian*, 17a), the step of Lucile's cry, the step of poetry's cry, because it amounts to walking on its head, like Lenz (25b–26b), with the abyssal sky below, this attestation is *transcendence*. For that very reason, it is antinomous for Levinas, aporetic for Derrida. Thus, poetry's responsibility, which refers to the responsibility of Derrida's "idiom" as well as that of Levinas's "saying without a said" in the place where the two meet, is another *Shibboleth*, a secret password, a hidden key that collectively and jointly opens for them the door of the constellation whose center is Celan, far, very far from Heidegger's poetics but without his shadow ever being very far away.

> The going out toward the other man, is it a going out? "A step outside of man—but into a sphere directed toward the human—excentric."[13] As if humanity were a genus allowing within its logical space (its extension) an absolute break; as if in going toward the other man we transcended the human, toward utopia. And as if utopia were not the dream and the lot of an accursed wandering, but the "clearing" in which man shows himself: "light of utopia. . . . And man? And the creature?—In such light."[14] ("Paul Celan," 44)

V.

The "light of u-topia" (*The Meridian*, 40b): one last time, Levinas places himself in step with his own books. In the space of a few paragraphs, he recalls the analyses of *Humanism of the Other* in his reading of Celan in proximity to *The Meridian*. Whence the light of this place from nowhere toward which poetry heads? What shadows, what obscurities does it dissipate? It comes from the fact that there is no more room in it for the gravity of affiliations. Poetry cannot be immured in one language; it cannot be appropriated by one particular culture that would claim it and establish it as its heritage [*patrimoine*] or, graver still, to which poetry would itself claim to adhere. It keeps its distance from every homeland [*patrie*]. Derrida already recalled this point, emphasizing in "Shibboleth" that, if Celan could inscribe Marina Tsvetaeva's statement that "[a]ll poets are Jews" as an exergue to his poem, "[a]nd with the Book from Tarussa," it was with the conviction that "there is no Jewish propriety," that this was "the incommunicable secret of the Judaic idiom" (Derrida, "Shibboleth," 49–50). The other, Celan tells us, should no longer even be thought of as a stranger, if the *stranger* is strange always in relation to (and for) a *proper* supposed to be self-identical that, in the name of *his or her* identity, would give the stranger that status.

> But I do think—and this thought can hardly surprise you by now—I think that it had always been part of the poem's hopes to speak on behalf of exactly this *strange*—no, I cannot use this word this way—exactly *on another's behalf*—who knows, perhaps on behalf *of a totally other*. (*The Meridian*, 31b)

Levinas, for his part, keeps the name stranger, but he displaces its meaning so radically that it accords at every point with the thought of *The Meridian*. Indeed, one will recall that, in a text in *Humanism of the Other* entitled, "Humanism and An-archy," Levinas takes the arrangement of a world in which each thing is in its place and in which humans dwell, no doubt in the sense that Heidegger gave to this term, as evidence of its inconsistency.[15] Thus conceived, the stranger is the plaything of technique and politics, which have not forgotten being, as Heidegger would say, but rather the meaning of *human*. The utopia of poetry, its non-place, is the reverse of such a world. Levinas, then, opposes to "dwelling" what he calls the "*incondition* of the stranger" (*Humanism of the Other*, 66, my italics), which one can believe, reading between the lines, describes point by point *The Meridian*'s lesson concerning the "passage to the other" and the "abandonment of sovereignty." Three things, then, deserve to be noted in concluding. First, this *incondition* signifies that the stranger cannot be circumscribed by any identification or, therefore, immured in any condition. Next, it cannot be reserved for a given category of individuals; it resists all partition. The Other, entirely Other, is defined by this *incondition*. Finally, and perhaps most essentially, the *incondition* of the stranger cannot concern only the Other. It cannot be recognized without turning upon one's own identity. It presupposes, Levinas says, self-alienation. This is how, paradoxically, it inscribes a "radical individuation" (*The Meridian*, 33b) in language. And this is how poetry outstrips us. In the same stroke, Levinas can interpret the line that gives Celan's speech its title—"a meridian"—in terms that make poetry "an unheard-of modality of the *otherwise than being*" (Levinas, "Paul Celan," 46):

> But the surprise of that adventure, in which the *I* dedicates himself to the other in the non-place, is the return. Not return as a response of the one who is called, but by the circularity of this movement that does not turn back, the circularity of this perfect trajectory, this meridian that, in its finality without end, the poem describes. It is as if in going toward the other I met myself and implanted myself in a land, henceforth native, and I were stripped of all the weight of my identity. A native land owing nothing to enrootedness, nothing to first occupation; a native land owing nothing to birth. A native, or a promised, land? (Levinas, "Paul Celan," 44–45, translation modified)

This native land is a land in which one comes and one responds. To whom? To what? To that other to which the poem dedicates itself in the secret sharing of its "incondition." To those eyes in the night, "scars in place of sight" whose calling and attraction Blanchot evokes in the last pages of his reading; to those eyes that demand that we come "even if it's nowhere, only there where—in the fissures-crevasses of drying—the incessant light (which does not illumine) fascinates" (Blanchot, "The Last to Speak," 85). To the dates of one arriving absolutely [*arrivant asbolu*], one concerning whom no one will want to determine in advance who they are or whence they come, because all determination of this order is an infinite source of violence. To come, to respond, to respond for the other, his or her outlook, face, and dates, to enlist before the call [*devancer son appel*]: Levinas, Blanchot, and Derrida—so close to the disaster of the Second World War, its trauma and caesura, one of the common and secret sources of their writing—were probably never so connected as when listening to the poetic word's injunction. In the secret of its encounter, the poetic word was the meridian of their constellation.

5

"that tumor in the memory"

(Levinas)

The test that violence constitutes for philosophical or literary writing is not only experienced in the present; it also implies the traumatic memory of those ordeals whose trace and wound continue to haunt that same present years or even decades later, whether or not writers were contemporary to it, if not immediate witnesses. There are many works that could be read from this perspective, but, as far as philosophy is concerned, Levinas's work seems to impose itself more than any other; none of the major books of the second half of the twentieth century is inhabited by the memory of the Second World War and, more precisely, by the extermination of European Jews in the Nazi camps to the same extent as *Totality and Infinity* and *Otherwise than Being: Or Beyond Essence*. And yet, a question that cannot be neglected remains suspended. Why, after all, should we remember the violence of history? By incessantly turning our gaze toward the past, captives of an impossible mourning, do we not ultimately risk being duped by memory? And, then, is the duping not primarily characterized by the deafness and blindness to present wounds that memory's monopoly so often supports? In "Nameless," a very short text from 1966, Levinas ignores none of this risk. If one does not want to deceive oneself, he says, one should take care to emphasize the actuality in which memory is inscribed. In broad strokes, this inscription recalls that

> [s]ince the end of the war, bloodshed has not ceased. Racism, imperialism and exploitation remain ruthless. Nations and individuals expose one another to hatred and contempt, fearing destitution and destruction. (119)

In other words, memory gets lost every time it makes its immurement in the past the blind reason for an active or passive *consent*—an indifference, a resignation, an encouragement—to murders in the present.

And yet, contemporary tragedies should take nothing away from the incommensurability of the lives destroyed and the suffering that they cause. It is up to memory, indeed, to avoid confusing everything and putting everything on the same plane. Undue reproaches and abusive analogies are forbidden to memory; they always come from memory's ideological or political implementation, as the often-abused reference to "fascism" and "Nazism" time and again exemplifies. If such approximations become the rule, not only is the historical method shaken; memory itself is wounded. This is the strange paradox to which the trauma of the past leads us: on the one hand, our relation to the traces of the past cannot abstract from the present; on the other hand, recalling the past is faultiest when it serves the interests and calculations of that same present.

In this way, if one wants to remember what the persecutions meant for the European Jews that suffered them from 1933 to 1945, one must recall the feeling of absolute abandonment that accompanied them. The least help, the least attention, no longer seemed possible from anywhere. Not only day-to-day life, then, became impossible; the world itself and belonging to the world seemed to have lost all meaning. For the persecuted Jews to keep or rediscover this meaning, it would have been necessary to raise indignant voices, to reestablish the broken links of responsibility through ubiquitous protest, and to reaffirm, in defiance of terror, the demand for solidarity and complicity that terror always aims to compromise. In "Nameless," which is one of the rare texts that he dedicates explicitly to these persecutions, Levinas recalls what makes the difference:

> One always dies alone, and everywhere the hapless know despair. And among the hapless and forlorn, the victims of injustice are everywhere and always the most hapless and forlorn. But who will say the loneliness of the victims who died in a world put in question by Hitler's triumphs, in which lies were not even necessary to Evil, certain of its excellence? Who will say the loneliness of those who thought themselves dying at the same time as Justice, at a time when judgments between good and evil found no criterion but in the hidden recesses of subjective conscience, no sign from without? (119)

Today, it is at times fashionable to jeer here and there at the militant action of intellectual protestors, their gatherings and petitions, when they take a stand against violence. This is to forget the weight of silence as it increases the terror due to the feeling that the violence bothers no one except those that suffer it, while others—the *rest* of the world—are distinguishable among themselves only by the degrees of passivity and activity of their "consent" to it. With respect to the Shoah, it is not in vain that this *solitude* and *abandonment* on a global scale are so often associated with an endless night that no glimmer of hope could pierce. Because it seemed solitude and abandonment had suspended the infinite network of moral and political relations that comprise the fabric of existence, they are part of its memory; they remain, they persist, they transmit themselves even as a "tumor in the memory" that nothing could efface: "the vertigo that grips us at the edge is always the same" ("Nameless," 120).

If it was legitimate for life to reclaim its rights, if it was necessary, as they say, to look ahead and build the future, then was it necessary to consider this "tumor" as a pathology? Assuming that the risk of a dark, if not thanatophilic, enchantment with the past exists, a legitimate attraction haunted by the call of the dead, did the memory of the persecutions have any alternative to giving in to its vertigo and dragging future generations into it? All the force of Levinas's essay comes from the fact that it ignores none of these questions, as if, beyond these few pages, his entire oeuvre (*Totality and Infinity*, *Difficult Freedom*, *Otherwise than Being*, and so many other texts) were engaged in them. As soon as it was a question of "children, who were born after the Liberation" (120), the question of memory became first and foremost a question of *transmission*. But what was there to transmit other than impossible mourning? Was not the greatest service that could be done for these children getting rid of this "tumor" once and for all so that life could finally reclaim its rights? Were they destined to carry in turn, indefinitely, the untenable burden of millions of victims?

To respond to these questions, one had to show that the memory of the horrors of the twentieth century is not hostile to life, or that life, then, was wrong to think it should make forgetfulness its condition and law, like anyone that asks us to "turn the page" in the name of the future or a given reconciliation.[1] This is Levinas's approach in "Nameless." His approach ignores nothing of the unnamable violence or the abyss into which the memory of it rushes, but it worries about what could be transmitted to future generations beyond the commemoration of the dead. What lessons should we retain from the past when its memory gets lost in the unbearable enumeration of unimaginable crimes? This is the question that ceaselessly haunts witnesses and survivors. The question cannot be separated from the work of Robert Antelme, Primo Levi, Jean Améry, Vasily Grossman, or Imre Kertész. It secretly inhabits, no doubt, Levinas's work. But nothing is certain! No self-assured assertion is acceptable on the edge of the abyss. Barely a hypothesis, a suggestion, like a murmur: "[w]e may, *perhaps*, draw from the experience of the concentration camps and from that Jewish clandestineness that has conferred ubiquity upon it, three truths that are transmissible and necessary to the new generation" (120, my emphasis).

I.

Three truths, then, could be drawn from the memory of the vertigo of mourning. Contrary to what one might think, the first truth does not concern the conditions of survival but, rather, the distinctive characteristics that make any life whatsoever a "human life." What is "to live humanly"? To respond to this question, we normally invoke the way advantages of culture permit men and women to introduce mediations in the satisfaction of the needs that nature imposes. We thus think that life is dehumanized when its mediations are compromised, and we know that the removal of mediations understood in this sense is never unrelated to the calculations of terror. In the concentration and extermination camps, all the testimonies concur to tell us that this removal was the executioners' primary weapon for stripping the victims of the feeling of their proper dignity and for proving to themselves that there was no limit to the victims' enslavement. We thus imagine that "to live humanly" is to live freely, singularly granting ourselves the means for these mediations with which we identify civilization: the variety of food and clothing, the diversity and singularity of shelter, not to mention tools. But Levinas puts forth the total opposite. "To live humanly," Levinas tells us,

> people need infinitely fewer things than they dispose of in the magnificent civilizations in which they live. [...] One can do without meals and rest, smiles, personal effects, decency and the right to turn the key to one's own room, pictures, friends, countrysides and sick leave, daily introspection and confession. ("Nameless," 121)

Thus, as the author of *Difficult Freedom* recalls in "The Case of Struthof" or in the contemporary text "Freedom and Command," tyranny not only knocks freedom from its pedestal; our conception of what constitutes the humanity of human cultures also finds itself completely changed. What, indeed, is culture? In what way could our idea of *the* human culture be affected by the memory we keep of the atrocities of the twentieth century? Or, rather, could it retain anything other than the obsessive and painful sign of its own collapse? No one today can ignore this resounding question that, although a familiar chorus, has lost none of its pertinence: how is it that one of the most imposing parts of human cultural capital—not to say, as some maintain, "European civilization's heritage"—has not protected the people of Europe from this return of the barbarity inscribed in memory like a "tumor"? The answer cannot escape the threatening pitfalls of the form of radical nihilism that consists in questioning the pursuit of this heritage and the necessity of its transmission, if not the very idea of culture, except by radically rethinking this idea. This is the first truth! If one understands "culture" as what makes life a "human life," one must recognize that the absolute destitution imposed by war—the murderous will to dehumanize millions of men and women, innocent victims, by abolishing all the mediations that attached them to existence with the most extreme brutality and cruelty—has brought to light another dimension, essential otherwise, of what makes the humanity of a life.

What is this dimension? In a later text entitled "Philosophical Determination of the Idea of Culture" (1983), Levinas will have given a decisive interpretation of it, but it is not excessive to hold that, in reality, all of his work supports and exemplifies that interpretation. A first means for understanding culture takes it to be knowledge, that is to say, appropriation, reduction of the other to the same. Culture is then culture of immanence, of human autonomy; it aims at a satisfaction such that no transcendence escapes it. As Levinas writes, it then "triumphs over things and men" ("Philosophical Determination," 181) even in practice conceived as the moment of knowledge. Another conception makes culture a dwelling of the world constituted by art as the creation of sensible forms of expression. There again, however, one does not leave immanence. The risk then is seeing art as culture's last word, as so many social practices and so much of the accepted discourse seem to confirm. The proof is that dwelling of this order always governs the system of values mobilized each time someone maintains that one person is "cultivated" and another is not. Whence the question posed by Levinas, which challenges this priority of immanence, the identification of culture as a possession, an acquisition, a comfortable "at home [chez-soi]," if not an inner-circle [entre-soi]:

> Is the culture of dwelling, in its artistic expression, not threatened with a break in terms of an absolute otherness which cannot be reduced to the Same and which invites to another Culture than that of knowing or of poetry? ("Philosophical Determination," 184)

There remains, then, a final and higher conception of culture, the relation with the other that Levinas names a "culture of transcendence" ("Philosophical Determination," 185). What is it about? First and foremost, a radical displacement. Culture is no longer understood on the basis of whoever possesses it or is deprived of it; it is no longer related to a blossoming or an individual formation or a collective heritage; rather, its essence is in its distribution [*partage*], and it is concentrated entirely in the connection that it creates. Thus, this third conception of culture could be retraced to the first conditions of that relation, the conditions without which it will always be a false pretense. Far from all appropriation and all reduction to the same, it manifests itself then as "responsibility for the other," and it is called by the epiphany of the other's face insofar as it expresses, first and foremost, his or her mortality. The "culture of transcendence," in this sense, is identified with the radical questioning of my own freedom by the death of the other. It returns the previously identified forms of culture to their correct value and truth. This is *the first truth* recalled by the terrible memory of wars: the entirety of culture cannot be constituted by food, clothing, or shelter, which are relative, or even by taste or knowledge [*savoir*], the assimilation of expertise [*connaissances*]. "To live humanly" is something else: namely, to assume, as far as possible, the responsibility for the care, help, and attention that the vulnerability and mortality of the other demand, which sometimes mean sacrificing one's own life, as all the rebels, partisans, and defenders against the ghetto have shown. The paradox thus pertains to the fact that this dimension of culture will have never been upheld—precisely by those rebels, partisans, and defenders—with so much clarity and evidence as at the very moment when the darkest forces were unleashed to dehumanize life.

II.

And yet, destitution and the suspension of all entitlements [*jouissants*] are not ends in themselves; there is no need to make a value out of detaching them. Thus, the second truth that one should draw from the memory of the wars, and more explicitly from the experience of the concentration camps, comes to complete the first. It must be specified, indeed, that the first truth could not support wartime heroism as the manifestation of a more authentic existence. Levinas undoubtedly knew the price of the idealization that exalts the virtues of war by forgetting that the values of peace are ends in themselves. One must always mistrust overly abrupt condemnations of what some call an everyday rut. Such a judgment—one cannot count the theories, philosophical treatises, literary pamphlets, or bellicose enthusiasms that bear the proof—ends up dreading the resulting atmosphere of peace, albeit very relative and very partial, in order to posit war as the essence of man in opposition to it. But each time such an essence is advanced, the result is always the same. In one way or another, it comes down to supporting or defending murder. By supposing that man were revealed to himself while "everything is permitted" and no burden of civilization weighed on him, one takes it to be evident that man is not, or at least not always, responsible for paying attention, bringing help, or providing care to the vulnerability and mortality of the other. When necessary, this bellicose conception prefers the warring, heroic, and murderous realization of the self over the ethical gestures and discourses for which the transcendence of the other calls. It begins by maintaining in good conscience that there are exceptions to the need for peace, and then—such is the logic of its consent—it makes these exceptions the rule.

> In not concluding, in a universe at war, that warlike virtues are the only sure ones; in not taking pleasure [*se complaire*], during the tragic situation, in the virile virtues of death and desperate murder; in living dangerously only in order to remove dangers and to return to the shade of one's own vine and fig tree. (Levinas, "Nameless," 121)

Hence, this should be the second "truth" of the memory of war: far from magnifying or idealizing the memory, this truth recalls the primary difference between, on the one hand, those who take pleasure [*se complaisent*] in violence and endlessly praise its intoxicating effect, those who are thus seduced and ravished by war because it seems to give them a goal in life, because they live it as freedom and, on the other hand, those that know the price of the obligations that war suspends, the bonds it breaks, the values it hinders, values that have no aspiration, consequently, other than the return to peace. It is important, in other words, never to evoke the time of terror without reviving the recollection of the acts and discourses that contributed, at the heart of the disaster, to keeping the thread of responsibility from breaking. War is never only or exclusively unnamable destructions; it is also gestures of hope, acts of faith in the return to peace, the persevering will to save what can be saved, here and there, of human dignity. Consequently, it is not true that men and women, in the darkest hours of their history, have no other outcome than ceding to the terrible spiral of murderous consents into which they are thrown. Violence and murder are not inevitable.

One sees the extent to which this second truth resonates with everything, moreover, that Levinas's thought ceaselessly stresses. If war does not authorize any recognition of "the virile virtues of death and desperate murder," it is because, no matter the rights that violence acquires there, *they do not efface ethics*. They cannot prevent the face of the other from calling to the responsibility of the I [*moi*] or, at the moment in which it inspires murderous temptation, from expressing again and again the "thou shall not kill" that constitutes the truth of its transcendence. In other words, there is no war—and no truth is harder to admit—that should make us despair of the necessity of ethics.

III.

But there is a third truth that measures the price of interior life. It resonates strangely with the "life of the idea" that, in the same era, Jan Patočka describes as the third movement of human existence. When one can no longer expect anything from politics because it has become synonymous with oppression, when entire peoples seem enslaved by terror and its calculations that make humanity despair, it is important to remember the unsuspected possibilities for resistance offered by "inner life." This is the final great lesson that comes to us from the memory of wars. No one has to capitulate before violence as long as he or she still can—and one always can—oppose it in consciousness. However dark the times, however brutal the condition of existence, it is not true that they eliminate all glimmer of hope, because it is always possible to resist in act or in thought. Partisans, rebels, resistant fighters are all figures of this possibility. But these figures also concern all thought that resists the wreckage of language and the ideas in the swamp of propaganda. It is up to them, Levinas writes, to find "a way to behave amidst total chaos as if the world had not fallen apart" ("Nameless," 121).

Because the declaration of war threatens to sweep away everything in its path, beginning with the law against murder, war measures the resources of "inner life" in a way that one cannot always grasp in the ordinary course of life. What I have elsewhere called "murderous consent" is another way to name this contagion. It means there is no longer anything to prevent women and men from accepting the murder of another, from resigning themselves or from encouraging it, from looking the other way and pretending to see and hear nothing of what the persecuted suffer, or from actively participating in the persecution. It is well-known that a time always comes when everything in the objective order seems to contribute to murderous consent: State rights, its discriminatory laws and decrees, its imposed quotas, its expropriations and expulsions, arrests and confinements, its deportations. No confidence can remain in any discourse or any initiative coming from this instituted order—with its stacks of institutions, agencies, and offices—except by remaining deaf and blind to the threats. This is when "the true inner life" as Levinas defines it reclaims its rights:

> The true inner life is not a pious or revolutionary thought that comes to us in a stable world, but the obligation to lodge the whole of humankind in the shelter—exposed to all the winds—of conscience. And, truly, it is mad to seek out the tempest for its own sake, as if "in the tempest rest resided" (Lermontov). But the fact that settled, established humanity can at any moment be exposed to the dangerous situation of its morality residing entirely in its "heart of hearts," its dignity completely at the mercy of a subjective voice, no longer reflected or confirmed by any objective order—that is the risk upon which the honor of humankind depends. ("Nameless," 122)

War and the violence that it sanctions will always have defenders. It can always be claimed that they respond to some historical necessity, which is also that of murder, to some imperative of civilization, to some collective obligation. They will always know how to enclose the reasons in the logic of institutions, and there is no limit to what these institutions can demand of or accept from them. Which is to say, in times of terror, nothing appears more clearly than the fragility and reversibility of the protections that these same institutions, or so we believe, are meant to assure. If humanity can then be preserved, it is without these institutions, "on the brink of morality" (122).

Levinas concludes these few, very intense pages by identifying this situation with the Jewish condition. Even if none of the victims of the war should remain foreign to the memory of this situation,[2] the "tumor" in memory is swelled first of all by the fate of the Jewish people exposed to the murderous madness of all the forms of anti-Semitism. This fate was exposed by "the screaming and howling of ruthless crowds," relayed by and themselves relaying further the virulence of anti-Semitic politics to the four corners of Europe,

> to find itself, overnight and without forewarning, in the wretchedness of its exile, its desert, ghetto or concentration camp—all the splendors of life swept away like tinsel, the Temple in flames, the prophets without vision, reduced to an inner morality that is belied by the universe. (123).

This inner morality is not the result of the solipsistic introspection of a subject folded back onto itself; it is the response to both a question and a call. The question: "To what does, to what can, humanity still cling when in times of peace these same screams and howls threaten at every moment—as Paul Celan, Imre Kertész, and so many others knew—to ring out once again, reviving again and again this same 'tumor in the memory'?"

To what can it cling if not to responsibility for the care, help, and attention demanded by the vulnerability and mortality of the other, expressed everywhere by the face of the other? To what can humanity cling, in other words, if not to the call for transcendence? Is this the reason of inner life, the matrix of human morality more original than all the civilizations and their metaphysical grounds? If this is the case, it follows that we have here one of the guiding threads that link works that Levinas held to be separate—his Talmudic readings and his major books, *Totality and Infinity* and *Otherwise than Being*—a tenuous thread in the middle of "nihilistic devastation" (123) to which one must cling. It also perhaps follows that we find here, "on the brink of morality" where "inner life" maintains its rights and does not imperil life when it reaffirms them, a figure that exemplifies the joint vocation of literature and philosophy, confronted with the test of violence, its trauma, or the haunting of its return.

6

On Shame

(Levinas)

Few concepts testify to the distance Levinas travels between *On Escape*, one of his very first essays, published in 1935 in *Recherches philosophiques*, and *Totality and Infinity*, which appeared a quarter of a century later in 1961, as much as shame, a concept so difficult to grasp in the ambivalences of such expressions as *to feel* shame [avoir *honte*] or *to* shame [faire *honte*]. These were not, as is known, just any years in the murderous history of that century: between these two dates, the domination of tyranny and terror had spread throughout the world and into the minds of men and women, such that neither the idea of freedom nor that of humanity could retain, if not the same meaning, at least the same assurance. By the time "peace" had come, it was no longer possible for thought to remain captive to problems that would neglect to carry such a painful burden. This impossibility measures the abyss that separates the different analyses of shame. As such, this impossibility cannot be separated from the question of violence or from the multiple detours that the "consent" occasioned by the death of others will have taken.

I.

There is nothing ethical or political, at least not directly, about the problem Levinas confronts in the 1935 essay. The problem concerns the signification of finite being. It is a matter of substituting the classical question of the "limitations of being," as they might describe the imperfection of the human condition, with the more original question of the "sufficiency of the fact of being" (51), the brutality of its affirmation and the weight, if not the gravity, of its irremissible character. The difficulty, *On Escape* tells us, derives not from our inability to exceed this or that limit in order to enrich or complete ourselves, but, much more so, from what we suffer as the impossibility of evading or straying from being. Thus, a need for escape, a desire to leave one's imprisonment, imposes itself. Now, nowhere do the chains of this sufficiency appear to be a cause for suffering more than in the identity of the I [*moi*]. The need to escape that manifests itself there, Levinas tells us, could not find any satisfaction that would appease the unease. Even if the pleasure that results would give us the illusion of leaving ourselves, it does not manage to "break that most radical and unalterably binding of chains, the fact that the I is oneself" (55).

The consideration of such a malaise introduces the motif of shame. One imagines easily what imposes it. If it is true that shame always constitutes the aporetic tribulation [*l'épreuve aporétique*] of the separation from oneself, in other words an impossible disintegration [*désolidarisation*] of actions or words that one wishes never took place, were never uttered, even when it is unthinkable to turn back, then shame agrees on each point with the impossibility of exiting that the gravity of being signifies. Thus, even when, estranged from ourselves, we would like to evade it, it is not possible for us to "de-identify." Which is to say that the first gesture made by the author of *On Escape* consists of freeing the notion from its exclusive link with morality by placing it on ontological terrain, even if it is in terms that already allow one to anticipate that this displacement will not constitute the final word of his analysis. As Levinas writes, from the moment shame is "founded upon the *solidarity of our being*, which obliges us to claim *responsibility for ourselves*" (63), we can assume, indeed, that it will be enough to change the nature of the link implied by the idea of "solidarity" and, moreover, the meaning and object of responsibility so that shame can no longer be thought in the same terms.

Nevertheless, in *On Escape* this step is not taken. Shame is essentially thought from the perspective of *self-relation*, even if the latter is dependent on the gaze of the other, on what one does or does not manage to hide from the other or to keep a secret, as the question of nudity exemplifies. Just as clothes shelter our intimacy, we wear masks in order to hide, including from ourselves, what we are. Even morality does not escape this rule. The conventions to which we bend and our pledges of loyalty to social codes are all garments with which we protect our social relations. We hide ourselves behind them, just as we veil our nudity. In the end, perhaps that is how we are duped, as Levinas suggests twenty-five years later when he opens the preface to *Totality and Infinity* with words that sound like a warning: "Everyone will readily agree that it is of the highest importance to know whether we are not duped by morality" (21). And it is also not a coincidence that Levinas evokes Céline's *Journey to the End of the Night* at this precise moment in his analysis in *On Escape* in order to suggest how our access to the world depends on "noble words" behind which we hide ourselves, words that Bardamu ceaselessly restores to their sad truth.

What, then, of shame? It occurs when the masks fall. When shame takes hold of us, writes Levinas, "we cannot hide what we should like to hide"; "necessity of fleeing, in order to hide oneself, is put in check by the impossibility of fleeing oneself" (64). In this sense, shame does not refer to a respect for decorum (which is supposed to prevent shame) or to a disrespect for decorum (which *should* provoke shame); rather, it refers to what the first tries in vain to conceal and the second reveals, which is in another way more essential: namely, the gravity of being or, to put it differently, the impossibility of the self to evade itself. Thus, one will not be surprised that, three years before Sartre makes it the title of his novel, this first arrival of shame culminates in a brilliant analysis of nausea. In more ways than one, Levinas's analyses sketch in advance the portrait of Roquentin in *Nausea*:

> In nausea—which amounts to an impossibility of being what one is—we are at the same time riveted to ourselves, enclosed in a tight circle that smothers. We are there, and there is nothing more to be done, or anything to add to this fact that we have been entirely delivered up, that everything is consumed: *this is the very experience of pure being.* . . . (*On Escape*, 66–67)

Ultimately, the irremissibility of shame, nausea, and being are closely confused. The first is one with the second, which itself is nothing other than the affirmation of the presence of being in its powerlessness and nakedness. Everything is said. Except that there results what one could call a strange "solipsistic" withdrawal of the analysis. From the moment it focuses on "self-shame before oneself," indeed, it largely leaves aside shame's interactive and intersubjective dimension, the very dimension emphasized, for example, by the extreme ambivalence and the complexity of the expression "to shame [*faire honte*]."

II.

You make *me* ashamed! Shame on you! You have no shame! How should one understand the reproach, if not the menace, that these interpellations contain? What should one think of the barely concealed violence, of the assured domination of which they are the instruments? To what cruel game do they belong? At the very least, they presuppose an indictment, a self-assured exercise of judgment, which sees right through the one it designates as a "shameful subject." If it is true that shame refers to being riveted to ourselves and to the agony of being unable to flee ourselves, then to remind whomever of the shame *they* must or *should* feel ("have you no shame?") consists of doubling their powerlessness. As soon as one addresses a shaming reproach to someone, one indicates to him or her, indeed, not only that he or she cannot evade what he or she said or did, but also that the gravity of self-relation that results, even if in the form of nausea, affects the relation that binds him or her to others. In accordance with its original meaning, shame is recalled to whoever might be tempted to forget that it is a dishonor, an insult, or an affront, that the "shameful" subject wounds him- or herself, even if unwittingly, at the same time that he or she offends others. "You make *me* ashamed" is the same as saying, "your shame reflects back onto the link that binds us to each other. It affects the friendly, filial, familial relation that we share in our existence."

So goes the violence of judgment. It imposes on the incriminated the burden of a freedom, which takes the accused hostage. The question that imposes itself is thus always the same: on the basis of what authority does one allow oneself to inspire, if not to demand, shame—"have you no shame?"—in the name of what knowledge or dogma does one grant oneself the right to do so? Shame, in other words, does not come solely from the irremissible presence of the self to itself; it constitutes, in every relationship, the weapon of a commandment. To shame someone is to command that they bend to a law. Thus, education, practice, and educational principles do not abstract from shame: learning propriety and the rules of hygiene; incorporating "manners"and other ways of "behaving oneself" at the table, in society, wherever one is in the eyes of others; making acquaintances, with its procession of evaluations; competency and its performances—all "work" to shame any shortcomings, bad grades, negative assessments, failures, weaknesses, defeats, etc. In Freudian terms, one could say that shame is a constitutive element of how the superego imposes itself on the ego. In Levinasian terms, this amounts to saying that more than one shame comes to be grafted, not without cruelty, on shame as he conceives it, namely, as the "radical impossibility of fleeing oneself to hide from oneself" (*On Escape*, 64). At stake is their strength and the fears that their political and/or religious culture instrumentalizes on the basis of a primary anxiety: shame belongs to the arsenal that transforms control of the ego into a repressive system. In its authoritarian uses, the ability "to shame" becomes the weapon of a sovereign freedom, always capable of exercising and experiencing the vertiginous pleasures of its domination. Does this mean that there is no shameful feeling that is not the effect of such power? Each time shame takes hold of us, it would have to be possible to turn back time, to look for the law of families, of profession, of social milieu that inspires shame in us and, behind that law, those who instilled us with respect for it (parents, priests, teachers, etc.), with as a guiding thread the idea of discovering the weight of inheritances as a historical mask of the irremissibility of being. After such a genealogical investigation, it is possible that the culture of shame would appear to us as the last refuge for norms to maintain their control over our lives.

When Levinas returns to the analysis of shame in *Totality and Infinity* twenty-five years after having written *On Escape*, however, this is not the direction he takes. War separates these two texts. And the meaning of the war—millions of swallowed lives, millions more mutilated forever, wounded, mourned, the memory of tortures and innumerable crimes, and finally the deportation and extermination of Europe's Jews—does not allow shame to be thought in the same terms as before. There is the painful shame of the survivors that the author of *Difficult Freedom* evokes, like so many others, in a text entitled "From the Rise of Nihilism to the Carnal Jew":

> Contemporaries retained a burn on their sides, as though they had seen too much of the Forbidden, and as though they had to bear for ever [sic] the shame of having survived. (*Difficult Freedom*, 221)

And then there is the necessary shame of the executioners and their descendants, which is as expected and hoped for as it is dreaded, because it is difficult to understand and because it neither erases nor forgives anything. Above all, however, too many crimes were committed in good conscience, too many murderers were convinced that the shameful feeling was on the side of their victims and that they were the righteous upholders of a just cause that granted them rights over the lives of others, too many for an entirely other way to understand and appeal to shame not to come about as an absolute necessity. From the moment that shaming someone for his or her actions or words—whether real, imagined, or fantasized—supposes an exercise of freedom, assured of the comprehension, knowledge, and powers that it recognizes in itself, that give it the illusion of *grasping* the other and with which it thus authorizes itself to level the accusation, "You have no shame!," it is this freedom that must be knocked from its pedestal. However, shame is still linked to the "impossibility of fleeing oneself" (*On Escape*, 64). On the contrary, the displacement effected by Levinas in *Totality and Infinity*, as well as in the contemporaneous lecture entitled "Transcendence and Height," consists of thinking the two perspectives together: if the shameful feeling can no longer be the effect of an accusatory freedom, it is because freedom itself stems from the self's inability to evade itself. Shame *happens to us* (here is the fatal blow) with and by *a* feeling that we take from our own freedom.

What is this feeling? The author of "Transcendence and Height" sums it up in the following terms, which are worth quoting at length. Shame takes a positive value whenever the consciousness we have of ourselves, the certainty that we have of our place in the world and of our ability to assert our rights and make our voices heard, to impose our presence, our will and our judgments, the need that we have to exist in the eyes of others and obtain their recognition and consideration is abruptly interrupted by the sudden sense of violence that this positioning and this affirmation of self incurs on the other.

> Instead of seizing the Other through comprehension and thereby assuming all the wars that this comprehension presupposes, prolongs, and concludes, the self loses its hold before the absolutely Other, before the human Other [*Autrui*], and, unjustified, can no longer be powerful. . . . The event of putting into question is the shame of the self for its naïve spontaneity, for its sovereign coincidence with itself in the identification of the Same. This shame is a movement in a direction opposed to that of consciousness, which returns triumphantly to itself and rests upon itself. To feel shame [*avoir honte*] is to expel oneself from this rest and not simply to be conscious of this already glorious exile. The just person who knows himself to be just is no longer just. The first condition of the first as of the last of the just is that their justice remains clandestine to them. ("Transcendence and Height," 17, translation modified)

Nothing in common here with the shame of one who says, filled with good conscience and with the best of intentions, "You make me ashamed" or "I am ashamed of you." No one, indeed, has the right to make himself or herself the righter of wrongs for our words and deeds in this way. Whether its violence is implicit or explicit, it is not unimportant that shame is marked on one's face, that it betrays itself by paleness or flushness, that it induces aphasia and paralysis. Like the censors, inquisitors, psychologists, moralists, and other didactic sermonizers from all countries and of all denominations, anyone who claims to do justice by demanding shame from whomever they reckon deserves it wages against their victims a war that is, in its essence, unjust. They reduce the victim to the mercy of their judgment; they ensnare him or her in the net of their vindictiveness, watching out in the stammering of the victim's excuses and the decomposition of his or her features the admission of *their* shame: *their* surrender. With the culpability that they demand, that they provoke and obtain, they measure the sway that they exert over their victim that becomes by that very fact an object of pleasure. They are at that moment duped by morality or by whatever other catechism to which they claim adherence. And that is why it matters that shame changes sides. For the reversal works as follows: whoever gives in to violence's blackmail, with all the forms of torture and cruelty it implies, should be the first to suffer the feeling they are trying to impose on others. Thus, over the course of a Talmudic reading entitled "Contempt for the Torah as Idolatry," Levinas recalls the extent to which the will to inflict the torment of shame is, at bottom, deadly. Commenting on a saying [*dire*] by Rabbi Eleazar Hamodai, Levinas specifies:

> Also very important is the seriousness attached, in Rabbi Elazar Hamodai's intervention [*dire*], to the act of putting the other to shame. Elsewhere the act of causing the face of another person to blanch is compared to murder. In *Baba Metsia 58b*: "Whoever causes the face of his neighbor to go pale with shame in public is compared to an assassin." The draining of blood causing the cheeks to pale would appear to be as horrible as bloodshed! ("Contempt for the Torah as Idolatry," 63)

III.

The culmination of the analytic reversal nevertheless remains for the 1961 major work, *Totality and Infinity*. Shame thus no longer comes from a self-introspection crushed by the weight of being, or from the other's judgment understood as an obstacle to my freedom to act and speak as I please, but from something else altogether. Significantly, it is at the moment where, studying the relationship between truth and justice, Levinas puts into question the privileges accorded to freedom that the experience of shame recalls itself to him. It is true that between 1935 and 1961 a major work appeared, which these pages ceaselessly confront: Sartre's *Being and Nothingness* (1943). Contrary to the Sartrean description of the other's existence, the analysis of shame allows for the contestation of the reduction of the other to his or her facticity. At stake is the demonstration that the other is not a fact against which our power and our freedom collide but, rather, the infinite object of a desire that, itself infinite, reveals the limits of this power and of this freedom to themselves. Assuming that the other is understood in any manner whatsoever as the object of power and freedom, it would indeed cease to be desired in its infinity. The other would be reduced to what our freedom thinks it can do and say about him or her, opening the door to every possible and imaginable form of violence. Nothing abstract here, although it is true that, in our most ordinary exchanges, this truth ceaselessly appears in all its nudity and that none of the relations that make up the fabric of existence escape from it. And so it goes when, in the memory we keep of a conversation between friends, it seems evident to us retrospectively that the words of advice given, the information shared or kept secret, the verbal jousting were nothing other than the mask of a force that sought to impose itself. The malaise that seizes hold of us is thus the sign that something was missed in speech and gestures. Like Celan's "Conversations in the Mountains," it reveals what was, at the heart of the encounter, a lack of reception and listening.

Shame must thus be understood as a symptom in the most acute sense of the term. It is the sign-effect of the murderousness that the exercise of freedom carries. Shame is caused by what it hides and, at the same time, reveals: the violence to the other's transcendence, understood as "perfection of infinity," that this exercise commits. Shame lays bare what we have the most difficulty admitting: the "consent to murder," the possibility of which secretly inhabits every act and every word that denies this transcendence by claiming an absolute sovereignty. Levinas summarizes in decisive terms:

> . . . it [the perfection of infinity] is accomplished as shame, where freedom discovers itself murderous in its very exercise. It is accomplished in shame where freedom at the same time is *discovered* in the consciousness of shame and is *concealed* in the shame itself. (*Totality and Infinity*, 84)

It is obviously not insignificant that, in the complex circuitry of *Totality and Infinity*, shame simultaneously involves the possibility and impossibility of murder. Shame is the efficiency of the other's face on my freedom. It puts my powers—including the power to interpret, classify, and judge these actions and words—in their just place. Shame recalls the constitutive violence of these powers, which always exerts itself against the singularity of the other that remains irreplaceable and undefinable. Such is the extreme radicalism of the Levinasian analysis of shame, which is anchored in the most concrete experience of the bankruptcy of freedom as soon as it is exposed to this singularity. It knows each time, it perceives in a more or less confused manner, it guesses even when it refuses to accept what it guesses, what it is capable of: the rights that it is willing to claim, the powers that it will always be tempted to use and abuse to affirm itself, to exist, to dominate.

If it is true that shame is shock, that it seizes hold of us, consumes us, that its ensuing malaise even engenders aphasia and paralysis, then this facultative shutdown provoked by the face of the other has the sense of a revelation. Shame translates and betrays the arbitrary and violent character of our "glorious spontaneity as a living being" (*Totality and Infinity*, 84). By chance, during a seemingly innocuous conversation or any given exchange, we discover that this shared meal, this friendly drink, this exchange of ideas, and all other forms of discussion that had desire and discourse as their vocation, in the sense where each are called by the transcendence of the other, went awry. But, at the same time, by the simple fact that it seizes us, shame also teaches us that we are not "condemned" to freedom but invested by it, and there exists a means for disengagement: the very one that the author of *Totality and Infinity* gives the name "ethics." It is thus that Levinas distinguishes himself from the analyses Sartre develops in *Being and Nothingness* and dramatizes in his theatrical works: shame is indissociable from a desire for justice because the shame that freedom suffers for itself discovers its own injustice. Consequently, of this hell that would be other people, shame is not, and could not be, one effect among others.

However, it is not a question of dismissing freedom but, rather, of submitting it to what Levinas calls the inversion of the "movement of thematization" (*Totality and Infinity*, 86) by folding it to the requirement that preceded it. The other is not an obstacle that keeps me under its gaze and judges me, but one whose *height*, understood as transcendence, commands me. The other eludes the knowledge that transforms what it targets into a pleasure and a possession. Hence, the inversion is nothing other than the movement by which the other constitutes an exception to this transformation. The inversion opens whoever desires the other to another knowledge that does not exist simply for itself. Shame, salutary and necessary, is the operator and the criterion of this other knowledge. Only those beings who have already been profoundly perverted by violence and never retreat from violence, those beings who are convinced they have all the rights over the life of the other, or at least over this or that group of determined individuals, can claim to evade shame.

7
a "balancing pole" over the Abyss
(Victor Klemperer and the Language of the Third Reich)

The power of totalitarian systems does not rest solely with the terror that they put into place, the terror that makes everyone fear for their survival and the survival of their loved ones. It is also distinguished by the hold they have over minds. There is thus no totalitarian system that does not begin by brigading universities, censoring presses and banning the newspapers hostile to it, muzzling the journalists, writers, professors, and other intellectuals liable to voice any opposition while making use of others. Yet, because every consciousness cannot be controlled permanently, because no organization or repressive apparatus is capable of surveillance over every word, much less over the thoughts of those submitted to the constraints imposed by these systems, such measures constitute only the most immediately visible part of their hold. It is not through these visible measures, in other words, that they manage to make millions of men and women feel, think, and reason in unison with the violence that distinguishes them. The efficacy of propaganda must be added. Yet, propaganda is effective only insofar as its semantic innovations, its turns of phrase, and its ways of saying and doing with a language understood by everyone end up imposing themselves as evident, to the point that they no longer upset or cause indignation in those that, more and more numerous, start reproducing them mechanically. The hold over minds is never so strong as when language itself is infected by ideological words. Now, the most dreadful part of this infection is the fact that it is insidious. The substitutions of one meaning for another, the shifts in the value of words, and the innovations imposed by such systems do not come about all in the same stroke through a prescribed reform. They occur unnoticed even by their first victims. In order to make an inventory of them, to list them, even to decrypt them, to measure them in all their gravity, one needs—one needed, consequently, in Germany, Italy, Russia, China, Japan, and Cambodia, everywhere that the government was conceived with a hold of this order—an intelligence endowed with competence and knowledge, an intelligence prepared for such inquiries by the habit of tracking all the ruses of language in texts, an intelligence that contains the force and courage not to concede to the new "spirit of the times." One needs, in other words, a philologist who keeps his eyes open and his ears listening like "a balancing pole over the abyss."

A performance by a tightrope walker on a rope stretched over the void with nothing for a balancing pole except the analysis of the transformations Nazi ideology inflicted on the German language! These are in fact the terms in which Victor Klemperer summarizes how, for twelve years (1933–1945) and in the most difficult conditions, he applied his philological competence, as a specialist in French Enlightenment authors, to a rigorous critique of the "linguistic violence" of the Third Reich:

> [i]t was thus the language of the Third Reich, both literally and in a non-figurative, philological sense, which I clung to with absolute determination and which became my balancing pole across the monotony of every ten-hour shift in the factory, the horror of house searches, arrests, physical abuse etc. etc. (Klemperer, *Language*, 10)

I.

Violence and language. There are three ways to understand what links them. In a first sense, one can indeed experience and describe all the transformations that a given ideology imposes on language as a violence: syntactical and semantic impoverishment, possible neologisms, sweeping simplifications and abbreviations. Language itself, then, is the subject on which this violence is inflicted. It is in this sense that, from the first months following the Nazis' rise to power, Klemperer observed the diverse linguistic phenomena attesting to ideological impregnation. The first phenomenon is the recurrent appearance of words that, although not new, nevertheless acquire increasing importance until becoming veritable leitmotifs of thinking. Three such words in particular hold Klemperer's attention: the verb *aufziehen* (to mount, to set up) and the two common nouns *Strafexpedition* (punitive expedition) and *Staatsakt* (state occasion).[1] The essential, then, is not only their increasing use but also what they connote and the way they act as a symptom. Indeed, they signal and engrave in language from the beginning the threatening power of the State, master of the artifices that it imagines and of the brutal means through which it imposes them. For all three come down to the State's absolute power of organization and orchestration—in other words, to its omnipotence. Hence, certain words that were until then not particularly distinguished from others by their use recall from everyone's lips the unlimited power granted to the State for making appear or disappear, for honoring or eliminating those, on the one hand, who serve it and those, on the other, who disturb it. We thus already have the premonition that this "violence" to language hides another, far more murderous. One realizes above all that this is the guiding thread for Klemperer's vigilance.

The same applies for the second and third phenomena that the author of *The Language of the Third Reich* notes just as acutely. The second phenomenon consists in words whose value Nazism inverts—beginning with "fanaticism." As a reader attentive to the philosophy of the French Enlightenment, familiar with the texts in which Voltaire denounces the murderous intolerance proper to all forms of exaltation and "fanatic" commitment,[2] the philologist does not overlook the threats involved in this inversion. From the moment the noun and adjective lose their negative connotation and acquire the commendable sense of "an inflation of the terms 'courageous', 'devoted', and 'persistent'" or, "to be more precise, . . . a gloriously eloquent fusion of all these virtues" (60), all the outpourings of anger, the calls for vengeance, the destructive expeditions characterizing the word find themselves legitimated.

The third phenomenon to be retained here, out of the many on which Klemperer lingers, concerns the punctuation and, more precisely, the systematic use of ironic quotation marks in practice among the thurifers of Nazi ideology. Indeed, the philologist notes the systematic practice of discrediting all divergent thinking, every word foreign to the means of these artifices. They endorse the idea that only one legitimate word and one legitimate thought exist: the one invoked in pages and speeches on end by the LTI (*Lingua Tertii Imperii,* Language of the Third Reich). Everything else, consequently, is in principle suspicious, undermined, subject to caution—and the punctuation is there as a reminder. If it is true that one must distinguish, in the neutral use of quotation marks, a neutral use and this ironic use, one must recognize, as Klemperer specifies, that "the ironic use outweighs the neutral one many times over. Because the LTI particularly loathes neutrality, because it always has to have an adversary and always has to drag this adversary down" (73). Which is to say that, behind the punctuation quibbles, violence stretches its shadow over language again and again.

More generally, these different operations imposed upon language all rest on one and the same presupposition and will: the idea that language, far from being in the service of a universal truth, expresses the "organic particularity" of "the spirit of a people." It is not the truth that matters but, rather, the way what is thought, written, and said with the words of language *serves* the interest of the "people" and the "race." Only the effects of the invocation or infuriated conviction count, attested to by the contrast between Hitler's "crude, often un-Germanically constructed sentences," their "conspicuous rhetoric"—which are for Klemperer contrary to "the character of the German language" (54)—and their enchanting power, their capacity for captivating the masses. Whence the philologist's indignation, his nostalgia for an authentic Germany, which is not without naïveté. Indeed, such indignation presupposes (which is problematic) an original purity of the German language to which the LTI would be foreign:

> [f]rom the point of view of the philologist I also believe that Hitler's shamelessly blatant rhetoric was able to make such an enormous impact because it penetrated a language which had hitherto been protected from it with the virulence which accompanies the outbreak of a new epidemic, because this rhetoric was in essence as un-German as the salute and uniform copied from the Fascists . . . (56)

Such are the limits of every denunciation that makes language itself the victim of violence, which occurs each time one laments its impoverishment or contamination by words that are foreign to it, whatever their origin. Such a critique presupposes, as the preceding citation seems to suggest, something like a prior "identity" of the language whose loss it sadly bemoans. Thus, Klemperer cannot resist the temptation to call upon a problematic "authenticity" of the German language, which the LTI, exemplified by Hitler's and Goebbels's rhetoric, would come to compromise. In truth, this compromise takes root much earlier, since he repeatedly puts German Romanticism on trial all throughout his analysis. Rereading the "Romantics" Ernst Moritz Arndt and Friedrich Ludwig Jahn, Klemperer finds in their thinking the origin of German racism (contrary to Germany's "essence" or "eternal properties"), which ultimately constitutes, as we will see, the most significant trait of the LTI and the raison d'être of all its artifices: "[t]hese racial teachings, twisted and distorted into a unique privilege of the Teutons and justifications for their monopoly on the human race, and which ultimately became a hunting licence for the most atrocious crimes against humanity" (137).[3]

II.

Yet, the epidemic remains. The second way to understand the link between violence and language pertains, indeed, to the contagion of the infected language, which in fact constitutes one of the most recurrent and also, no doubt, painful motifs among Klemperer's notes. It is the book's lament and its most apparent subject: "Watch men assume as their own these connotations, these murderous expressions, with no distance or reflection, denying all critical spirit!" This is the warning of the philologist who, inversely, adopts the position of a vigilant overhang, "above the fray," as the only one that allows for identifying and recognizing the LTI for what it is, along with the violence proper to it. As Klemperer says, "[b]ooks, newspapers, official communications and forms issued by administrative departments all swam in the same brown sauce" (12), including speech, not only official public speeches but also the speech punctuating the most intimate exchanges with trustworthy beings. Thus, Klemperer does not have words bitter enough to express his indignation when faced with the capitulation of people that, although linked to them through the bonds of friendship or professional esteem, he saw resorting one after the other to the murderous clichés of the LTI, like Beranger observing the metamorphosis of his co-citizens and loved ones into rhinoceroses in Eugene Ionesco's play. Nothing seems capable of shocking them, moving them, revolting them any longer. Everything that they read and everything that they hear ends up coming from their own mouths, stamped with a seal of incontestable obviousness that comes from, Klemperer writes for pages on end, a veritable "intoxication," if not "poisoning."

> Nazism permeated the flesh and blood of the people through single words, idioms and sentence structures which were imposed on them in a million repetitions and taken on board mechanically and unconsciously. [. . . Nazi language] steeps words and groups of words and sentence structures with its poison. Making language the servant of its dreadful system, it procures it as its most powerful, most public and most surreptitious means of advertising. (15–16)

Which is to say that the subject on which violence is inflicted is no longer language itself but, rather, the indifferent people that hear and reproduce it almost mechanically—the entirety of the men and women that this powerfully orchestrated machinery gathers in order to submit them to its hold. This is why the capitulation is both moral and political. It frees political convictions from all moral considerations. From the moment the LTI governs the sentiments of those that it has intoxicated, ruling their entire "moral being," no connection, no friendship, no solidarity, no knowledge shared among friends or colleagues in philology resists the betrayals that it makes possible, even if unconscious or half-conscious. But who betrays whom? First of all, the men and the women who give in to the furies of the LTI betray themselves, disowning what they had loved, subscribing individually to discriminating judgments. As they perceive and conceive nothing of the wounds that they inflict upon the first victims and on whom they impose the evidence of their convictions, they disown them in turn. If Klemperer's book is much more than a scholarly work on the language of the Third Reich, it is because it is punctuated with stories all recounting the same *surprise,* the same *disappointment,* and the same *rupture* in relations. It is always in the various encounters, in the exchanges that it interrupts, that the poison of the LTI manifests its hold not only over the mind but also, in the same stroke, over the heart of those with whom communication is from then on no longer possible. All the bitterness of this "paralysis" of moral sentiments is summarized in a few words: "The sole purpose of the LTI is to strip everyone of their individuality, to paralyse them as personalities, to make them into unthinking and docile cattle in a herd driven and hounded in a particular direction" (23).

III.

And yet, the two preceding points are not sufficient for characterizing the link between violence and language proper to the Third Reich. As long as language is the subject of violence, the latter is understood, indeed, in a sense that remains metaphorical despite everything, as when one speaks of "wounds" inflicted upon language or of a "tortured" syntax. The fact that the contagion spreads to the entirety of the people and touches all categories of the population, the fact that therefore no one escapes its automatisms, says nothing of what makes up its extreme radicality, which pertains to its effect—nothing less than the legitimation of the violence itself, a violence whose subject is no longer language but those that Nazism stigmatizes, excludes, despoils, and ends up assassinating: the Jews. This is no doubt the most decisive point: the proper of the LTI—and it has perhaps no other objective in the end—is to make the entirety of the German people the subject, at once active and passive, of a common murderous consent, namely, the consent that allows for designating the Jews as the enemy that, as the duty of the people and as the responsibility of those that govern them, must be fought by any means necessary. Indeed, everything prior announces nothing other than this sedimentation of the unacceptable that makes the State's anti-Semitism legitimate, acceptable, if not even desirable, in the eyes of the Germans. With the same pain, all Klemperer's stories agree in this sense. They show how language introduces into the customs the radical (and ultimately murderous) separation between the "Aryans" and the "Jews" through expressions such as "alien" to the species, "of German blood," "of inferior race," "Nordic," and "racial defilement."[4] If it is true that the vocation of the philologist's work is to discover directly in language what language symptomizes, the work ultimately brings to light before any other consideration the preparation, the announcement, and the legitimation of the violence of murder *in advance*. Everything in the LTI implies, Klemperer says, "this promotion of murder to the status of a profession" (31). And he specifies a bit further on: "The hysteria of language should one day be studied as a phenomenon in itself. This perpetual threatening with the death penalty!" (31).

Murderous consent, we know, is the *eclipse* of the responsibility for the care, help, and attention for which the vulnerability and mortality of the other calls—everywhere and for everyone. At best, it consists in a resignation or a habituation to the other's suffering, and at worst, in the encouragement of it. In so doing, it divides humanity into two parts: those whose call will be heard and those who are denied the simple right to be heard. On the one hand, Klemperer's linguistic and philological analyses thus converge to recall the following: the LTI's work, its impoverishment of the language, its simplifications, abbreviations, and shortcuts have no other end than targeting the object of this eclipse in a logic of discrimination, exclusion, and persecution that leads to extermination. On the other hand, the stories with which he enamels these reflections are recorded to testify to the unfortunate success of this enterprise of desensitization and dehumanization of the "people": those that he tries to remind of this destructive logic, like a wedge driven into their enthusiastic participation, have no eyes for seeing it and already no ears for hearing his complaint.

At stake, in other words, is a reversal that turns shared compassion, solicitude, care, and attention into indifference, if not, more frequently still, unbridled hostility. The entire question, then, concerns understanding what drives this reversal, which Klemperer attempts—and it is an understatement to stress how much—from cover to cover, as if for him the only means for piercing the enigma of this capitulation that reverses friendships and unties all (or almost all) the ties that make up the tissue of existence were understanding what happens *with* and *in* language. Three of these driving factors can thus be highlighted: faith, blindness, and shamelessness. The author of *The Language of the Third Reich* lingers longest on the first, the second and third being only its most manifest consequences. Klemperer emphasizes this faith on several occasions; the following phrase repeatedly comes from his interlocutors' mouths even when defeat seems inevitable and the catastrophe acknowledged: "I believe in him."[5] Whatever the background of those that utter it, the authoritarian (and in the same stroke threatening) proposition that always closes off all discussion, attesting at the same time to the ravages of the LTI, expresses nothing other than a profession of a faith in Hitler's person, raised to the rank of "Germany's savior." I emphasized above the extent to which the first effect of the LTI was what I have called elsewhere "the sedimentation of the unacceptable."[6] The pedestal on which it rests is itself a concentrate of sediments: it gathers together the qualifiers systematically attached to the Führer's name that make each of his decisions and each of his actions incontestable, turning the judgment that announces, comments upon, or explains those decisions and actions into Gospel. As the philologist recalls in a captivating chapter entitled "Personal announcements as an LTI revision book," the wording of obituaries announcing the death of a soldier on the front testify to this sedimentation: "[h]e died for his beloved Führer," or again, "He fell believing in his Führer to the last" (121). Everything that Hitler could have ordered, everything that Goebbels could have relayed with respect to Hitler's thinking and his will, the accumulating violence and crime were thus justified and exculpated in advance by the almost religious faith driving the LTI from one end to the other. Such is perhaps, in the end, the most radical conclusion to which Klemperer's analyses lead: what turns the LTI so deeply murderous is nothing more and nothing less, in the end, than the allegedly sacred character of the speech it relays.

> From 1933 to 1955, right up until the catastrophe in Berlin, this elevation of the Führer to the status of a god, this alignment of his person and his actions with the Saviour and the Bible, took place day by day and always "went like clockwork" and it was impossible to contradict it in any way. (112)

A blindness, which owes much to faith, is the second driving factor of the murderous consent that eclipses the responsibility for care, help, and attention for which the other's vulnerability and mortality call. Such blindness is even intrinsically linked to faith the moment that the adverb "blindly," in the same spirit as "fanatic," as the LTI's critique recalls, designates "the ideal manifestation of the Nazi spirit with regard to its leader [*Führer*] and respective subordinate leaders [*Unterführer*]" (151). Nevertheless, the adverb should be read literally. To act, to obey an order, and to follow *blindly* are expressions that not only testify to unconditional loyalty; they also indicate that this act of allegiance, the proof of an unshakable faith, demands one "to blind oneself" in the proper sense of the term, that is to say, to make the decision, in all awareness, not to see or to *pretend not to see*, to look away or close one's eyes. Thus, this adverb, which the philologist calls "one of the linguistic pillars of the LTI" (151), inscribes murderous consent in the heart of the linguistic apparatus. If it is true that revolt, goodness, critique, and shame[7] count among the relief roads allowing one to respond to murderous consent and to propose an alternative to its nihilistic hold, the language of the Third Reich systematically blocks them and erases the possibilities of a "witness for the human,"[8] saved or restored, that each of them offers. The LTI clearly indicates that there is certainly no place for any of these "human" ways of responding to or opposing the violence.

Another word from the LTI also testifies to the same situation and perhaps designates the preliminary condition of the blinding, if not the preparation that makes it possible: *gleichshalten*, "to force into line" (154).[9] Being forced into line is, indeed, nothing other than the disciplinary constraint of a mechanized and automatized behavior, a generalized goosestep that dissolves every singular step into the rigorously regulated order of a collective "forward march," in unison with an army ready for battle. Like all the other mechanical metaphors that Klemperer brings into relief, beginning with the one that exalts "the motor running at full tilt" (156) in human work and effort, the expression *gleichshalten* thus deliberately carries into language the negation of any invention of a proper singularity and engraves that negation in the hearts and minds of those that let themselves get carried away by the rhetorical flights. We are nevertheless familiar with this road of necessary inventiveness. A gesture of revolt, an indignant protest would suffice to attest to it, just as a gesture of gratuitous goodness or unexpected offers to help could manifest it, to say nothing of the courage for the truth that runs the risk of critique. For twelve years, over the course of which the Nazis expanded their hold over Europe, Klemperer never missed an opportunity to observe the slightest sign that, throughout his encounters, seemed to him to manifest an attestation of this order. Each of them appears in his diary as a blessing, a source of joy and comfort, a reason—always fragile and reversible—for holding on.

There is nevertheless a sign that is never encountered, so to speak, a sign, expected perhaps, whose erasure Klemperer's book measures, confirming the LTI's hold over the subjugated people: the absence of shame. The fact that an entire part of the population (neighbors, colleagues, yesterday's friends) were stigmatized, humiliated, persecuted, pursued, and treated as outlaws should have incited a feeling of shame in the people (the alleged "Aryans") in whose name these crimes were committed, the shame that one feels when faced with what men and women can inflict upon others. Throughout the stories punctuating the philologist's reflections, one indeed crosses protests here or there, germinal critiques and revolt formulated in veiled terms, gestures of discrete goodness, like the apple set on the machine in the workshop,[10] but never any sign of shame, never the least manifestation of a dissociation [*désolidarisation*] with the racial politics put in place by the Nazis. This erasure of shame, which opens the door to all crimes, is the effect, the result, and, from the point of view of its ideology, the most powerful success of the LTI, the calculation of its language and the reason for its artifices. It confirms its hold on the population through the motif most proper to it (the motif that distinguishes it from every other system of propaganda): "the Jewish war." In fact, all its elements converge to create an ineradicable syntagm: the initially popular basis in the most primitive and most regressive "race consciousness," the pseudo-scientific foundation that the Nazis attempted to give it, the vociferations and imprecations that make up the style proper to the LTI. "The Jew," ultimately, is the central word of the LTI, the pillar on which the entire edifice rests, the proof in language that "[r]acially motivated antisemitism, for Hitler initially a feeling resulting from his own primitiveness, is the central concern of Nazism, well thought-out and carefully developed into a coherent system":

> *Der Jude*—the word is even more prominent in everyday Nazi usage than "*fanatisch*," but even more common than the word "*Jude*" is the adjective "*jüdisch* [Jewish]," because it is the adjective above all which has the bracketing effect of binding together all adversaries into a single enemy: the Jewish-Marxist *Weltanschauung*, the Jewish-Bolshevist philistinism, the Jewish-Capitalist system of exploitation, the keen Jewish-English, Jewish-American interest in seeing Germany destroyed: thus from 1933 every single hostility, regardless of its origin, can be traced back to one and the same enemy, Hitler's hidden maggot, the Jew . . . (176–77)

In the preceding pages, we have chosen to make the legitimation of violence inscribed in the heart of language the guiding thread for a reading of Klemperer's book. It culminates here. For twelve years, tirelessly, the LTI nourished the supposed "Jewish war"—providing the excuse for persecuting and exterminating the Jews. The insulting epithets, offensive words, defamatory accusations were ceaselessly repeated, sedimenting the unacceptable, swallowing all the shame of the crimes that they legitimate.

IV.

Nevertheless, if one wants to make the denunciation of the murderous consent that language authorizes, if not facilitates, the guiding thread for reading Klemperer's reflections on the LTI, the denunciation finds its limits in the geopolitics accompanying his philological analyses. The fact that elements of this nature should be taken into consideration in a meticulous study of the language of the Third Reich is not at all surprising, since it is well known that world cartography and speculations on the origin of peoples constituted one of the central axes of its propaganda. Klemperer thus recalls that at the heart of Nazi ideology was the conviction that Nordic men, Germans first of all, make up the essence of Europe—including Greece, where every effort was made to find such origins in the Hellenes. Whence the idea that Germany had as its historical mission the defense of Europe against the two dangers threatening it, in the south (Syria and Palestine) and in the east (Bolshevism), Goebbels going so far as to invent the repulsive idea of "the onslaught of the Steppes" (162), threatening the European continent with the forces of Asia.

These elements are well known. What surprises most, then, is that the philologist, far from limiting himself to putting these Nazi constructions into relief, acts as a political commentator and substitutes another geopolitics for them: the geopolitics that consists in making Moscow "the focus of European thought" (162) and making Russia the bearer of "the European torch" (164). Comparing the "mechanization of man" implemented by the Nazis and the mechanization that he cannot ignore as a constitutive element of Soviet ideology, he does not have words strong enough to praise the latter. While the mechanization comes from an "enslavement of the mind" (157) in the case of Nazism, mechanization is identified with the mind's liberation with respect to Stalinism. If it is true that both of these "totalitarian systems" are characterized by a profusion of technical metaphors used to designate the power of the people in movement, Klemperer affirms without hesitation that they designate slavery for the German metaphor and freedom for the Russian metaphor. Some ten years after the Moscow Trials, when numerous travel narratives had already begun to testify to an entirely different reality of the Soviet system, such an illusion calls for three remarks.

The first remark is that the philologist opposes the LTI here. Because Nazi propaganda ceaselessly depreciated the image of the Soviet Union, Klemperer persuades himself that he reestablishes the truth by taking the opposite position, without suspecting for a moment that the reality is entirely otherwise and that the Stalinist terror had no reason to envy the Nazi crimes.

The second remark is that, despite everything, some elements of this murderous reality had already leaked out by the time *The Language of the Third Reich* was published (in 1947). Published in the part of Germany controlled by the Soviets, the praise of the system is therefore questionable at the very least. It presupposes the bias of not seeing, not hearing, the will to disbelieve anything that might stain the ideal image of the USSR that the philologist creates for himself: a murderous consent.

Finally, the last remark: in these few paragraphs dedicated to Bolshevism and its language, Klemperer reiterates what he already affirmed in the first pages, namely, that "nothing brings us closer to the spirit of a people than language."[11] In so doing, Klemperer could not have had the same relation to Russian (its history, literature, idiolects, and sociolects) as he had to German. He could not perceive, from a distance, what constituted the equivalent of the LTI in the Soviet system. In a sense, his "illusions" confirm, in reverse, the scope and the difficulty of the work undertaken year after year in order to decrypt the language of the Third Reich. The task could not have been completed by just anyone; it required that particularly trained ear of which Nietzsche speaks in the preface to *Twilight of the Idols*, the exceptional competences of an analyst. It required above all exemplary courage to brave the threat and to risk his life by procuring newspapers, books, and other documents (damning evidence) forbidden to Jews. Finally, it required, despite everything, keeping an unshakable trust in the virtues of knowledge, so disparaged, and in the force of truth in order to face the lies and the terror.

8

Duped by Violence?
(A Reading of Sartre)

It is of the utmost importance to know if violence dupes anyone that fails to denounce violence by minimizing it or anyone that ventures to justify it. Few philosophers, witnesses of the fall of colonial empires, have taken on the task of dismantling the trap of the first of these two pitfalls as much as Sartre. For this minimization is always a mystification. It pretends not to see; it relativizes, puts off, finds pretexts and excuses for what it cannot ignore. This minimization attempts to avoid the most evident manifestations of colonial systems by, for example, distinguishing the "good" colonies from the "bad" or by finding social, economic, and psychological causes in "rebellion," which are meant to dismiss the problem's political dimension. Whence the guiding thread that ties Sartre's committed [*engagés*] texts together: the intransigence of demystification without concession. It presupposes tracking the discourses and images that maintain the "benefactor" myth of colonization by rerouting the proclaimed "benefits" ("civilization," "literacy," "modernization") to the truth of the system that establishes them. To that end, it implies making the system appear as such, with its history and its own coherence, by traversing all the violence that belongs to it as such: passive and present. This traversal is writing's combative responsibility: the meaning of its commitment.

I.

1954. Prefacing Henri Cartier-Bresson's book of photographs, *From One China to the Other*, Sartre recalls the extent to which the photographs gathered in the book contribute to demystifying the most accepted images of China, images whose picturesque character is only the recto of the violence that they warrant: the violence of a scornful characterization that is, Sartre writes, and remains today "the civilized form of massacre" ("From One China to Another," 22). Perpetuated in the majority of the printed, reproduced, and diffused images with respect to China, as Sartre emphasizes, is indeed nothing other than the apparently innocent but nevertheless dreaded form of a "colonial mentality" whose only effect, under cover of curiosity, is to trace a line of demarcation that cannot be crossed between "us" and "them," keeping foreign peoples at a distance and frozen in their distant exoticism. One must thus, in Sartre's eyes, greet Cartier-Bresson's approach as decisive. Cartier-Bresson's approach consists in substituting what Sartre calls "materialistic" images for these suspicious clichés of complacency, images whose vocation is not to separate, to characterize, or to enclose the other in his or her supposed difference but to gather, to approach, and, finally, to produce a sentiment of solidarity. "Images, when they are materialistic, bring men together, that is to say when they begin at the beginning: with bodies, with needs, with work" (26).

Now, what is said here of images also holds for writing: because words are, along with images, the first vectors of violence, they cannot be deserted, abandoned to the calculations of those that make use of them in order to mask an oppressive system or, better still, to maintain the illusion that the system can survive on its own at the cost of a few adjustments. There again, one must mistrust any thought that, with a good consciousness satisfied with the imbalances in the world, blindly reproduces "differences" by recalling that the perception of them, far from being "natural" or "immediate," is always the fruit of a historical, political, and social construction. With respect to the miserable condition that includes four hundred million Chinese, hungry Italian day laborers, and work-exhausted French peasants, "cultural" differences are thus "secondary" and incidental. A few months after Sartre writes these lines, he actively commits to the analysis and denunciation of the colonial system. The Algerian War, which does not leave his thoughts during the years that follow, is only the beginning of his commitment. The idea of a transnational solidarity, then, still inhabits his reflections. In order to emphasize, no doubt, that Cartier-Bresson's snapshots are not in the least posed or artificial but also to indicate what they in the same stroke reveal concerning a common "humanity," Sartre writes: "At a hundredth of a second we are all the same, all of us at the heart of a human condition" (26). This is the album's "message [*faire-part*]." But what will become of this solidarity once the colonial system's violence has been traversed? Could it lead to a different perception of what gathers and what divides? Once all pretenses to unity have been brought to light, if the first effect of this violence amounts to digging an uncrossable ditch between colonist and colonized, what will the alternative be: an unprecedented gathering or a new division that changes the relation of force and reverses the roles? Such is the test constituted by this "traversal." From the first texts in 1956 on the Algerian War to the prefaces that he writes for Frantz Fanon's *The Wretched of the Earth* and for *Discours de Lumumba*, Sartre's tone ceaselessly hardens in the pains taken to highlight what the colonial system irremediably and irreparably created: a fracture in humanity. It is then that, beyond the violence that is proper to the colonial system and that condemns it, the question is raised concerning the violence that its reversal calls for and justifies. If the first violence comes from a murderous consent, the mechanism of which Sartre endeavors to dismantle, how is one to name the legitimation of the second?

II.

1956–1957. Traversing the system's violence, then, Sartre retains two essential and constitutive phenomena of this test: on the one hand, the racism consubstantial to it; on the other hand, the torture that, during the Algerian War, exemplifies in its most radical form the crimes to which the same system is prepared to consent in order to keep itself in place. For the first phenomenon, it is a question of showing that racism is an intrinsic consequence of colonialism, in other words, that one does not go without the other and that it would be illusory to think it could be purged from the system. Everything contributes to its implantation, to its sedimentation in the hearts and minds not only of the colonists but also of the citizens of the mainland that it ends up infecting: "Racism is inscribed," Sartre writes in the article on Albert Memmi's *The Colonizer and the Colonized*, "in the events themselves, in the institutions, in the nature of the exchanges and the production" (58–59). And he continues: "Racism is *already there*, carried by the *praxis* of colonialism, engendered at every instant by the colonial apparatus" (59). Which is as much to say that racism cannot be attributed to some idiosyncrasy: in question is neither a malicious feeling nor a "malicious disposition" that some morality lesson or some appeal to the universality of human rights would suffice to correct while maintaining the system more or less the same. There is nothing incidental or secondary about racism, and it is above all not an epiphenomenon of colonization linked to differences of custom and culture. So, anyone that denounces its manifestations while holding to an explication of this sort in reality does nothing but maintain what they would condemn. For reasons that they will have trouble admitting, they refuse to push their reprobation to what should nevertheless appear as its inevitable conclusion: the uncompromising refusal of a system that does not engender racism by chance but, rather, because it needs racism in order to remain in place. One will understand that, fifty years later, Sartre's demonstration has lost none of its pertinence, since it is true that, today still, the same people barely hide their scorn for, if not hatred of, formerly "colonized" peoples, immigrants in the mainland, while they show their nostalgia for the colonial empire by complaining that its "benefits" have been relegated to the syllabus of a history course in public schools. Such nostalgia is no doubt part of what makes this thought, in a world that racism has not ceased to infect, our heritage even today. Sartre's combative writing will remain a model as long as there are men and women in Europe and elsewhere that not only profess racial inequality but also call for racial separation, symbolic or real, in European cities and countrysides to which racism has been displaced and installed in a lasting way, as long as there are men and women who deny the right to vote for those to whom they ceaselessly promise it.

Now, in what does this system consist? If comprehension without concession is the condition *sine qua non* of a *traversal* of the system's violence, a traversal that consists neither in minimizing the violence nor in accommodating any aspect of it, all in bad faith, it is because only this traversal allows for showing how any reduction of "the Algerian crisis" to an economic, social, or psychological problem is insufficient. It alone, in other words, allows one to approach the crisis in the only dimension that measures up to this violence—namely, its political dimension—and to understand by that very fact the legitimacy of the reclamation of independence. This is, as is known, the step that Camus will not have taken, and one understands better here what an incomplete traversal of violence signifies when it is checked and held back, at the threshold of the most difficult observations, by scruples over loyalty and affiliation.[1] With unequaled severity, Sartre wants to recall the following: first, the history of French Algeria is a gigantic expropriation whose only effect, since the middle of the nineteenth century and under the cover of a so-called "development" of the lands, was concentrating "European land ownership at the expense of Algerian ownership" ("Colonialism is a System," 41). The stake of the expropriation consists in allowing mainland industries to sell off [*écouler*] their products in the new market created by the colonist community that, at the same time, resells to the mainland the product of the lands that were stolen from the colonized people, who never receive the promised benefits [*en voient la couleur*]. Their needs are thus sacrificed, and and their impoverishment, exacerbated by unemployment due to the mechanization, is ineluctable. Sartre, then, has no trouble developing the consequences of a procedure that takes the opposing view of colonization's official discourse, whose lies and pretenses, hypocrisy and denial of misdeeds, still have supporters today. He reveals the strategy of making Muslims illiterate, not to mention the prejudice of considering Arabic as a foreign language, which Derrida will recall many years later while invoking his childhood in Algeria in *Monolingualism of the Other*. In one sentence Sartre sums up what is essential in the text that he dedicates to Memmi's *The Colonizer and the Colonized*: "Colonialism denies *human rights* to people it has subjugated by violence, and whom it keeps in poverty and ignorance by force, therefore, as Marx would say, in a state of 'subhumanity'" (58).

This is the logic, as Sartre borrows it from Memmi, that leads to racism: for the system described here to work, it is imperative that the colonized and the colonizers do not have the same rights, contrary to the demands of universal principles such as the Declaration of Human Rights, principles on which the mainland prides itself. Exploitation presupposes, in other words, the separation of two very determined and hermetic categories of individuals between which an indelible hatred then sediments. The irremediable, the irreparable: a large part of the texts Sartre dedicates to decolonization will consist in taking their measure. If hatred constitutes its motor, it is because, to begin, the colonist is destined to hate the colonized for at least two reasons. On the one hand, the colonist cannot complete the dehumanization without losing his or her own identity. Without the power that the colonists exercise over those that they colonize, they would be nothing. On the other hand, they cannot assimilate the colonized or grant them the rights that they grant themselves without, there again, ceasing to be the colonists that they are. Thus, the only possible outcome is a bidding war of scorn. As the distinction on which the system rests becomes compromised, the system is essentially destined to become harder and harder, more and more racist and brutal in order to maintain it. This is why, Sartre explains, there is no oppression without "hatred of the oppressor towards the oppressed" ("Albert Memmi's *The Colonizer and the Colonized*," 60). The impossible dehumanization of the latter ends up dehumanizing the former, the oppressors themselves becoming prisoner of the image of the oppressed that they forge for themselves. Incapable of understanding what is happening, they are fixed in mechanical reflexes, regulated like clockwork by the system's ideology. No matter the cost, it seems vital to them that the distinctions remain effective and, therefore, that the colonized seem subhuman. We are familiar with what these mechanisms, displaced from the colonies to the mainland, become in the decades that follow. They grant Sartre's analyses all their force in recalling that ordinary racism is not idiosyncratic: even today, racism comes from the rage for maintaining class distinctions between immigrant populations and the most destitute and most fragile categories where these same distinctions, related to their reciprocal conditions of life, turn out to be less and less pertinent and manifest. Being haunted by a breakdown in distinctions thus produces a bidding war in the racist demand for distinct rights and obligations. One understands the temptation of governments to make "the best use" of it: not knowing how to protect the conditions of existence of both or to guarantee everyone minimal security, they can at least see to it that the distinctions remain by fueling the source of racism.

III.

1957–1958. At the beginning of this chapter, I mentioned that Sartre isolates two constitutive phenomena concerning the test constituted by, for him, the traversal of the colonial system's violence. If the first phenomenon is racism, the second is the torture that is no doubt, along with arbitrary executions, the culmination of systematic recourse to violence, but which also reveals, as a symptom, the perversity of the mechanisms implemented by the colonial apparatus in order to make all the mainland citizens consent to that same violence. Sartre forcefully denounces, indeed, not only the practice of torture in itself; he denounces at least as much the murderous consent that the practice's semidissimilation, the lies, and the doubts maintained with regard to it manage to produce. Two factors, then, contribute to the implementation of murderous consent, and their articulation must be grasped.

The first factor comes from a political and military strategy. Recourse to torture, indeed, is not something that happens by accident or chance as an epiphenomenon of war, something derivative or over-the-top, excessive zeal; it is programmed. Understood as the dehumanizing method of interrogation that it is, it constitutes the acme of the "dehumanization" invoked above. Thus, military authorities and their intermediaries on the mainland must deny the evidence at all costs. All methods are good for making any denunciation appear as a rumor and for sewing doubt in the populace.

Here, the second factor intervenes, the factor to which Sartre, thinker of shame and bad faith in *Being and Nothingness*, gives most of his attention. What is this factor? It is the complicity and guilty complacency to which people are driven by this strategy that allows them to pretend to doubt, not to know, to be too uninformed, to lack sufficient proof in spite of the mass of testimonies, in other words, to comply with the semicomfort of false incertitude. For torture to become the object of murderous consent, it is not only necessary for the authorities to strive to half-deny and half-legitimate it as a necessary exception in their public strategy; an intimate strategy must take over: the trite arrangements every person makes with the violence that he or she prefers not to see or to pretend not to believe, the trite sentences, the conclusions of arguments that he or she repeats to maintain the doubt, in other words, the tortuous meanderings of a path taken by bad faith. Sartre recalls this in an article ironically entitled, "You are Wonderful":

> That is where the lie is—and the excuse for the lie: yes, we lack evidence, so we cannot *believe* anything; but we do not seek this evidence because, *in spite of ourselves, we know*. What were the demoralizers asking for? That and nothing else: an ignorance that is excusable but more and more unforgivable, which progressively demeans us and each day brings us closer to those whom we should condemn. (67)

Yet, no one is meant to ignore violence, unless they are duped by the lies that it maintains. Everyone knows deep down that the comfortable refuge in semi-ignorance is unsatisfactory and guilty. For, when information circulates, it is within the reach of anyone that wants to know. For those who ordinarily remain suspicious of all contamination of politics by moral principles, the observation is implacable: from the moment ignorance is always false or rigged, from the moment the doubts are not real, from the moment we credit only the lies that we really want to believe, such consent becomes an "enterprise of demoralization" and makes everyone collectively, by their silence and their passivity, accomplices to the crimes committed in its name. It is at this moment that torture most clearly reveals the test that it constitutes, not for those who suffer it and its irreparability, but for those who do nothing to stop it, remaining complacent in their feeling of impotence and taking refuge in hesitation. This test is the test of nihilism. Indeed, Sartre shows the way torture undermines the confidence of anyone that this consent turns into an accomplice of the values, the sentiments, and, generally, all the links that gather them within the same community. It is not insignificant that in the two texts he devotes to torture—"You are Wonderful" and "A Victory"—Sartre takes the risk of speaking of France and the French with a capital letter.[2] Because the violence is committed in the name of a certain idea of the Nation, its place in the world, its prestige, power, and sovereignty, the violence compromises the attachment to its affiliation. Every collectivity exposed to criminal acts perpetrated in the name of its security, of its place or its grandeur, experiences this fragility in the relations that make up a society's framework. Sartre's analyses could thus be transposed to many other scenes throughout the four corners of the world. The result, then, is a sense of shame, to which the author of "You are Wonderful" returns on a number of occasions:

The fact is that we are ill, very ill; feverish and prostrate, obsessed by her old dreams of glory and by the sense of her shame, France is struggling in the midst of a vague nightmare which she can neither flee nor decipher. Either we see clearly or we are done for. ("You are Wonderful," 64)

But the "demoralization," in which this test of nihilism concretizes, goes further still. The "demoralization" throws suspicion not only on determined members of a given community, leading each to wonder deep down about what others know or refuse to see, what they justify or refuse to endorse, and the extent to which their complacency with the crime extends; it is the possibility of recognizing in a common "feeling of humanity" a common value that the "demoralization" comes to question in the most radical way. This is torture's entire scope: accepted by a population that, a few years earlier, suffered occupation, arrests, already the whole question of deportations and arbitrary executions—and Sartre makes all the parallels—torture makes one doubt the human. And it is then, at the test's culminating point, that the temptation to cave to the fascination with the inhuman appears—as if what murderous consent revealed were nothing more or less than the inhumanity of the human, as if unveiling it should, in the final analysis, have no other effect than contributing to our disillusion. We thought that the extreme violence that humans are prone to inflict on each other was an accident of history. Torture, which has always been among such violence, teaches us that this is not at all the case. As Sartre writes so insistently in the article he dedicates to Henri Alleg's *The Question*, "it is the inhuman in us which is our truth":

Deep in their stupor, the French people are discovering this terrible truth: if nothing protects a nation against itself, neither its past nor its loyalties, nor its own laws; if 15 years are enough to change the victims into torturers, it is because circumstances alone dictate. Depending on the circumstances, anyone, at any time will become a victim or a perpetrator. ("A Victory," 76)

Consequently, stupor turns to despair: if patriotism must thrust us into debasement, if there is no safeguard anywhere, at any time, to stop nations or the whole of humanity from falling into inhumanity, then why indeed should we take so much trouble to become or to remain human beings: it is the inhuman in us which is our truth. ("A Victory," 77)

Is this the last word that torture should inspire? Must one cave to the fascination with "the abyss of the inhuman" (79)? It is here that, confronted with violence, writing testifies to its whole vocation. For Sartre then shows that this abyss is a trap into which everyone falls when they forget to see that the acceptance of or habituation to violence comes from what I have elsewhere called "the sedimentation of the unacceptable." Behind torture lies a criminal system that must be denounced and combatted and that, to that end, demands to be analyzed. Words exist for doing so, phrases that must be linked, first, in order to expose the practice in broad daylight, then in order to describe all its gears, to retrace the decisions that authorize or tolerate it, and finally in order to counter all the arguments put forth to justify it. Thus, the vertigo of the "abyss of the inhuman" dims out behind the vocation that writing takes on. Such is Sartre's homage to Henri Alleg. His testimony is a counterword that restores the inhuman to its proper place. One needed, the author of "A Victory" writes, "the calm courage of a victim, his modesty and his lucidity, which awaken and demystify us" (79). But the damage is done. Torture leaves traces, and it irreparably produces a radical hatred before all. Following Sartre's texts on the colonial system in chronological order, in rhythm with the events that provoke them, it seems that the systematic practice of torture, even more than racism, produces the consciousness of an irremediable rupture. It leaves no place and no chance for words, for reconciliation, or for any form of dialogue.

IV.

1961. The break is confirmed in the long preface that Sartre writes for Frantz Fanon's *The Wretched of the Earth*. The crisis of the colonial system, as it entails an exacerbation of racism and the explosion of violence exemplified by torture, is not an epiphenomenon in European history, a secondary accident; the crisis discredits it further and becomes the symptom of its loss. None of the values proclaimed as a title to exemplarity resist—beginning with the universal humanism that the crisis finally discredits. Supposing that one recognizes any value in humanism's words and, for example, in the respect for human dignity or for human rights, the uprising of "colonized peoples" reveals that, indeed, it is not the Europeans that could allow such peoples to recognize these values as their own but, rather, the most radical rupture with their way of incarnating them. In other words, the condition for such recognition had to lie in separation rather than assimilation. In order to be "human" in the sense Europeans give to the term, they had to turn their back on Europe. One might thus think either that these values are relative and do not at all concern colonized people or that they are effectively universal, in which case Europe, contrary to its ideology, was the least capable of carrying its truth. For the history of its constitutive relation with what it itself had defined as its "alterities" revealed that it had itself ceaselessly scorned them. Racism, torture: so many contradictions that forced the image that Europe had constructed of itself to explode.

> [S]ince the others are making themselves human beings through their opposition to us, it appears that we are the enemies of the human race; the elite is revealing its true nature: a gang. Our cherished values are losing their sparkle: looking at it closely, there is not a single one that is not stained with blood. If you need an example, remember those grand words: "How generous France is!" Generous, us? What about Sétif? And those eight years of ferocious war that have cost the lives of more than a million Algerians? And the torture? ("The Wretched of the Earth," 170)

> We sent the troops to Algeria where they have remained for seven years without effect. The violence has changed direction: when we were victorious, we employed it without appearing to be corrupted by it: it decomposed the others, while for us human beings, our humanism remained intact; united by profit, the people of the mother country baptized the community of their crimes "fraternity" and "love"; today, that same violence, everywhere obstructed, returns to us via our soldiers, is internalized and takes possession of us. ("The Wretched of the Earth," 171)

But if the preface to *The Wretched of the Earth* marks a turning point, it is not only because it describes the collapse of Europe; following Fanon, it draws a final consequence: contrary to every apology for non-violence, the demand for sustaining without reserve the violence of the "colonized peoples" or at least abstaining from its condemnation. Such is the paradox of traversing racism and torture, as well as the forms of oppression and humiliation that characterize it: because the hatred that it sediments in the hearts and minds of those that the system forces to live in terror can have no other outlet than violence, the condemnation of the same system cannot denounce it, no matter its manifestations. Any other attitude, moreover, is suspected of complacency. Compromising with the irremediable, it ends up adapting itself to what it could not manage to remove through legal means, supposing that it even intended to do so. Above all, however, minimizing the suffering and the "dehumanization," it refuses to take measure of the ditch that hatred has dug, incapable of admitting that, precisely for these reasons, it is impossible for the "victims" of colonization to put an end to the oppression in any other way.

But that is not all. For in this essay, which is intended as an homage to the legitimate uprisings of the people in order to put an end to their servitude, the most radical propositions resonate as a veritable "murderous consent." Carried away by the conviction that violence is legitimate, that it constitutes a just inversion of the relation of forces after decades of scorn and killings, Sartre, anxious to share the people's anger, proliferates formulations that exalt it as a process of "man reconstructing himself" (166). Taking up Fanon's formulations, Sartre wants not only to show that *all* means are good for expelling colonialism; he also maintains that violence is the only means that the colonized have for "liquidat[ing] the colonial darkness within and outside them" (166), that is to say, the only means for existing—in the strongest sense of the term—and for creating themselves as humans. The problem, in other words, is not only political; it is equally existential. The problem is inseparably both. Violence is thus recognized as both a necessary arm and a reason for existing.

> We knew this truth, I think, but we have forgotten it. No gentleness can efface the marks of violence; it is violence alone that can destroy them. And the colonized cure themselves of the colonial neurosis by driving out the *colon* with weapons. When their rage explodes, they recover their lost transparency, they know themselves in the same measures as they create themselves. [. . .] For, at this first stage of the revolt, they have to kill: to shoot down a European is to kill two birds with one stone, doing away with oppressor and oppressed at the same time: what remains is a dead man and a free man . . . (166)

There is thus violence and violence: violence of the colonists and *all* the military and political apparatuses that sustain them; violence of the colonized or, more generally, all the oppressed of Earth. If the first violence is condemnable and should be fought, the second is legitimate and authorizes all means necessary to wage that struggle. Such reasoning is problematic for at least two reasons. First, it forbids distinctions that war ethics, supposing that one recognize its pertinence here, nevertheless demands. It is not true that *all* means are valid, even for a legitimate and necessary emancipation, unless by emancipation one understands a collective vengeance against an enemy that is itself collective and undifferentiated. No matter its origin, terror has innocent victims. Whoever refuses to recognize that nothing can legitimate violence that strikes blindly is *duped* by that same violence—except by maintaining, as is perhaps the case here, that every colonist deserved to die for the generic motive of a substantialized affiliation. The second reason for which Sartre's analyses are problematic pertains to determining the criteria that permit one to maintain this distinction between violence and violence once the possibility of calling for nonviolence has been discarded. If it can no longer be a question of moral principles, then what is in question? politics alone? the situation? the meaning or direction [*sens*] of history? Everything that makes the political inheritance of Sartre a controversial legacy pertains to these unresolved questions.[3] But this is also no doubt what continues, fifty years after the end of the colonial empire, to inscribe that inheritance in the present moment.

9
"the spirit of storytelling"[1]
(A Reading of Kertész)

> This century, the twentieth century, is like a firing squad in continuous service.
> —Kertész, *Journal de galère*, 210

> And if we examine whether the question of the Holocaust is a vital question for European civilization, European consciousness, then we find that the answer is yes. Because the very civilization within the frameworks of which the Holocaust occurred must reflect on it. Otherwise it too will become a civilization of accident and mishap, no more than a debilitated organism drifting helplessly towards annihilation.
> —Kertész, "The Holocaust as Culture," 75

Every relation to history in the early twenty-first century implies and bears the memory of last century's murderous wars. Undoubtedly, these wars do not comprise the entirety of history, and our attention is perhaps legitimately solicited by many other parts of the past, however we recall them, but the wars are indissociable from the way history files and maintains its trace in the orientation of our existences. To think history, indeed, is not only to understand the development of past events by staging the different types of causality that might account for it; nor is it exclusively an attempt to find a meaning in the becoming, to grasp a movement, progression, or any progress whatsoever, whether of reason, law, freedom, or democracy. It is just as much a reflection on how our relation to the past *affects* us individually and collectively. It is to grasp the nature of the faculties and emotions that are at work in the perception of the past and the consequences that result from it. The question is thus of knowing [*savoir*], on the one hand, if these affects depend on the work of historians and, on the other hand, if such interrogations still fall under what one calls a "philosophy of history." Indeed, it is less a question of determining the terms and conditions of our knowledge [*connaissance*] of the past—scholarly or vulgar, informed or intuitive—than of understanding the place that knowledge occupies in our lives, even if we have no awareness of it.

But the affect of history cannot be separated from the memory of crimes. Before any critical examination, this affect comes from—for everyone—the progressive and brutal consciousness of this violence. There is a mysterious moment in the genesis of every individual where the possibility of radical evil, whose horrors and terrors the twentieth-century wars exemplify, becomes evident.[2] From a random story, testimony, documentary, or work of fiction (but does one ever know retrospectively, with infallible precision, when it began?), at the whim of an encounter, or perhaps from school, there comes a moment *when one knows*. Regardless of the degree of clarity or confusion of this knowledge [*savoir*], history forces its way into life as a plurality of stories about "good" and "evil," as obscure and imprecise as these notions must remain.[3] In the service of a calculated representation of "good" and "evil," it undoubtedly happens that political, ideological, or religious forces intervene in its implementation, that some interest, in other words, is a stakeholder in this intrusion of the past into life. But however powerful it may be, however many intermediaries, however many instruments of propaganda and diffusion of which it makes use, no force is fully able to control or exhaust the passage of the past into life. It can certainly impose its own lies, even by means of terror, yet there always comes a time when history is restored, when the mild and sometimes secret force of stories and testimonies prevail over their falsification, refusal, or confiscation.

Literature is this force. There is no denying it: the role twentieth-century history plays in our lives is inseparable from the books, testimonies, or novels by Primo Levi, Robert Antelme, Elie Wiesel, Jean Améry, Tadeusz Borowski, and Charlotte Delbo, as well as those by Eugenia Ginzburg, Yury Dombrovsky, Varlam Shalamov, Vasily Grossman, or Aleksandr Solzhenitsyn, and still so many others.[4] Literature is also this force in the belatedly recognized work of Imre Kertész—as much for the force of the stories as for the violent resistance it generated—not only because *Fatelessness*, *Kaddish for an Unborn Child*, and *Fiasco* pertain to this force and make the obstacles that this force must overcome in order to be accepted an element of the story, but also because no one has explained, if not theorized, more thoroughly than Kertész the role literature and, with it, the imagination play in our individual and collective consciousness of "good" and "evil," the memory of which history engraves and maintains in the existence of each of us. Tirelessly, in *Fiasco*, but also in his *Galley-Boat Log*, in a series of essays collected and published under the title *The Holocaust as Culture*,⁵ and in an extensive interview with editor Zlotán Hafner entitled *Dossier K.*, Kertész will have attempted to comprehend the recourse [*recours*] that literature constitutes and the succor [*secours*] it brings to take control of the most unbearable historical reality.

I.

In a lecture dated from the early 1990s entitled "The Enduring Camps," Imre Kertész's point of departure is the observation that the experience of radical evil, constituted paradigmatically by the death camps of the Third Reich, has a dimension difficult for history to grasp. Even if it were possible for history to record all the facts, the way the memory of them is *inscribed* in our lives and *orients* our existence eludes historical investigation. Nor is a "philosophy of history," in the classical sense of the term, capable of accounting for it. Because it is not possible to find the least rational or theological justification in these "facts," they would have no *value for us* as a testament to the World Spirit, in the sense Hegel gives to the term, or as a manifestation of divine will. We do not live *with* their memory in order to attest to one or the other, and this is not the way we learn, as children or adolescents, what happened in the regimes of terror, beginning with the unimaginable deportation and extermination of millions of people in the death camps. It is not in this way that, overnight or more gradually, without always being able to say when and how, our awareness changed entirely. In other words, we are answerable to no spirit or God when the memory of radical evil irrupts into existence.

But then to whom or to what are we obliged? To men and women themselves? And what does this debt or duty mean? Kertész's response is not simple, and it could lead to confusion, since the terms he puts forth can themselves be abused (in fact, they have been) and used in an opposite sense than the one he gives them with strictly inverse intentions. It must first be said that this memory reaches us by way of a plurality of stories from which a law arises, a law to which the testimonies offered by these stories bend, *each one singularly and irreplaceably*, at the same time that they institute it *communally* in existence. Clearly, this law is no more scientific than juridical. And yet, any attentive reader of these stories knows that this law secretly commands the reader's existence from the moment the law maintains alert vigilance against its transgression. In an expression borrowed from Thomas Mann, the author of *Fatelessness* names this law "the spirit of storytelling":

> Allow me to name this law, in my confusion and for lack of anything better, according to an expression borrowed from Thomas Mann: simply, the spirit of storytelling, which not only directs our spirit, but which we also nourish with our own life, and would not exist without doing so. ("Enduring Camps," 44)

But what is the "spirit of storytelling"? First and foremost, that which in it and thanks to it becomes constitutive of a "myth." This is the hidden imperative that governs a story's writing and to which we ourselves are obliged to bend. The law to which stories submit prescribes that they converge in the constitution of a myth. Clearly, it is of the highest importance not to misunderstand the meaning of the terms. Kertész by no means supports—and who would, except the most criminal of ideologues?—that the extreme violence, the testimonies of which occupy our memory, are "mythic" in the sense of "falsified" or "fabricated." Nor does the myth in question signal toward a foundational terror that would find in this function the dubious legitimation of a history of origins. Even less does it suggest that in the horrors recounted there is anything mythical whatsoever in the sense contrary to "historical truth." So, what constitutes this myth? And how, from the day it begins to haunt us, do our lives bend to its grip? How does *one live* the history of wars?

At stake, writes the author of *Kaddish for an Unborn Child*, is a "secret and common decision" ("Enduring Camps," 44). This decision is not the matter of one person alone. Everyone named so far, and everyone that would have to be named in turn, would be familiar with this decision. There is nothing arbitrary about it, either. Rather, if one can talk about a "spirit of storytelling," it is in the sense that this decision is the reflection of a "spiritual necessity" that renders it imperative for everyone and calls upon his or her responsibility. What is this about? Nothing more than sharing—as the major reason for the memory of wars—"stories about good and evil." This is how our singular lives are reminded of history. It is a gift of literature made to us by the exemplary witnesses of writers and poets—and here we should add to the names already mentioned the names broached in previous chapters: Paul Celan and Osip Mandelstam—a gift of words that concern "good" and "evil" and thereby have the force of law.

> The horizon of our everyday life is determined by these stories that are, in the end, stories of good and evil, and our world defined by that horizon is filled with incessant murmurs concerning good and evil. I would venture an audacious claim: in some sense and at some level, we live exclusively for the spirit of storytelling. This spirit that constantly forms in the heart

and mind of each of us has taken the spiritually impalpable place of God: this is the imaginary gaze we feel upon us, and everything we do, we do in the light of this spirit. (44)

Because "good" and "evil" can no longer be appropriated either by an ideology or theology, because their delimitation is always suspect since it serves political interests and is always susceptible to becoming murderous consent, they could find truth only in literature. This does not mean that literature is the refuge of values that would be otherwise devalued. No recycling, no reclamation, is at stake. It simply means that these stories give the highest proof of the truth of "good" and "evil." If this were not the case, totalitarian systems and authoritarian regimes, all governments and politics that attempt to impose their absolute version of good and evil, would not fear as a threat the "spirit of storytelling" and the force of myth that it opposes to their lies. Indeed, there is no method they are not ready to employ in the attempt to curb the intrusion of history—which is to say, the memory of crimes—into life, in the attempt to deny, in other words, that existence is haunted by the past in any other way than within the strict limits and according to the ideological orientations prescribed by these systems and regimes. The whole force and singularity of Kertész's oeuvre comes from having taken the measure of this situation twice over. On the one hand, as we know, with *Fatelessness*, Kertész will have made *his own* singular and irreplaceable memory of the camps, a memory recovered and above all completed in what he always insisted on presenting as a novel,[6] a part of the murmur that constitutes the myth. On the other hand, with *Fiasco*, Kertész will have made the censorship and obstruction of his book's publication as much a part of the "spirit of storytelling." No one more than Kertész will have put into perspective this redoubling of violence constituted by the confiscated memory of wars when it attempts to deprive the people of the literary voices that share the only stories of "good" and "evil" that escape the grip of this confiscation.

Consequently, when men and women deprived of their freedom are denied history, the lack is sorely felt more in this "spirit" than in the work of the historian. If it is true that the memory of the destruction, deportation, and extermination of millions of men and women cannot be thought independently of the voices that share our lives and speak to us about good and evil, the repression or deliberate extinction of these voices, as one snuffs the flame of remembrance, never signifies anything other than the potentially murderous willingness to abandon what literature might teach us or tell us about good and evil. Sometimes people complain that their murmur is incessant. We have already seen and heard everything about the regimes of terror and their work of destruction. It is necessary, they say, to turn the page, to stop indulging in the painful reminder of the wars of the twentieth century. But it is not possible for this murmur to stop. It would amount to wanting to silence history, to repress the spirit of storytelling, to kill myth and thereby to leaving the field open to the incomplete constitution of an "imposed truth." Kertész, like Paul Celan before him, will have always been alarmed by these desires for silence and oblivion,[7] just as one should be unsettled today by a political will that, wherever it is at work, intends to rewrite history in its own way and control education under the guise of "national identity." Kertész recalls in an essay entitled "The Holocaust as Culture":

> The dictatorship of the proletariat did not like people to speak of the Holocaust. It silenced all such voices or forced them into schemas of conformist euphemisms. If one were nonetheless bold enough to entertain the notion that Auschwitz was, after the Crucifixion, the most significant event for humankind which had traumatically fallen, so to speak, through European ethical culture, and if one were to wish to approach these questions with the appropriate seriousness, then one could count on being condemned from the outset to complete solitude and isolation. One could assume that one's books would be printed in limited numbers, if at all, and one could be confident of being banished to the margins of literary and intellectual life, thrust into the silence of official critical opinion, much like solitary confinement. In other words, once sentenced to death himself, the author could now expect the same sentence to be passed over his work. (71)

But why literature? It is always to be feared that history (even more so when it is prescribed), History with a capital-H and Philosophy with a capital-P make do, translate, summarize, interpret, and select the *plurality* of murmurs according to their own criteria; in other words, it is always to be dreaded that they will do violence to what makes the singularity of each murmur. But what makes this singularity? Language, first and foremost. The force of these murmurs, the force they bring and lodge in our lives, is always the invention of a language. This is why history, beginning with the history of the wars of the twentieth century, cannot be separated from literature. This is what binds the "spirit of storytelling," and the myth that constitutes it, to its fate. This is what the stories of "good" and "evil" that engage our responsibility require: *the poetic language* of Paul Celan and Osip Mandelstam, the prose of Primo Levi and Varlam Shalamov. As Kertész repeatedly recalled about *Fatelessness*, he had to invent a language *for* Auschwitz, if not reinvent Auschwitz *in* language:

"But you can't mean to say that you invented Auschwitz?"

"But in a certain sense that is exactly so. In the novel I did have to invent Auschwitz and bring it to life; I could not fall back on externalities, on so-called historical facts outside the novel; everything had to come into being hermetically, through the magic of the language and composition. Look at the book from that point of view. From the very first lines you can already get a feeling that you have entered a strange sovereign realm in which everything or, to be more accurate, anything can happen. As the story progresses, the sense of being abandoned increasingly takes hold of the reader; there is a growing sense of losing one's footing" . . . (*Dossier K.*, 9)

II.

But we must go further. Why do we have a *vital need* for these stories? Why, so to speak, do we breathe beneath their gaze? Because secretly at stake in them is the responsibility called for everywhere by the care, help, and attention that the vulnerability and mortality of the other demands. If one talks of "spirit," it is indeed to indicate that the stories in question do not give life to history at the heart of our existence solely for the aesthetic pleasure they could produce or only to respond to a need for knowledge. To put it otherwise, it is not in this way that the "logic, the moral horror and villainy, the incommensurable torments, the monstrous teaching" that frame these stories have become "an integral part of the European spirit." As Kertész writes, for them to reach "the proportions of a turning point in the history of mentalities," it was necessary for catastrophe to touch "vital organs" ("Enduring Camps," 46). What are these organs? What was destroyed that had been "vital" to such an extent? The answer comes quickly; it primarily concerns the executioners, but undoubtedly also anyone who more or less actively encouraged or assisted through their passivity or silence the murder of millions of men and women: a contract was broken—a contract that binds people to each other in a mutual responsibility demanded by their vulnerability and mortality. Ultimately, the "spirit of storytelling" consists of the reminder, whose warning remains vital, of *a massive and monstrous breach of contract, the wound of which European consciousness has not ceased to bear—and it is not certain that it should.*

It is time to take a peek at the two co-authors of the century's Grand Guignol, the Communist and Nazi movements. The spirit of storytelling considers that they have breached their contract, in other terms, that they are criminals. The atmosphere of crime is seriousness, Kierkegaard said.

> I spoke about breach of contract because, ever since the vision of the law appeared in the burning bush of European moral culture and then was engraved in stone in the form of words, we measure every event from the standpoint of these words and every act is evaluated in light of the contract. (46)

Literature's force amounts to engraving in one's heart "the spirit of storytelling" in order to protest against this breach. It undoubtedly happens that literature itself strays or gets lost in the neighborhood of ideology, that it calls on crime, or that it supports a murderous voice. Poets and writers are no more immune to a breach of contract than anyone else. But when this occurs, they also renounce the vocation of literature. They make themselves outlaws or, put otherwise, they turn away from *their law* for the worst, as the spirit of storytelling distinguishes it, bears it, and teaches it. This is why there is no place (and there will never be a place) for an "anti-Semitic literature" or a "racist literature," that is to say, for a racism and anti-Semitism that would don literary robes in order to gain acceptance. What exist, on the contrary, what have always existed, are the anti-Semitic and racist provocations to breach the contract, provocations that believe they can build their opposition to the "spirit of storytelling" into a universal law—it is the denial of "good" and "evil," as Vasily Grossman, Varlam Shalamov, Primo Levi, Jean Améry,[8] Imre Kertész and so many others narrate the distinction, in favor of murder erected in the need of history.

And it is true that nothing better exemplifies such a breach than racism and anti-Semitism. It is important to ask how every existence acquires revulsion to this breach—especially when we witness, as is the case today, the resurgence of the most xenophobic passions, as if suddenly "the spirit of storytelling" hung at half-mast, as if the voices that carried it for more than half a century had become inaudible.[9] Wanting to understand, as we do in these pages, the place that the memory of the wars of the twentieth century occupies in our lives, there is no doubt that the living inscription of such a revulsion—which is allergic to the criminal breach of contract that racism and anti-Semitism call for as their deepest desire against a specific set of individuals: Jews, Gypsies, "Arabs," "Blacks," etc.—no doubt thus that, marked and engraved in consciousness, such a refusal to consent in any form whatsoever to the murder of the other is the first and most vital stake. We spoke above about history forcing its way into life. With its intrusion, the "invisible hand" of all the stories concerning "good" and "evil" is at stake. Leaving their indelible mark, they put in one's heart, in words and images, the memory of these breaches of contracts that, without exception, all the crimes of history are—and they thus recall the prohibition of murder to those who would be tempted to forget it or compromise with the responsibility that it activates:

Regardless of how we analyze it, the smoke of the Holocaust casts its long, dark shadow on Europe and at the same time its flames have etched an indelible mark in the sky. In this sulfurous light, the spirit of storytelling reiterated the words carved in stone; it has placed ancient history in this new spectral light, made real the parable, revived the eternal passions that speak of human sufferings. (50)

In a later essay entitled "Weimar Visible and Invisible," Kertész insists on the fact that the contemporary artist cannot take his or her art seriously if its inspiration remains foreign to the suffering whose call is heard everywhere. It is up to the artist, he says, to identify with those who suffer, as if this identification were part of a contract to which he or she were held responsible. Consequently, literature most often finds itself on the side of history's "vanquished" or forgotten. Literature recalls to memory the attention, care, and help that their vulnerability and mortality demand. Such is ultimately the function of the spirit of storytelling. It is not only a question of upholding a duty to remember. It is not exclusively toward the victims of the past that it turns. Unlike history (*this is its spirit*), literature builds a bridge between the two shores of suffering, the shore whose recollection [*souvenir*] it engraves in memory [*mémoire*] and the shore whose call (*this is ethics itself*) must not be denied or ignored. It struggles against oblivion only by opening everyone's existence to the possibility of a protest against violence and injustice. Through the stories of the past, literature gives us the eyes and ears to see and hear these stories of "good" and "evil" that make our present. Kertész ceaselessly repeats it:

> Today suffering befalls man [. . .], and art is today a solemn protest against this suffering; it could not be anything else. ("Weimar Visible and Invisible," 108)

> The Holocaust is a value, because through immeasurable sufferings it has led to immeasurable knowledge, and thereby contains immeasurable moral reserves. ("The Holocaust as Culture," 77)

III.

And yet, we most often see and hear nothing, or almost nothing, even though we are persuaded that we do. The scope of the "incommensurability" of the sufferings that make up the framework of the stories must be measured anew if one wants to understand why the memory of the wars in the twentieth-century requires literature's help. In an essay entitled "Long, Dark Shadow," Kertész indicates this from the beginning to everyone that came to hear him speak: "The problem, dear listeners, is the imagination. To be more precise: to what extent is the imagination capable of coping with the fact of the Holocaust?" (171). In other words, if it is true that, "in Auschwitz, good and evil are not for one instant confounded," this nevertheless does not mean that it is easy to imagine them *as one should*, that is to say, as is necessary for their image to take root in life in order to become a part of what Kertész himself calls "our ethical culture" (171), if not its very pedestal. There are, writes the author of *Fatelessness*, at least three conditions for both literary and cinematographic representations of the Shoah to be up to the task and the stakes, that is to say, as Kertész emphasizes in his essay "Who Owns Auschwitz?," three conditions for them to avoid becoming kitsch. First, the representation should ignore nothing of how the idea of humanity did not escape unscathed from the human destruction at work in the death camps. If it had escaped unscathed, the camps would not occupy the central place that they are granted in "the spirit of storytelling," and they would not constitute "an indispensable image in . . . collective myths" ("Long, Dark Shadow," 171), measuring up to this unsettling [*ébranlement*] that is also a censor in history. Next, the representation cannot misrecognize that this extreme violence constitutes a possibility of "human nature," which will or will not be realized depending on conditions proper to public and private life. Representation strays, in other words, if it reduces the evil to the perversity of only a few people, especially, then, if it concedes to a fascination with the executioners to the detriment of the political conditions (the totalitarian systems) that produced them. Finally, it is necessary for the representation to bring to light the universal scope of the destructions, such that consciousness and memory of them "exceed" the fate of the "communities" implicated (the communities of the murderers and of the victims), however one circumscribes them.

Yet, even though one would avoid being kitsch—and one knows that this is far from always being the case, even less so, indeed, for cinema—the question of the imagination remains nonetheless. "Why literature?" we are asking in this book. Because no concept is suitable for the massive and systematic character of the crimes, of the forced labor, the starvation, the deportations, and, finally, the planning and organization of the extermination of millions of men and women in the death camps, to say nothing of the humiliations, degrading treatments, and experiments that made history last century. Because consequently, Kertész specifies, "of the Holocaust"—but one should say the same of all the genocides that are so difficult to conceive and "to penetrate"—"we can form a realistic notion only *with the help of aesthetic imagination*" ("Long, Dark Shadow," 172, my emphasis). The imagination thus comes to help thinking, philosophers, histories, anybody. But it does so only through the test of an aporia. For it, too, stumbles from the lassitude of counting.[10] Where thinking gets lost in the abstraction of the mass crimes and their victims, it must take up the challenge of accumulation. It must (*this is its ethic*) give an image of what really happened, which nevertheless remains *unimaginable*.

> When piled up, images of killings are distressingly wearisome; they do not trigger one's imagination. How can horror be the subject of an aesthetic if there is nothing original in it? In the place of exemplary death, the facts can only serve up mountains of corpses. ("Long, Dark Shadow," 172)[11]

This is why the task is interminable. It is not possible to fancy one has imagined [*se figurer avoir imaginé*] *once and for all* the unimaginable. There is no, and there will never be, a final narrative. The page on murders and consents to them will never be definitively turned. Thus, "the spirit of storytelling" is the spirit of this very incompletion, which constitutes the universality and immortality of the myth. Nevertheless, the expression should not mislead us: the invocation of "aesthetic imagination" presupposes no "aestheticization" of the Shoah, no plaything, no pleasure; it presupposes a burden.[12] Stumbling on the unimaginable, expression calls the imagination up to the incommensurable. Because the victims cannot be confused in an anonymous mass or summarized in an abstract number, what it gives to imagine, what it thereby engraves in one's heart is first and foremost what Kertész himself ceaselessly called "the ethical result [of the Holocaust] as it is reflected in the global consciousness" ("Long, Dark Shadow," 172). And this result is both an impossible and an eternal mourning, an interminable ceremony, the memory of crimes and with it, as its sharpest point, the refusal of all the murderous consents that are still today and will continue to be the framework of history. This is what the myth pertains to insofar as the "spirit of storytelling" constructs it: it nourishes on the flame of memory that all these deaths singularly demand. Hence, one conceives better how the problem [*l'épreuve*] of the imagination is aporetic: it asks us to substitute for the mountains of corpses a few faces, a few names, a few recounted lives where terror's only objective was to efface them. Such is its ethical truth. It knows that numerical abstraction does not measure the incommensurable and that it has no chance for engraving our hearts.

> As we have seen, only through the power of aesthetic imagination may we gain a notion of the Holocaust. More precisely, what we imagine in this way

is no longer just the Holocaust but also its ethical result as it is reflected in the global consciousness, that black memorial whose dark brilliance—so it seems—continues to glow inextinguishably in that universal civilization which we call our own, to which we belong. ("Long, Dark Shadow," 172)

Nevertheless, this impression is never assured, and one will always fear that its relays weaken, that its lights fade. Thus, the unacceptable can return to assault consciousness; violence, murder, and all the accompanying consents can, because of political interests or a proclaimed meaning or direction of history, reclaim rights that they do not have. Beyond the spirit freed from them, this is no doubt what ultimately makes each story, in the same way as one of Paul Celan's poems, a bottle thrown into the sea or an outstretched hand.[13]

10

"Surviving": The Novel

(A Reading of Kertész's *Galley Boat-Log*)

> Berlin—that monstrous symbol of absurdities, of our disorderly, walled-in life, which has not ceased being the past, which came to a standstill somewhere and whose sole occupation is to swallow up the future: the present is the apathetic poverty of survival. Yet the direction of this survival is completely unsure; it may be advancing in time yet it is still not steering towards anything—at least not perceptibly. People fill in the cracks between the stones materially as it were, like some sort of stifling, squishy mass: they queue up in shops, at cafés and restaurants. [. . .] It is incomprehensible how every night does not bring massacres, arson attacks, blood baths and pillaging, then in the morning everyone would go to work.
>
> —*Journal de galère*, 87–88[1]

I.

Kertész deposits these impressions in his *Galley Boat-Log* during a trip to East Germany in 1980. It would be another ten years or so before the Berlin Wall falls and the totalitarian system ceases to weigh so heavily upon even the smallest deeds and gestures of existence, spreading its shadow beyond the home and the workplace onto storefront windows and restaurant patios in the city streets. Already for twenty years, Kertész has measured its disastrous effects very irregularly throughout the pages of his *Log* in the course of a reflection that inquires into both the means for "reappropriating" this confiscated life and the possibilities that novel writing offers from this perspective. From the 1960s on, an expression accompanying his first novel suffices for him to summarize the situation concerning the mutations that this confiscation induces in the lives of men: "the functional man."[2] Four traits characterize the negation, if not even the degradation and mutilation, that this reduction of man to his function connotes. The first is the identification of the individual with the place that society assigns him or her and as it manifests itself in the ensemble of predetermined, ordered, and controlled facts. Forbidding all deviance, all deviation, all invention that escapes their rule, it constitutes the suffocating and threatening form taken by the submission of man to modern life's modes of organization in a totalitarian society. This is why these imperious and imperative "facts" are understood as "absurdities," like those with which Kafka's characters collide. The word returns again and again in the first pages of the log in order to signify the diktat of a thoroughly censored life, which is the most common and most visible mark of the violence exercised by totalitarian systems on those that it submits to its yoke. "Conforming to the necessity of facts," remaining within their external determination as if there were no way to escape them: this is the *absurdity*. It deprives humans of all possibility for "living their own reality"; it no longer allows for the "existential experience of life," even if that experience is tragic. In Kertész's terms, the absurdity makes one "fateless":

> Conformity: When a person does not seek concordance with reality but with the facts. What is reality? In a word, ourselves. What are the facts? In a word, absurdities. The link between the two, briefly put: a moral life, fate. Alternatively, there is no link, which means an acceptance of facts, a series of chance events and adjustment to those events. He will never be able to reassemble his alien life from the unknown, perilously sundered fragments. (*Journal de galère*, 17)[3]

But the conformity that thus constitutes the first trait of functional man would be nothing if it did not turn into "slavery." The proper of the reduction of men and women to their "function" by the totalitarian system is that the type of "absurd" determinations that implied by the reduction are always made against their "natural dispositions," against everything that they know, perceive, and feel. This reduction, then, compromises in advance any idea of freedom—every project, in the Sartrean sense. The possibilities that it leaves and the choices that it authorizes are so slim that an irremediable feeling of shame results for those that find no way out: the shame of "living here," as Kertész says, and in the same stroke the shame of growing accustomed to the subjection imposed, of finding excuses for it, of inventing refuges for oneself. Such is the second characteristic of this reduction. The third touches upon the power that the reduction gives to the masses. "Functional man" is never alone; he has for himself the number that justifies all his denials and renunciations. He is therefore in principle opposed to anything that might signify a disagreement with the general consent to the diktat of facts held to be incontestable.

There remains one more trait that specifies the nature of this consent. In the course of his trip to Dresden, Kertész already noted how the "[n]ever-ending boredom" and the "never-ending humiliation" characterizing functional man's life could become threatening as soon as "[a] smile, a gesture of politeness, however natural, elicits bafflement and aggression" (*Journal de galère*, 92).⁴ Transformed into a slave, Kertész writes, man misrecognizes the possibility of "humanity . . . between one person and another," all the dreariness of a daily life crushed by the facts makes man "unpredictable, underhanded, and inclined to destruction" (91–92). This is why any force could take hold of him and transform him into an arsonist or murderer overnight. One is not dispossessed of the power "to live his or her own reality" in vain; one does not become a *stranger* to one's own existence without a considerable price to pay: the essence of functional man manifests itself in the resignation to murder, the acceptance, encouragement, or promotion of it, the fascination with it. Following the example of Camus, whom he was reading assiduously at the time, Kertész thus knows with an absolute certainty that *murderous consent* is the most convincing sign of our era's nihilism, that it has for a long time substituted for marvel at the world and respect for life. This is the nature of its violence, and this is the reason the author of *Fatelessness* can write that his reflections, no matter their subject, always bear upon Auschwitz and that, even if he is apparently speaking of something else, his thoughts are always on the extermination of European Jews or, rather, that the extermination of European Jews speaks through him (32). The *Galley Boat-Log* comes to a close in 1990; the Berlin Wall has fallen; the hold of totalitarian systems seems to belong to the past. And yet, their murderous specter remains: "Murder happened in that era," that is, the era of marveling at creation,

> not as a common bad habit, an infraction, a "case," but as a form of existence, a "natural" attitude that one adopts and that one applies to life and to living beings; murder as philosophy of existence and the murderous attitude constitute without doubt a radical change—whether sign of the times or sign of the end of times matters little. One might object that extermination is not a new invention; yes, but the *continuous* extermination carried out systematically for years, for decades, and thus becoming a *system* . . . is a recent invention, if it is not the most recent of all. For, and this is where the novelty resides, it is *accepted*. The murderous form of existence shows itself to be possible and livable: it is thus *institutionalizable*. (236–37)

II.

The camp at Buchenwald, "the installation of the red ignominy" (*Journal de galère*, 247), its fall, its reestablishment—these events that, for Kertész, mark the advent of "fatelessness" in the twentieth century represent the greatest fiasco of "humanist ideals" imaginable, which no one had imagined belonging to the essence of civilization. Like a tumor in the memory,[5] they recall that the "reduction of human life to vegetative survival" is always possible (247), even when here and there—turning their heads, closing their eyes, and covering their ears—the majority of men and women of the time, no matter their level of education or their attachment to these *chosen* ideals, continue to have children, go about their business, and distract themselves. A strange paradox results: on the one hand, there is no established morality to which one could still adhere, because there is no morality that is not sooner or later transformed into a "license to kill," bringing a mortiferous culture to the hearts of men. Because there is no crime whose authors have not found some moral alibi to invoke as a justification, "ethical life"—which in principle turns against life (sometimes destroying it)—is suspicious from the beginning. In these conditions, nothing seems less adapted to the "de-realization" of functional man than the traditional moral and rational universe. The classical position of the moralist, which supposes that one can be the "master and possessor" of one's existence naturally and that it is within the power of everyone to project their existence into its own situation, is untenable; the moralist's judgments on the world are vain and without object. This is why, despite the debt that he recognizes with respect to philosophies of existence, Kertész ceaselessly takes his distance from Sartre's thought and in particular from his doctrine of freedom.[6]

On the other hand, however, the need for "human transcendence" signified by "ethics" has never been so manifest. Because the man or woman is dispossessed of his or her existence (and because this dispossession is linked to the possibility of murder), no task is more urgent—but also, to be sure, more difficult and improbable—than responding to the "ethical" demand of making (or remaking) "one's life one's own life." What is in question can thus be clearly defined: the possibility for the individual submitted to the pressures of totalitarian society to reappropriate common history at the same time as his or her own existence—that is to say, to manage to exist as a *singularity* despite all the murderous specters of the past and the terror of the present. It is no coincidence that Kertész cites Simmel in *Galley Boat-Log*: "[t]he only proof that our form of existence is not coerced on us by others is *our irreplaceability* by others" (cited in *Journal de galère*, 41).⁷ This reappropriation, which is ethics itself (the *only* ethics that holds up and the *only* ethics that counts), is the only chance of "surviving" in a world that makes collectivity a madness and a weapon of intimate destruction. Yet, like all ethics worthy of the name, like all commitment that refuses payment with all too easy moral and metaphysical words, it is not evident. Opposed, threatened, exposed to all the obstacles and all the forms of hostility described in a novel such as *Fiasco*, this ethics is the object of endless worry, and it constitutes a lifelong search. More precisely, it demands a particular aptitude that Kertész repeatedly calls "existential genius,"⁸ which appears most often in the form of a questioning because nothing guarantees its possibility:

> Shame of living here. Considering that I accepted slavery—considering simply that I live. [. . .] Am I definitively marked with the seal of the epoch and of the place despite the fact that I deny all moral cohabitation to the point of hating myself, indeed, to the point of suicide? By remaining here, I withdrew myself from the tragic, that is to say, from fate, and I submitted myself to the comic, to a stately fate full of chance. Even if my work expresses precisely this comic, the shame of participation and enslavement. This is what resounds almost like a justification. Is existential greatness possible here? Is it possible to live one's unique existence profoundly, to live one's life consciously? Such is the fundamental question. And my answer is no doubt: yes. (111–12)

We will soon see what allows Kertész to answer this "fundamental question" so affirmatively; we will see, in other words, how "existential greatness" allows the individual to "hold out as an individual" and by that very fact to resist the shame of slavery or, further, to escape what the author of *Galley Boat-Log* does not hesitate to call "the mire of inexistence" (163). In the 1980s, as Kertész began keeping the journal more regularly and taking stock of a life, existential greatness measured itself according to its results, recalling the adage that Nietzsche made a vital imperative: "Become who you are."⁹ Translating *Birth of Tragedy* at the time, Kertész adopts the adage, specifying that the problematic of individuation, which constitutes one of the guiding threads of Nietzsche's book, is *his* problematic. "Finally, I succeeded in escaping that impersonal fate," he writes in September 1983. "I thought and constructed myself. Despite everything. By working at the very bottom of the mine, silently, teeth clenched" (148).

III.

Impersonality, functionality, slavery: one must begin again on the basis of their manifestation if one wants to understand the conditions of survival. Indeed, they cannot be separated from a joint denial of language and truth—or, rather, from abandoning the examination of truth as it might be expressed and discussed in language, in a plural and contradictory way, as a "vital value." In totalitarian societies, "murderous consent" is inseparable from renunciation of the truth, the cult of its illusion (in the form of imposed dogma), and ruses of organized lies. Thus given over to the force [*puissance*] of those with the power [*pouvoir*] to manipulate it, language is first an immurement. For totalitarianism, language is the medium of absurdity and the instrument *par excellence* of enslavement and stigmatization of life. Such that nothing determines what Kertész calls "the existential conditions of the existential structure" more than this lingual vacuum (43–44). If it is true that freedom is *what* does not exist, as the author of *Galley Boat-Log* often repeats throughout the 1970s, the words we say, the expressions that do not belong to us, the automatisms and mechanisms imposed upon us are the manifestation *par excellence* of this inexistence. At the same time, language opens a breach through which the spark of a possible freedom glimmers. "One does not know where or when the fuse will light," writes Kertész, "but one moment it will make the breach an abyss that will swallow the totality" (44).

Nevertheless, we know the name of this breach, the recurrence of which in Kertész's *Log* recalls its omnipresence in Kafka's *Diaries*, to which Kertész often refers: writing—writing understood "as a survival technique." Because one refuses to accept ready-made language and ideas, perceived and lived as an unbearable violence (the violence of inexistence itself), "one starts to write," Kertész says in 1965, "like someone trying to convalesce from a severe ailment, to master his mental illness—at least as long as he keeps on writing" (20).[10] If Kertész can answer affirmatively to the question posed above concerning the possibility of an "existential greatness," if he can have the slightest feeling of having escaped the shame of inexistence, it is not by manifesting an exceptional talent or genius—there is no form of self-satisfaction in his answer—but by elaborating, thanks to writing, this "survival technique" that will have allowed him to avoid wasting away and thus to hold on. In the 1980s, the two motifs—the motif of writing and the motif of life *as* survival, hence, of the health [*salut*] of life—are in fact indissociable, Kertész says, "like in times of war or natural catastrophe." To write is first and foremost to give oneself the means for "staying alive" without expecting anything from anyone (above all from opposing armies, political authorities, or cultural institutions), thus sheltered from every form of compromise with the existing powers. This is why it is first a question of a *private* affair that cannot be evaluated in terms of publicity or recognition (which, as we know, will have come late), of success or failure. But it is also what gives his concern, understood as "self-representation," an undeniable ethical scope. The trap of totalitarianism, indeed, is to immure people within a deceitful system of false representations that give them the illusion of a relative freedom and a real mastery over their life understood as the realization of their inner and outer activity. The system makes them believe that *their* words, *their* thoughts, *their* acts constitute sufficient proof of their freedom and mastery, because they are really *theirs*. It puts them to sleep with a calm confidence in life that accommodates itself to all the murders. Writing becomes ethical in its opposition to this slumber in a bed of lies and imposters. When one makes writing a demand, writing allows one "to reappropriate" one's life—or at least to prevent one's existence from falling outside oneself while doing nothing *to save* it.

> To separate my ethical being from my aesthetic being, the existing from the creative. My problem is that they are inseparable. But at least knowing that my creative being is a product of my imagination and an arbitrary representation that I myself have created (or if one prefers: metaphysical hygiene), it is nothing real or necessary. [. . .] Knowing: the creative being is enslaved to the existing being; to uproot it from existence each day for a few hours; otherwise, the necessity that nourishes it risks wasting away. —The talent, the genius, etc.; nonsense; creation is not a divine grace that comes from the outside but, rather, a vital function, a means for staying alive. (173–74)

IV.

And yet, writing to *save oneself* is not sufficient. Indeed, nothing of what has been said up to this point suffices to describe the *singularity* of the self-invention that characterizes Kertész's work: writing a novel whose nature and structure are thoroughly determined by the necessity of "reappropriating" a confiscated life. Yet, one must not go astray. This is why the *Galley Boat-Log* is enameled with reflections that bear less upon literature in general than upon the existential significance of writing a novel that amounts to elaborating the only model of a novel appropriate to this form of de-individuation and dispossession of existence proper to functional man. Two names suffice to characterize this form, two names that Kertész adopts to describe what, for him, *Fatelessness* and *Fiasco* represent and the place they occupy in their era: the "structural novel" and the "atonal novel." The novel must be structural by virtue of the absence of fate characterizing functional man. Indeed, this absence signifies that the individual's psychology, character, and metaphysical ideas or vision of the world have no importance. All that counts is the way the individual's existence is "linked—positively or negatively—with the Structure, whether bestowed on or expropriated from it" (27).[11] And if this is a requirement, it is because the novelist cannot or can no longer cheat with this "fatelessness" that constitutes both the legacy and the mark of totalitarian systems for at least two reasons. Already, he or she can no longer adopt the position of a *deus ex machina* observing the moral and metaphysical tribulations or the psychological deferrals of his "characters" from the outside and on high like an omniscient judge. All sovereignty of this order is not only illusory; what is more, it changes nothing in the inexistence of whoever pretends to believe in it. In other words, the novelist that, following the example of Sartre, deludes him- or herself with such an illusion reappropriates nothing of his or her existence and life. They miss the point. The following paradox results: if it is true that the objective of novel writing is a "radical individuation," this individuation can be produced only by a relative "erasure" of the individual from the novel's material. This is the meaning of "not cheating with reality"! It means that one cannot (can no longer) give the "character" a density, a depth, a freedom, a "tragic grandeur," while at Auschwitz "the greatest trauma for the people of Europe since the Crucifixion" (32)[12] is sanctioned by their irremediable loss. This is why the only point of departure possible is fatelessness. Novel writing confronts first and foremost fate's structural absence (which is the effect of external forces and determinations and which, for that reason, bears both the weight of the past and the gravity of the present). And only because it is absorbed in this confrontation, refusing all pretense, all fleeing or evasion, the writer that refuses to *lie to him- or herself* can have the chance, however minimal, to reappropriate his or her life. In other words, because he or she does not fear testifying against the individual, countering all naïve humanism, he or she will perhaps be able to make it pierce through once again.

The second reason for demanding a "structural" novel is that, after Auschwitz, it is the only way for a writer to be totally "committed" in his or her fiction, not in the Sartrean sense of a commitment that judges fates with a moralizing, that is, exterior omniscience but in the sense of a total presence. This is the demand Kertész retains from his reading of Kafka, but also of Proust. They are the ones that made the novel, *par excellence*, a process thanks to which "one reappropriates one's life." And the author of *The Castle* knew better than anyone, as Kertész repeatedly emphasizes, the extent to which one risks one's life in the "attempt." If it is true that Kafka's stories and novels (*The Metamorphosis* and *The Trial* first of all) are haunted by the necessity of reappropriating a hindered existence, it is not insignificant that, at least in the two cases just cited, they end with the death of the one engaged in this search, sometimes unbeknownst to him.[13] For the author of *Fatelessness*, this outcome is exemplary: it no doubt shows the cost of giving writing the objective of this reappropriation, but it also indicates the extent to which this reappropriation is necessary and what the benefits are, namely, an oeuvre that would finally be "imprinted with existence." Thus, writing specific to the novel—the very writing that mobilizes all the forces of whoever dedicates him- or herself to it—is a race against death to find the path of *his* or *her* life in time.

> The incalculable importance of the novel: it is a process thanks to which one reappropriates one's life. The alleged crisis of the novel is not due to its uselessness but, rather, to the fact that writers do not know their duty, the fact that they are amateurs or charlatans. Not everyone can be Proust, Kafka, or Krúdy. But from the moment they existed, we should know what the only possible object of the novel is: allowing one to reappropriate one's life, to relive it, to fulfill it for a single and sublime instant before dying. (147)

"Fate and novel": Kertész does not hesitate to write that therein lies the *truth* of his life—the truth that therefore, as so many pages witness, will have ceaselessly made him suffer in a strange proximity to Kafka's work, but also the truth that will have saved him from inexistence by keeping him "alive." Ultimately, even death here finds, if not a semblance of meaning, at least the sense of its reprieve. And here again, the memory of Auschwitz spreads its shadow over writing, as the most overwhelming fact is not only that millions of beings were murdered but also that at least as many beings "did not understand their death" (145)—which is to say, they had no chance, even as they believed it to be necessary, to settle the account of their erased existence.

Yet, the author of *Fatelessness* and *Fiasco* does not present novel writing only as "structural"; it should also be "atonal." How is this to be understood? As a complement to its structural character, this adjective's significance leads us once again onto ethical terrain. Once again, it takes into account the radical rupture (at once ethical and aesthetic) represented by the death of European Jews in the death camps. Indeed, if it is true that one of the most characteristic traits of the great European novel was until then its moral tonality, whatever its nature—a *basso continuo* that gave the work its "fundamental note"—the "atonal" signals that this possibility has since run dry. If there was always a moral behind every novel, explicit or hidden, announced or not, this more or less secret reference and this more or less sincere guarantee are no longer possible. They have been carried off with the ashes, if not of humanism, at least of the illusion of it. Hence, the paradox (yet another) is that precisely this atonality restores an ethical dimension to the novel. And it has this effect for at least three reasons. First, it is consequently subservient to no preexisting tonality, that is, to no preconstituted vision of the world. The novel depends on nothing and no one. Second, in so doing, writing escapes all analytical frameworks. Its object cannot be immured in any category; it remains what it is: "a unique, inexplicable, and inconceivable phenomenon, an adventure and an existence whose place is beyond all analysis" (74). Against every possible reduction, it thus preserves its irreducible singularity, which is the only path possible for a reappropriation of confiscated life. Third, freed from all dependence, the necessity from which novel writing stems is anchored in a resolution whose imperative and subjective commandment constitutes the very essence of ethics. Thus, in 1979 while working on *Fiasco*, Kertész can write:

> But my resolution—with respect to the novel—is so firm that it seems to be an order coming from somewhere else; it makes me totally independent of the anxiety, fragility, and petty weakness that I am. My relation to the word is exclusively subjective and ethical. That is where I draw the passion that fills me with the insatiable desire to name things. I do not want to see the world rationally for it to see me rationally in turn; I do not desire balance. I want existence, opposition; I want fate, but a fate that is mine, that I share with nothing and no one. I want bridges burned and the sensation that has shaped my mood for days: "There is no turning back." (80–81)

V.

One would have to analyze this resolution and put it into perspective for each of Kertész's novels. To conclude, I will linger upon one that was published in 2003: *Liquidation*. None of the recurring themes of *Galley Boat-Log* are absent in the novel, like the mistrust of metaphysics and "ethical categories" that one of the characters judges to be "rocky in the extreme" (*Liquidation*, 54). One also finds in the novel the conviction that, "physically and morally," woman or man living in the era of catastrophe remains "an utterly vulnerable being" deprived of fate, a being for whom—as the deceased writer affirms, the writer whose novel, apotheosis of his life, cannot be found—"there can be no return to some center of the Self, a solid and irrefutable self-certainty," a being that is "lost" (54–55). Above all, however, the story implements a vertiginous *mise-en-abyme* with the "ethical" demands, if not principles, of the structural novel. It stages a play whose dialogues have rigorously the same object as the novel itself: the search for a lost work, the legacy of a deceased friend that could gather the enigmatic meaning of his existence interrupted by death. The work thus speaks of nothing other than the existential necessity of reappropriating life, but here the writer himself is no longer concerned; rather, it concerns those that shared a life, the women that loved him, the friend and editor that he addressed—as if this unfinished life had been deposited into their hands and confided to them for safekeeping. Everything thought in the first person singular in *Galley Boat-Log* thus takes on a plural form in the novel. At stake again and again is not only the insurmountable difficulty of transforming life into a fate and filling the vacuum of existence after Auschwitz but also—and this constitutes the singularity of *Liquidation*—the way this difficulty affects all the relations composing the fabric of existence. At stake is the distribution between, on the one hand, faith in writing as health and, on the other hand, its impossibility in a world where murder remains the fundamental tonality. Thus, the friend and editor declares:

> But I believe in writing—nothing else; just writing. Man may live like a worm, but he writes like a god. There was a time when that secret was known, but now it has been forgotten; the world is composed of disintegrating fragments, an incoherent dark chaos, sustained by writing alone. If you have a concept of the world, if you have not yet forgotten all that has happened, that you have a world at all, it is writing that has created that for you, and ceaselessly goes on creating it; Logos, the invisible spider's thread that holds our lives together. (97)

But nothing is simple because in the novel—which follows the memory of the *auto-da-fé* that Kafka had demanded of his friend Max Brod—the writer named, like in *The Castle*, only with a capital letter (B.), a survivor of the camps around which the entire narration turns, asked his ex-wife before committing suicide to destroy the evidence, and the friend searches in vain for traces of it. He chose to program the erasure of the narrative thanks to which he could have ultimately concluded his story and acquitted himself of the past, thereby indicating the impossibility of such an acquittal. The deprivation is thus redoubled. It concerns not only B. himself, who will not have left any story, but also his friends, his editor, his legatee, all of whom are left orphaned by this untellable story. And yet, Kertész's novel exists.

If it is consequently true that the writer, object of the narration, is linked to the structure negatively (which leaves him no other outcome than the double disappearance of himself and his work), if it is true that his existence, in other words, *escapes* him even in and beyond death, the writing of *Liquidation*, for its part, reverses the meaning of that same structure. It announces what it wins and saves from the verge of collapse, as close as possible to danger: nothing other than life itself, nothing more and nothing less than the force of living given by attachment to the truth contrary to all the lies and all the compromises, contrary to all the illusory pretenses and excuses. These last two entries from *Galley Boat-Log* testify:

> To be the savior, not of "humanity"!, but of nothing but one's own life, in order to grant oneself absolution, one needs a whole life of constant and incredibly intense inner work. Man has an appalling life—history—and he has a powerful narration of the world, much more sage than he, in which he is transformed into divinity, into a Magi; this narration is as marvelous as historical or "real" life is incredible. (274–75)

> [A] good artist has no choice but to speak the truth, and to speak it radically. That does not prevent him from staying alive, because the lie is not the one and only condition of life, even if many see no other possibilities. (275)

11
"a profound feeling of protest"
(A Reading of Singer)

> My religion goes hand in hand with a profound feeling of protest. Once in a while, the old Jewish hope for the coming of the Messiah awakens in me. There must come the time for revelation! How long should we wait? My feeling of religion is a feeling of rebellion. I even play with the idea of creating (for myself) a religion of protest. I often say that God *wants* us to protest. He has had enough of those who praise Him all the time and bless Him for all His cruelties to man and animals.
> —*Conversations with Isaac Bashevis Singer*, 115–16

It is during a reflection on the use of philosophy in literature and on the relationship his characters have with major "human ideas" that Singer, who makes no mystery of his beliefs, discloses this secret [*confidence*], which concerns as much the "blindness of man" as "God's permanent silence" (115). In a few words, this secret recalls that if, as Singer has repeatedly said, the first care of the writer and storyteller is to entertain readers, this care is nevertheless not unrelated to the search for truth. This is why, Singer adds, he would never make a man or woman the protagonist of a novel if this care had never crossed his or her mind. And yet, Singer also specifies, nothing is more tedious than the generalizations, digressions, and demonstrations into which even the best novelists sometimes lose their characters. A being, in fact, does not reduce to what he or she thinks, and it is not altogether certain whether or not a being can best be described and known through his or her reflections. Assuming that the search for truth would be *protest*, the latter could be neither exclusively nor principally declaratory. Protest cannot be summed up by remarks with a universal vocation, but rather in irreducibly singular looks, directed words, facts, and gestures. If there is a "task of the storyteller," it is to make protest appear in the variable fabric of the exchanges and relationships, meetings and separations, that give to each existence its exemplarity.

I.

In Singer's work, as is well known, this task is inseparable from recompositions of memory. As he often repeats, the essential part of his inspiration will have been drawn from the faces, expressions, and words that brought the Krochmalna Street of years past back to him and from the stories heard from chance visitors. Whether in *The Family Moskat*, *Scum*, or *In My Father's Court*, to cite only a few books,[1] Singer revives an incomparable gallery of characters, as if it were the responsibility of the survivor-storyteller to offer these characters the possibility of still *remaining* beyond the tragic disappearance of the world to which they belonged. This remembrance is already in itself a protest: first, against the incommensurable cruelty of destruction and, second, against the redoubling of this cruelty in oblivion—as if literature, playing on our ignorance, had the power to disrupt in its own way the conventional relationship between the living and the dead, as if the essence of literature's "entertainment" pertained to the pleasure of evading the weight of mourning and history while reading. In *Scum*, the small world of Krochmalna Street wakes up to find an elderly Hasid pass by with his velvet hat, long beard, and *papillotes*; a knock on the Rabbi's door and in walks Moshe Blecher, Reb Chayim Gorshkover, or the milkman Reb Asher—and we might believe, for an instant, that nothing is over, that all these colors and sounds, the smells from the kitchen, cholent or bread fresh from the baker's oven, these movements, these comings and goings, were merely frozen in time, suspended, waiting for the magician that could reanimate them by just waving the wand of literature. It is no coincidence that Singer's universe, haunted by the existence of supernatural powers, is full of spirits, phantoms, goblins, and ghosts. When something disappears and could come back again, who knows where it goes? Who knows what time is made of? Everything happens as if the protest responds to a call that only it would hear. One thus thinks of what Singer recalled to Richard Burgin regarding the feelings he experienced while writing *The Family Moskat*:

> I said to myself, "Warsaw has just been destroyed. No one will ever see the Warsaw I knew. Let me write about it. Let this Warsaw not disappear forever." Just like Homer (forgive me the comparison), who was the greatest of them all, felt about Troy, I felt about Warsaw in my own small way. (*Conversations*, 73)

The protest echoes the following melancholic page from the end of *Shosha*:

I tried to engrave in my memory each alley, each building, each store, each face. I thought that this was how a condemned man would be looking at the world on his way to the gallows. I was taking leave of every peddler, porter, market woman—even of the horses of the droshkies. I saw in each of them expressions I had never noticed before. Even the horses seemed to know that this was their last journey. There was knowledge and consent in their large eyes, dark with pupil. (257)

But the call that demands memory and protest against forgetting is also the call of language. If it is true that one of Singer's most singular traits is his unconditional attachment to Yiddish, he undoubtedly finds one of his most profound motivations in resistance to the erasure of what was once for him an "origin," a country, a history, a culture, and an education. To write, time and again, in a language that so many forces were striving to reduce to a "dead language" was still the most faithful and effective way to protest against this persecution. The whole force of his work is there: it will have never declared the duty of memory, never expounded endlessly on its demand, but, more than its incantation, it will have repeated the practice of it. Book after book, throughout the stories and by the magic of restored dialogues, his work will have put that duty into practice by giving it the evidence of a language and, with it, a rescued culture. Humboldt's idea that every language contains a world was rarely shown to be more exact. In his acceptance speech for the Nobel Prize for Literature, recalling the "quiet humor" and the "gratitude for every day of life" that seemed to him to characterize the idiom of his childhood, even when it was "the idiom of frightened and hopeful Humanity," Singer will have made this humor and gratitude, as well as this hope and fear, a common heritage (*Nobel Lecture*, 15). And if it is true that every translation is challenged to bring a bit of the source language's world into the target language, Singer's readers, throughout the world and in their own languages, *in their own way*, have become heirs of the Yiddish language. If one someday had to draw the impossible typology of the major works of the second half of the twentieth century that have been haunted by the extermination of Europe's Jews, next to all the major works that have told the story of the persecutions, deportations, and extermination, all the survivor testimonies, then, that have stood against forgetting, then a separate place should be reserved for Singer's works, which turned back time, brought to life and revived what had been destroyed, made it survive, inscribing joy, the emotion of remembering, at the heart of mourning with its grand bazaar of passions, of small strengths and great weaknesses.

II.

But the protest is not only that of literature, as such, against the violence of history. Directed this time against the weight or absurdity of social conventions and against the stringency and complications of the law, protest also resides, otherwise, within the very interiority of tales and novels. One cannot count Singer's characters, who are defined by their trite arrangements or their transactions with the commandments and precepts of the morality of the community, their distance from the paths traced in advance, their will to independence or their break from religious obligations. Such is the case for Yasha in *The Magician of Lublin*. From the first pages of the novel, Singer is pleased to point out not only that the protagonist "spent his Sabbath talking and smoking cigarettes among musicians," but also that,

> [t]o the earnest moralists who attempted to get him to mend his ways, he would always answer: "When were you in heaven, and what did God look like?" (4)

For others, "liberation" is commensurate with the system of constraints and prohibitions within which they have been brought up. Such is the case, among so many others, for Tsutsik, the protagonist and narrator of *Shosha* who recalls at the beginning of the novel how often, for as long as he can remember, he had always heard his father declare, about everything and nothing, "it is forbidden":

> Everything I wanted to do was a transgression. I was not allowed to draw or paint a person—that violated the Second Commandment. I couldn't say a word against another boy—that was slander. I couldn't laugh at anyone—that was mockery. I couldn't make up a story—that represented a lie. (5)

Finally, it is especially the case for Singer himself who, like Yasha, never misses an opportunity to express his skepticism against this inflation of laws to be observed, Singer writes, as one passes from the Bible to the Mishnah, then to the Gemara or to Maimonides. In a general way, it is the authority of tradition, incarnated by the fathers, that is contested. In his interviews with Richard Burgin, the author of *Shosha* stresses how the study of the Law complicated lives of Hassidic Jews so much that they no longer had any time to occupy themselves with anything outside of religion and were reduced to live with their families in poverty. But it is especially in the succession of stories that comprise *In My Father's Court* that the numerous chapters put into perspective, with as much tenderness as irony, the comical situations, if not aberrations, that result from the strict respect for dietary prohibitions, rules for marriage and divorce, and, more generally, the constant desire to remain pure.

And yet, Singer specifies, "a morally neutral human being is a monster" (*Conversations*, 6). Consequently, his protest does not stand against morality, which is never foreign to the characters in his novels, but against their confinement within dogma and rules that ignore everything about life, beginning with the attention, care, and help for which everyone singularly calls. Thus, in the major autobiographical work, which magnifies the figure of the father and pays homage to that of the mother, the Law is not totally erased but moves into the background. Whether it is a question of Rabbi or Rabbetzin, the parents of young Isaac, knowledge of the texts is important; it frames, occupies, and illuminates their lives, but it is not the essential thing. What is emphasized, what moves the son, is first and foremost the comfort needed by the men and women who appear before his father's court—and the humanity with which these men and women are greeted, listened to, and counseled is highlighted from the start. Judgment, if there is any, never takes refuge behind principles. It takes into account each person's weaknesses and sufferings and remains attentive to flares of passion without always condemning them; judgment seeks the most appropriate solution, the most judicious response to appease them. Finally, it flows forth as much in speech as in the gestures and acts that give rights to the vulnerability of each person.

This is why morality cannot be reduced to a set of abstract commandments. Assuming one would want to talk about an "ethic of protest," it responds to a plea for help—and it could not be given or described in advance. It is not a matter of going against the rules, or necessarily of revolt, but of inventing the uncertain pathway of a *supplement* that is, on its own, a concentration of humanity. Each time, it is unpredictable and miraculous; it defies the calculation of the interests of reason; it engages a responsibility that, again, remains incommensurable; an interruption of love cannot explain it either. If it is true, as Singer recalls in the opening pages of his interview, that the writer transmits a truth that comes from his heart, then this truth occurs entirely in the exemplarity of the gestures and actions that take on this challenge. This is the meaning of protest! The possibility of such a truth is what literature brings to life despite our major and minor miseries, what it reveals in the interstices of human passions, what it snatches from the cruelty of human beings, what it opposes to the violence of history.

One would find numerous examples in Singer's tales and stories, but it is perhaps in *Shosha* that he most clearly displays that possibility. The storyline of Aaron (Arele to his family, Tsutsik to his friends) conjugates two protests. The first is the chaotic invention of a singularity in and by writing; it assumes a one-way departure from childhood lessons and precepts; it is translated into a wandering between contradictory attachments, loves, and loyalties; it gives right to the great game of human passions and emotions in all their grandeur and pettiness; it refuses to confine life within shackles of morality. But this is not what illuminates the novel. This protest may well be vital to someone who feels they are suffocating, but it is little compared to the protest that gives the story its true scope. While everyone should coax him to leave Shosha and follow Betty to America, Aaron/Arele/Tsutsik honors his commitment never to leave her. The responsibility he feels toward her, the attention he gives to her fragilities, the care he has for her fears and anxieties transcends any interest he would have in running away from her. He knows that any abandonment would be fatal, *so he stays*. Thus, the second protest, which one imagines to be painful, is the loyalty to *an* attachment and *a* promise despite all the violence of the world and the cruelty of history.

III.

But there is still a third way to understand the feeling of protest that Singer confesses. Indissociable from the other two, it concerns a certain idea of literature. At least two tendencies are challenged by the author of *In My Father's Court*. The first is to idolize the writer, making him one value among others within a given system: "the worship of the trademark" (*Conversations*, 37). Once again, the argument of authority is challenged. It concerns, this time, rising against the hegemony of criticism that imposes on a given era a determined taste, admiration, cult that requires, for example, that one unconditionally praise to the skies the work itself less than the names Proust, Joyce, or Kafka. The second tendency is to enclose writing within stylistic research and, more generally, within a labor over language that takes precedence over every other concern [*souci*]. Singer returns to it repeatedly in his conversations with Richard Burgin, regretting that literature loses in such labor what one could call the "ethics of storytelling":

> Our discoveries in literature should not be so much in words, phrases or style as in the new phases and new facets of human conduct. The writer who all the time ponders his style makes no discoveries. (51)

What is this "ethic"? The author of *Satan in Goray, Old Love, Crown of Feathers*, and many other novels and novellas will modestly say that he gets it from his brother Joshua, who supposedly taught him to substitute all desire to interpret and explicate things in life, such as shame and cruelty, with the care to "make them as alive as possible" (9). In Singer's case, one knows that such a concern plunges into the roots of childhood, to what was in his childhood attention, curiosity, wonder, desire to break into the complicated and mysterious world of adult passions. Moreover, here lies one of the most singular traits of *In My Father's Court*: it grants this "ethic of storytelling" the perspective of a child. The autobiographical narrative not only assembles memories; it reconstitutes the genesis of an intelligence turned toward others, an intelligence moved by faces and silhouettes, attitudes and postures, idioms and gesticulations: the refusal of all vain and useless introspection.

"To bring to life," "to give life"—we have thus returned to the first meaning we gave to the "feeling of protest" that Singer confesses. There should be no doubt that, for the author of *Shosha*, and for many others alike, the wounds of memory should never close, and what the blindness of men have taught him about the human condition cannot be erased or forgotten. Consequently, in a number of places, the work retains a sensible trace of the fear of history, even if it always does so between the lines or indirectly. When questioned about *Shosha*, about the "Hitler tragedy" whose threat escalates as the story progresses, Singer in fact states that it could not be "seen as it was" because this threat's endpoint—the Shoah—is "beyond the pale of literature" (139). All that could be recalled retrospectively, after everything had been destroyed, after everything had disappeared, was the ignorance or premonition of catastrophe while life, caught in the grip of anxiety and incomprehension, still continued. All that could be described, further back, was the *world before*. In other words, if there could exist a protest against death, however vain, that avoids fleeing into solitude or folding back onto the self, its only solution was to recover something of these lost moments. This is the "ethic of the storyteller," faced with the test of violence, of its memory and traces: to retie the threads of life by turning once again—never once and for all—to the noises and clamors, the flavors and colors, the anger and tenderness of the large-small Jewish microcosm of Krochmalna Street. To see them, to see them again, again and always, despite all the sadness and all the sorrow of the world, through the bewildered eyes of a child.

12

"And nobody here knows who I am"

(Emigrant Voices: Arendt, Sebald, Perec)

> We actually live in a world in which human beings have ceased to exist for quite a while; since society has discovered discrimination as the great social weapon by which one may kill men without any bloodshed; since passports or birth certificates, and sometimes even tax receipts, are no longer formal papers but matters of social distinction. It is true that most of us depend entirely upon social standards; we lose confidence in ourselves if society does not approve us; we are—and always were—ready to pay any price in order to be accepted by society.
>
> —Hannah Arendt, "We Refugees," 273

In the book *Ellis Island*, which was adapted from the film he made with photographer Robert Bober, Georges Perec reports—among other testimonies of arriving at the island and the numerous formalities, protocols, and exams that accompanied an immigrant's entry onto American soil—one woman's testimony that describes the linguistic conditions of this reception in the following terms:

> And then they took me to Ellis Island, there was a crowd of people there and they talked and talked, one talked like this, the other talked like that, they all spoke a different language, but to me, to me they spoke English. / GP: You didn't speak English back then? / Mrs. G: No. Only "yes" and "no." (150)

Ellis Island can thus be imagined simultaneously as an airtight door increasingly difficult to open—for the imposition of new conditions and restrictions never ceased from the date it opened on January 1, 1892, until the day it closed on November 16, 1954—and as a veritable Tower of Babel, requiring translators and interpreters to help overcome, if not the first of the many losses every exile signifies, at least its most immediately paralyzing ordeal [*épreuve*]. One needs only to look at any of the photos of the immense registration hall, also known as the "stockyard" due to the metallic fences that compartmentalized the room and demarcated its walkways, in order to remember in the space of an instant what an exile's first steps at the end of a long journey must have been like: the impossibility of making oneself understood, of comprehending and responding in one's native language, the foreignness of *the language of others*, and the sudden certitude that *one's* language—which, as Hannah Arendt reminds us, signified a certain proximity—was no longer of any help for the majority of the activities and procedures of everyday life.

As we know, this experience, with the confusion, disorientation, and fear that it entails, does not belong to the past. Other emigrants[1] have replaced those that had fled the regimes of terror, pogroms, or poverty in Europe. They are no longer knocking solely on America's doors; they no longer land on the shores of Ellis Island. Early in the morning they hurry into endless lines at the doors of national consulates, members of the European Community, and a few other communities, with the likelihood of being denied and left with no alternative than to risk their lives in improbable, clandestine journeys. With the calculated denial of this primary responsibility for the care, attention, and help demanded by the vulnerability and mortality of immigrants, the airtight doors through which immigrants—whether legal or illegal, if not criminal—are required to pass today rival the brutality and cruelty of yesterday.

But the violence does not stop there. Should they make it to the end of their journey, and even assuming that their situation could be sorted out and that, at best, they acquire the necessary authorization to remain on this soil, to live and to work there, *immigrants are never safe*. This is undoubtedly the major lesson of the texts that Hannah Arendt dedicated to emigration in the years following her own exile to the United States. However, this quasi-statutory "insecurity" informs us not only of the common conditions of existence of refugees or exiles around the world. It constitutes an unavoidable element in the necessarily critical analysis of State sovereignty. Put otherwise, if we want to understand the dogma and fantasies that accompany the perception of this sovereignty and the different forms of attachment to which it gives rise, including the most violent, there will always be a certain violence or fraudulence at work within the neglect or denial of what the persistent status of emigrants teaches us about them.

I.

For Hannah Arendt, as for so many other thinkers, artists, and refugees of her era, this demand could be satisfied only through a critical and historical questioning—as well as a political analysis—of what had managed to pass as both the condition and the purpose of welcoming foreigners, immigrants, refugees, and, more generally, all those whose presumed identities were circumscribed by membership in a community perceived as a minority: namely, their *assimilation*. "Foreigners," "refugees," "immigrants," and every other type of minority were acceptable only to the extent that, in order to assimilate themselves, they could manifest the will, desire, and ambition to merge into the same, which is to say, to reduce or dissolve their alleged previous identity in order to integrate better. But with what, with whom, exactly? In what fantasy of belonging? If the question, as we will see, recurs throughout Hannah Arendt's texts, it is also a matter of dogma, as vague and uncertain as it is, that has lost none of its relevance today. Nearly everywhere, assimilation particularly requires learning the host country's language as proof of the effort of "goodwill," the "sincerity" of the desire, or the "seriousness" of the ambition. It is even, here and there, a discriminatory condition, the object of an exam or test.

And yet the idea of assimilation is not at all obvious. It is torn between a particular fact, for which the concept is everywhere inadequate, and an ideological imperative that this inadequacy renders, by definition, potentially murderous. For there is never a reduction to the "same" for at least two reasons. The first is that the "same" is itself undetermined. What identity are we talking about when we invoke the necessity of assimilation? How do we distinguish it? Who circumscribes it? What are its criteria? Precisely because the answer is always ideological, because it feeds on the characterization of people or on any other equally rash attempt at a definition, the "same" is never revealed. It is much more a matter of the imagination, of fantasy—it depends as much on circumstantial affects as on their ideological, religious, and/or political instrumentalization.

The second reason pertains to the fact that identity cannot be decreed. It is neither replaceable nor substitutable. No one is able to decide this change one day, once and for all. As will be seen later in a reading of W. G. Sebald (a story taken from his novel *The Emigrants*, as well as passages from *Austerlitz*), the identity of emigrants, refugees, and exiles cannot be thought according to anything other than their heterogeneity, which is to say, their splitting or division, and their discontinuity. It comes from that which is lost and returns without waiting for it, from what is forgotten and remembered in turn. It is always spectral.

The fact is thus impossible to settle with complete rigor. Everything about it is fragile, both the "same" and "other," that which is supposedly lost and supposedly acquired, the "substituted" as much as the "assimilated." Yet, herein lie the tragic limits of assimilation; in precisely this way it gives rise to ideology. As soon as it becomes the subject of a defense, its satisfaction, indeed, is always found lacking. In each instant it can reveal itself to be "insufficient" and, as such, can give rise to new requirements until the time when, finally, it will be considered impossible. Such is the double face of assimilation's violence. On the one hand, it promotes, if not demands, reduction to the same as a proof of allegiance that must thus be paid in sacrifices and renunciations—like sacrificing, for instance, one's mother tongue. On the other hand, assimilation takes hostage everyone that it submits to its law. It imposes blame on everyone for never belonging enough to whatever it decides to promote or defend as the "same." For Hannah Arendt's generation, the anti-Semitic persecutions that began in the 1930s, which badly mired all the previous generations' dreams of assimilation, undoubtedly constituted an experience of this order. It is no coincidence that, across various texts written in the 1940s, Arendt continues to rewrite the history [*histoire*] of their disillusion—as is the case in a 1933 essay, "Original Assimilation: An Epilogue to the One Hundredth Anniversary of Rahel Vernhagen's Death":

> Today in Germany it seems Jewish *assimilation* must declare its bankruptcy. The general social anti-Semitism and its official legitimation affects [sic] the first instance of assimilated Jews, who can no longer protect themselves through baptism or by emphasizing their differences from Eastern Judaism. [. . .] For assimilation is a fact, and only later, in the context of defensive struggle, does it become an ideology; and ideology one today knows cannot maintain itself because reality has refuted it more fully and unambiguously than ever before. Assimilation is the entrance of the Jews into the historical European world. (*Jewish Writings*, 22)

Yet, once again, this ambivalent logic is not relegated to the past. Assimilation is everywhere divided between the impossible interiorization of restriction, with respect to its exclusive or discriminatory aspects, and the violence of required commitments. On the one hand, traces of his or her past identity always remain in the life of the emigrant—his or her clothing, religion, language, family ties—the substitution or disappearance of which nobody can decree because nobody can measure the secret life of the emigrant's past identity and its possible returns. On the other hand, even if it could be imposed, the reduction of belonging (the Jew, the Arab, the Italian, etc.) remains exposed to the risk of being, or of becoming once again, insufficient in the eyes of the law, in the rhythm of governmental changes and the vicissitudes of history.

II.

The tragic consciousness of this failure radiates a diffuse unease on every page of Hannah Arendt's texts. She summarizes the experience of all those who had found an adoptive homeland in this or that European country and who, under a given decree or villainous law, found themselves stateless overnight. The blackmail and fear that this new status imposes on all those it subjects to the uncertainties of that law undoubtedly constitutes, for them, the new face of Europe: a suppression of rights, expropriations and dispossessions, the prohibition of practicing a profession, and arbitrary internments. This is the sense of the war that generalizes for millions of men and women the absolute absence of protection, the murderous abandonment that this status signifies. Arendt recalls in a 1941 text entitled "Active Patience":

> [t]oday—except for Britain—there is no European nation that has not robbed a larger or smaller number of its citizens of their citizenship, driving them into exile, leaving them to the goodwill or bad will of other countries, without consular or legal protection of any kind. (*The Jewish Writings*, 139)

It is important to draw two major political consequences from such a state of affairs. The first concerns the truth of citizenship. Indeed, the mass of "stateless persons" makes clear that, far from resting on a natural base, far from finding its basis in a more original belonging, citizenship is always, first and foremost, the effect of a political will that gives itself the power to grant, deny, confirm, or suppress citizenship according to its own interests. The paradox is that, at the moment millions of men or women find themselves with stateless status because the States have decided that they did not meet the criteria to obtain or retain the rights conferred by citizenship, their new status brings to light the vanity and artifice of these criteria. Their stateless status shows these criteria for what they are: the result of an arbitrary decision. Since citizenship is subjected to so many uncertainties, since it is subjected to the fluctuations caused by changes of regime and government, since, finally, yesterday's naturalization can be remitted the following day, there is evidence that nobody is immune to losing what they thought was assured.[2] What is citizenship, with regard to history? Not an inalienable right that one would receive by birth, but a grace that is given and can be withdrawn. Such is the nature of the blackmail that constitutes the true face of national State sovereignty. The State is never so cruelly and brutally sovereign as when it decides who is—or who can—become a citizen and for whom it is impossible. One thus thinks of the story Jacques Derrida tells in *Monolingualism of the Other*, which recounts the conditions in which he lost his French citizenship in Algeria under the Vichy regime, while being expelled from school, and the conditions for this citizenship's reinstatement. And one should read, from this perspective, the long text that Arendt devotes to "Why the Crémieux Decree Was Abrogated."[3] In other words, because all naturalization is fragile and reversible, because there is no Constitution strong enough to assure that a given political force, under the double pressure of ideology and opinion, will not be tempted tomorrow to turn back on what was granted yesterday by infinitely complicating, for example, the renewal of identification documents, citizenship and the rights it confers remain, everywhere and under all circumstances, the stake and subject of a major political struggle that simultaneously acquires a universal meaning, if not vocation.

What is this politics? Hannah Arendt will not only have offered a formulation of it whenever the question of refugees, exiles, and stateless peoples imposed itself on her. She also will have outlined it in broad strokes throughout the eminently political reading she proposes of Kafka's *The Castle* in the essay she devotes to the author of *The Trial* in 1944. What does this interpretation teach us? First and foremost, it teaches us that, if it is true that the proper of the hero of *The Castle*, K., is the desire to fight only for "those things to which all men would seem to have a birthright" ("Kafka," 99), he insists that these things are granted to him *as a right* and not *as a favor*. He thus refuses to bend to the obscure rules that try to make his residence permit dependent on the goodwill of the authorities, whose power, desires, and intentions are always the subject of a fantasy. If it is consequently the case that the conditions of K.'s residency fall under the minimum requirements for human existence, that minimum should not be subject to the vagaries of a decision as arbitrary as the decision embodied by those same authorities. "He is willing to satisfy all necessary application procedures in order to obtain his residence permit, but he does not want to receive it merely as a favor" (99).

Such an attitude cannot but cause surprise and disapproval, since it is a matter of a struggle against the current of all the forms of resignation and consent that are imposed on the village. The villagers do not understand why K. refuses to admit that life is essentially a matter of grace or disgrace, benediction or malediction. Long ago they deserted the requirement to exercise the right to "a basic human life in the world" (99, translation modified). Their only horizon of expectation is one of the happiness or misery that is accorded to them without their ever being able to know why they received the lot or fate that would be due to them. By contrast, K.'s "political" project, Arendt tells us, is to "create and obtain on legal grounds even what is simply part of human life" (100). He owes it to himself, against all odds, to fight so that the simplest, most basic human demands are met.

Written during the war, it seems that Arendt's interpretation of *The Castle* makes the novel a parable for the situation of the foreigner, whose exile subjects him or her to an interminable waiting for rights. For if it is true that the issuance or denial of these rights should never be a benediction or malediction of the State, the exact opposite nevertheless happens for all the refugees, migrants, and other exiles of all times, including those in well-seated democracies that profess respect for human rights while cutting that same respect off at the doors with the hostility that they reserve for the newcomers who flock to their borders. Kafka's story, then, bears no other lesson than the following one, which has dramatic consequences: in fact, there is no sovereign Nation-State that does not use these rights as its supreme weapon by reserving for itself the power to grant or deny these rights depending on its interests. The word "grace" itself is not employed by accident. It evokes not only the divine will that uses it; as the very essence of the sovereign, it signals the power to order the execution of those condemned to death or to save them. It recalls that such power always, ultimately, plays with the vulnerability and mortality of those who still require attention, concern, and care.

III.

The major force of Arendt's texts lies in ignoring nothing of this vulnerability and mortality, beginning with the 1943 essay entitled "We Refugees," an essay written in the first person plural—"we"—which is a rare event when one thinks of the extreme reticence of the author of *On Revolution* with respect to every declaration of belonging and attachment to a people or collectivity in any form. What is this vulnerability? First of all, it is vulnerability of a loss. A community of emigrants is first of all a community of loss, and there will always be a certain violence in wanting or pretending to ignore it. If State violence has a face, it is probably still here and there—as in China, the United States, or Iran—the death penalty, but that face is everywhere else the reduction of the immigrant question to a problem of quotas, to the element of an economic and political compatibility, in the denial of "losses" to which each emigrant's story testifies, on its own, in a singular and irreplaceable manner. This is where the "sedimentation of the unacceptable"[4] begins each time it is a question of immigration: that the singularity of mutilated lives and, hence, the losses are erased in it. Nobody seems to care about knowing who these emigrants are that have been chased from their homelands by poverty, war, or persecution, as if they had lost nothing, as if the separations counted for nothing, as if their voices did not reach us to recall the worries, the lack of a "sense of the world," every time there is an eclipse in the responsibility for care, attention, and help demanded everywhere by the vulnerability and mortality of the other.[5]

In Arendt's essay, as in Georges Perec's evocation of the arrival of immigrants to Ellis Island,[6] the reminder of what has been lost is a matter of primary importance. Against any façade of optimism, this reminder gives to Arendt's and Perec's reflections an anxious, pessimistic, if not melancholy tone:

> We lost our home, which means the familiarity of everyday life. We lost our occupation, which means the confidence that we are of some use in this world. We lost our language, which means the naturalness of reactions, the simplicity of gestures, the unaffected expression of feelings. We left our relatives in the Polish ghettos and our best friends have been killed in concentration camps, and that means the rupture of our private lives. (Arendt, "We Refugees," 264–65)

But the author of "We Refugees" describes not only loss but also the constraint of the dissimulation and the "trouble of identity" that results. The emigrant, Arendt explains, is not distinguished only by the fact that he or she has left everything, lost everything, and must rebuild everything, but also by the demand to forget who he or she was and from where he or she came. Hospitality, if there is any, is always conditioned by the demand for the immigrant to interiorize the pressure to break or rupture with the past and with the lost identity. This is, in the last resort, the truth of what is required everywhere and in all circumstances in the name of assimilation or integration as a pledge of allegiance or a promise of commitment. Put otherwise, violence exerts itself not only on the borders of those States that detain, turn back, and expel newcomers; it perpetuates itself internally within the random conditions of these constraints, always capable of being reinforced, complicated, rigidified by new prohibitions. As one knows, their pressure does not emanate exclusively from political authorities and police forces; it proceeds just as much from public opinion, for which the foreigner must forget him- or herself *as* foreign. It is up to the refugee, the newcomer, the exiled whom we are kind enough to welcome (this is what is then repeated to him or her in all its forms) to hide from him- or herself and from the others who he or she is in order to be accepted—which is to say, to silence in him- or herself and among others the "voice of the emigrant."

> [W]e already are so damnably careful in every moment of our daily lives to avoid anybody guessing who we are, what kind of passport we have, where our birth certificates were filled out—and that Hitler didn't like us. We try the best we can to fit into a world where you have to be sort of politically minded when you buy your food. [. . .] The less we are free to decide who we are or to live as we like, the more we try to put up a front, to hide the facts, and to play roles. We were expelled from Germany because we were Jews. But having hardly crossed the French borderline, we were changed into *boches*. [. . .] It is the same story all over the world, repeated again and again. In Europe the Nazis confiscated our property; but in Brazil we have to pay 30 percent of our wealth. [. . .] In Paris we could not leave our homes after eight o'clock because we were Jews; but in Los Angeles we are restricted because we are "enemy aliens." Our identity is changed so frequently that nobody can find out who we actually are. (269–70)

And yet, these voices are not doomed to silence. Like those of survivors, these voices often take their time and, after lengthy detours, can make themselves heard by whoever wants to hear them, for themselves, with their own fragility and vulnerability, as German writer W. G. Sebald does by collecting their echo in *The Emigrants* (1992) and *Austerlitz* (2001). Perhaps it will be remembered that, in each case, these narratives have in common the interlacing of two stories: the story of the *encounter* between the narrator and the living or posthumous traces of a relative, a friend, an acquaintance that the anti-Semitic politics of the Third Reich and the extermination of European Jews forced into exile, and the story of the broken fate, the separations, uprooting, and the wounds of memory that these same traces reveal. Intermittent conversations, fragmentary stories, interspersed with long absences thus—like a thread that links them together—merge with group photos, photos of monuments and landscapes, portraits that revive in the heart of the pursuit *the memory of what was lost*. But nothing is obvious or immediate; the buried memories of violence, intimate and reserved, give themselves fragmentarily only to whoever wants to take the time to pursue the trace. And nothing forbids the thought that, despite friendship or kinship, the voices of the uprooted that Sebald gathers might have never pierced the walls that adjoin indifference on one side and melancholy on the other. Consequently, these encounters and the investigation that accompanies them, the solitary journeys, the hotel rooms, the gathered testimonies find a supplementary vocation. They are not only, in the secret of the encounter, in the sharing of dates and places, a witness to the human, as Paul Celan would have written; they also highlight how, in a spectral manner, the violence of history destroys the lives of the uprooted from within. For those who would like to forget, according to the geographies of vulnerability in which it is convenient for them to take refuge, they recall that *all* life of exile, refuge, or statelessness is exposed to the spectrality Levinas called, for his part, a "tumor in the memory" ("Nameless," 120).[7]

What should thus come to mind is the tenuous thread that ties together Sebald's books, Arendt's voice (when she makes herself the spokesperson for emigrants in "We Refugees"), and Perec's "histories of wandering and hope": *suicide*.[8] Voluntary death, the impossibility of still believing in the possibility of a "basic human life in the world" (Arendt): the author of *Ellis Island* evokes suicide in the course of a page that recalls that, between 1892 and 1924, three thousand applicants for immigration took their own lives on Ellis Island, at the end of their journey, after having suffered increasingly discriminatory tests and the various registration formalities that decide either their entry or rejection (*Ellis Island*, 20). Arendt, for her part, devotes a long analysis to suicide in "We Refugees" in order to relativize—if not to counter—the optimistic image of a successful immigration, happy to have escaped from terror to this new Eldorado.[9] Whether at the end of the journey or in the first months, even in the first few years, after being uprooted, both Arendt and Perec tell us that exile is inseparable from a relation to death that leads exile to the only truth that does not lock it within the shackles of ideology and the calculations it provokes: namely, the vulnerability that exile signifies. But it is up to the author of *The Emigrants*, finally, to measure the most intimate recesses of the fissure that leaves its mark on all exile. Indeed, as we have seen, his stories are distinguished by the temporality in which they are inscribed. In every instance, there must be time for the word to free itself, when such is the case, or for truth to surface. Each "emigrant word" seems to conquer a voluntary silence that could have lasted decades, and it takes all of the narrator's patience as a witness, memoirist, or archivist to interrupt the silence and pierce its secret. However, this secret always has the same object: the historical and intimate events that will have made a proper place, a homeland, a motherland an impossible place. This impossibility, intensified by the memory of the dead, creates the pain of exile and corrodes time. This impossibility rushes each of these characters into an endless melancholy, the outcome of which can only be their own disappearance, like photographs that end up maintaining not so much the memory of the world, but its erasure, if they do not themselves call us to join this erasure. Thus Paul Bereyter's photo album that the narrator peruses:

> Again and again, from front to back and from back to front, I leafed through the album that afternoon, and since then I have returned to it time and again, because, looking at the pictures in it, it truly seemed to me, and still does, as if the dead were coming back, or as if we were on the point of joining them. (Sebald, *The Emigrants*, 45–46)

Must this be the last word? There is undoubtedly another—and even more political—reason to bring attention to these tragic destinies, real or fictitious. This other reason takes the form of a hypothesis: what if their audible-inaudible voices were ultimately, today, the veritable "specters" that haunt not only Europe but the totality of the world? What if the emigrant's audible voice told us, first and foremost, the truth of the world even as many forces contribute to making it inaudible? What is this truth? One last time, it is worth turning to the texts Arendt wrote during the war. And among the many texts I would like to cite, I will focus on the article that dates from December 25, 1942, "What Is Happening in France?" The text's opening already grabs the attention of its readers: "This means you!" Arendt writes (*Jewish Writings*, 176). In question is a resistance—more specifically a revolt—manifested by an admittedly minor part of public opinion against the mass deportation of Jews orchestrated in Vichy's France; it is also a question of the support and help that some chose to give at the peril of their own lives. It would be wrong, Arendt explains, to assume that compassion alone accounts for this opposition and attention. And relativizing their meaning by reducing them to the expression of an affect would be to miss their scope. For the meaning is elsewhere—it is political. This care, attention, and help that are brought to the vulnerability and mortality of beings that suffer discrimination, the active contestation of those measures that first weaken and then directly threaten their existence, the disobedience that results, translate the "human responsibility for others" (176) into political will. Because they could not be contained within the borders of a State, this responsibility and this will have a double effect. First, they return the Nation-State to its proper limits, including when it takes itself for a State subject to laws. Second, they draw the contours of another relation to the world, an emancipation and solidarity that find their foundation in this attention and help, against all the tenants of Realpolitik. Who then knows whether or not the voice of Arendt, spokesperson for the emigrants and the persecuted of these dark years, should not be taken up again in favor of the foreigners of our time:

> For a society to attempt to protect us against measures taken by the state, for a people to revolt against its government for the sake of foreign Jews, is so new to Jewish history that one can be certain it will take at least twenty years before this new reality makes its way in the heads of our practitioners of realpolitik. (177)

13

On Fear of Dying

(Three Russian Stories)

Fear will not have had much of a chance in twentieth-century philosophy, crushed as it was between two major concepts, from two different fields, that will have monopolized all attention: *anxiety* and *terror*, two screens or two obstacles whose scope and raison d'être must be measured. On the one hand, in the wake of Kierkegaard's *The Concept of Anxiety* and Heidegger's existential analytic of Dasein, philosophers of existence will have concentrated on anxiety, relegating fear to the rank of accessory emotions; on the other hand, the theoretical discussions bearing on the justification or the condemnation of violence in the name of an idea of history or revolution will have made terror the key concept in the analysis of authoritarian and repressive systems, beginning with totalitarian systems. As a result, "fear of dying" and all the manifestations that betray it were for a long time, if not foreign to all theoretical reflection, at least *secondary*, irremediably *secondary*, with regard to what anxiety before death imposed on the ontological-existential plane and to what terror's conflation of trial, indictment, and defense imposed on the historical and political plane, as if fear were too individual, too subjective, but also perhaps indefinitely suspected as a weakness, a lack of courage and resolution, thus too ambivalent to be given the consideration it deserves. Consequently, one will have also missed the encounter between these two large fields of investigation comprised by the existential analysis of the relation to death and the political analysis of the effects of the regimes most threatening to the security of life. The first will have neglected the irreducibly political dimension of our threatened and threatening relation to death; the second will have minimized the subjective character of the effects of terror on every singular existence, that is, the way it affects the bodies and the minds in the bundle of relations—to oneself, to others, to the world—that comprises the singularity of all subjectivity.

And yet, there are so many imaginary variations on fear! For this is the paradox: while anxiety and terror captivated the attention of philosophers, the experience of fear ceaselessly imposed itself not only as an object of literature but also, even more so, as one of literature's major driving forces. The experience of fear is already inseparable from the emergence and momentum of literary genres to which one must give their due; fantasy literature, horror novels, all the stories of specters, apparitions, phantoms, the living dead, bloodthirsty monsters picked up by cinema—all have indelibly composed the imaginary of fear. Above all, however, it is up to the literature—narratives and testimonies, but also plays and poems—that confronted terror and took as its object the possibility of a perception of terror that was less abstract than the perception that reduced it, rightly or wrongly, to a political means. Yet, literature did so precisely by vindicating what constitutes the most immediate, most quotidian, most invasive translation of terror, which drives those that suffer its yoke to the verge of madness: namely, a fear at every moment for oneself and one's loved ones, the fear of being arrested, imprisoned, tortured, deported, and, ultimately, executed. One might say that, in a sense, philosophy will have long ago left this fear to literature, as if the stakes were not there, but one can also say that, on the day that literature will have caught up with thinking and imposed its testimony of fear, nothing will have been as it was. It will perhaps have required the narratives of Solzhenitsyn and Ginzburg (*Journey into the Whirlwind* and *Within the Whirlwind*), of Dombrovsky (*The Faculty of Useless Knowledge*), but also the poems of Mandelstam and, retrospectively, a reading in reverse of Kafka's prophetic novels, beginning with *The Trial*, for another approach to terror to be imposed: the approach that grants rights to what terror does to the life of the living by immuring them in an obsessive and paralyzing "fear of death."

There is, from this point of view, a striking example: Merleau-Ponty's essay *Humanism and Terror*, written in 1946 and published in book form in 1947. As its title indicates, indeed, this essay refers explicitly to terror, as the Moscow Trials exemplify it, by drawing upon a very critical reading of Koestler's novel, *Darkness at Noon*. One can assume, then, that the book ignores nothing of the politics of terror implemented by the Stalinist regimes, and nevertheless, by interrogating its legitimacy, the book strikingly misses what in reality invalidates all the justifications that it proposes in the name of revolution, namely, the most concrete—the most phenomenological, one might say—analysis of the fact that such politics means first and foremost, not a confrontation with history, but the extreme violence of the invasion of fear: fear of others, without exception, from the most familiar to the most foreign, fear of informers, of their insinuations and their denunciations, of murderous rumors and traps, fear everywhere and every moment.

From where, then, does such a denial of fear come? Is it because fear is suspicious from the beginning, as if the philosophies of existence that valorize the anxiety of nothingness and the political theories that interrogate the meaning of history and the violence for which it calls both considered that it is undignified to fear death? In other words, is it because this fear lacks both the meaning of existence and the meaning of action and history? And if this is the case, what is the counterpoint or counterweight offered by literature? All fear, no doubt, is not synonymous with violence, but it is so each time that, for various reasons, it can be traced back to "fear of dying," where this fear leads whomever it seizes to the verge of madness. In the following pages, I will attempt to respond to these questions by closely following what we learn from three stories whose common ground is belonging to literature of the Russian language and tracing a path in it: Tolstoy's "Memoirs of a Madman," Tendriakov's "Parania," and finally, in more detail, Mandelstam's "The Egyptian Stamp."

I.

I had gone out into the corridor thinking to escape from what tormented me. But *it* had come out with me and cast a gloom over everything. I felt just as filled with horror or even more so.

"But what folly this is!" I said to myself. "Why am I depressed? What am I afraid of?"

"Me!" answered the voice of Death, inaudibly. "I am here!"

A cold shudder ran down my back. Yes! Death! It will come—here it is—and it ought not to be. Had I been actually facing death I could not have suffered as much as I did then. Then I should have been frightened. But now I was not frightened. I saw and felt the approach of death, and at the same time I felt that such a thing ought not to exist.

My whole being was conscious of the necessity and the right to live, and yet I felt that Death was being accomplished. And this inward conflict was terrible. I tried to throw off the horror, I found a brass candlestick, the candle in which had a wick, and lighted it. The red glow of the candle and its size—little less than the candlestick itself—told me the same thing. Everything

> told me the same: "There is nothing in life. Death is the only real thing, and death ought not to exist."
>
> I tried to turn my thoughts to things that had interested me—to the estate I was to buy, and to my wife—but found nothing to cheer me. It had all become nothing. Everything was hidden by the terrible consciousness that my life was ebbing away. I needed sleep. I lay down, but the next instant I jumped up again in terror. A fit of the spleen seized me—spleen such as the feeling before one is sick, but spiritual spleen.[1] It was uncanny and dreadful. It seems that death is terrible, but when remembering and thinking of life it is one's dying life that is terrible. Life and death somehow merged into one another. Something was tearing my soul apart and could not complete the severance. (Tolstoy, "Memoirs of a Madman," 786–87)[2]

What does Tolstoy's story teach us about the anxiety of death, the fear of dying, and the terrors through which they manifest? First and foremost, it teaches that they are inseparable, tightly knotted together, and that, consequently, the relation to the prospect of one's own death cannot be analyzed independently of what gathers together the anxiety of nothingness, the fear of losing one's life, and the terror of the unknown in a way that remains for everyone irreducibly singular in what constitutes the most mysterious part of the genesis of his or her subjectivity. The passage just cited, indeed, recounts one of the two crises that lead the narrator who experiences them to the verge of madness. As the story begins, a story that presents itself as the "memoirs of a madman," the one who is going to launch into a long anamnesis of the pain [*mal*] that lies in wait for him, haunted by its always imminent return, barely escapes psychiatric internment, which was presented as a possibility, as we learn very quickly, because of repeated anxiety attacks, but also because of the fear of their return and the night terrors that accompany them, which are the most visible manifestations of this pain. More precisely, however, this anamnesis seeks not only to reconstitute the history of these attacks; it also seeks to understand the complex origin of the knot that, in our apprehensiveness before death, binds the first experiences, the first interrogations, and the first nightmares of childhood to the agitations of adolescence and the passions of adulthood. The story reminds us, in other words, that we have grasped nothing of this apprehensiveness or of the violence proper to it as long as we have not explored the different strata that constitute the imaginary of our relation to death, as if the story warned us, a few decades in advance, that it is useless to focus on anxiety and set it on an ontologico-existential pedestal if it is in order to forget our fears that divert it from nothingness by finding an object for it, even if that object is anxiety itself. For this is what Tolstoy teaches us: there is nothing in this relation that is more dreadful than the anxiety attacks that accompany not so much the certainty of death's imminence as the absolute consciousness of the finitude of all life. Thus, it is anxiety itself that causes fear, and its repeated attacks lead the author to the verge of madness because they are a permanent threat. Life, at bottom, is less paralyzed by the anxiety of death than by the very concrete fear of the attacks it provokes, a fear that Tolstoy describes with a preciseness and finesse that no existential analytic, immured in its ontological clauses [attendus], could achieve.

> I had suffered all night unbearably. Again my soul and body were being painfully torn asunder. "I am living, have lived, and ought to live, and suddenly—here is death to destroy everything. Then what is life for? To die? To kill myself at once? No, I am afraid. To wait for death till it comes? I fear that even more. Then I must live. But what for? In order to die?" And I could not escape from that circle. I took up a book, read, and forgot myself for a moment, but then again the same question and the same horror. (789–90)

It is this fear that, ultimately, pushes him into this politics of waiting and opportunism [attentisme], indifferent to everything that had until then given meaning to his life (his house, his family, his business and belongings), which finds relief only in religion. There are, of course, other possible solutions, and literature ceaselessly plays with the possibilities that it manages to invent, not so much in order to substitute fear for anxiety as to give it an object other than that anxiety itself, just to give us something else to fear.[3] Since it is a question of Russian literature, how can one avoid invoking all the stories of specters, the living dead, or resuscitated cadavers that, at the borders of the real, ceaselessly play with our childhood nightmares, giving fear this other object: Alexander Pushkin's "The Undertaker," Nikolai Leskov's "The Ghost of the Engineers' Castle," Fyodor Sologub's "The White Dog," or the stunning story from Leonid Andreyev entitled "The Burglar." These stories all have in common the fact of proposing, not without humor, if not a distraction at least a playful and terrifying alternative to the solitude of the anxiety and apprehension of its attacks, which teaches us no less about the complex strata, the imaginary constructions, the passions of the body, and the illusions of the senses constitutive of our relation to death.

II.

While political philosophy analyzes terror from the point of view of its historical necessity or the internal logic of a revolutionary process that owes its survival, as a process, only to the elimination of all opposition, it always runs the risk of reducing the victims that result to effective opponents. Most of the time, it ratifies the justification given by unscrupulous proponents of that same terror and the functionaries that it recruits: the justification consists in seeing in terror only the means of the process's survival, identified with the purity of its principle, the infallibility of its ideology, the rigor of its objectives and the political line chosen to attain them. Thus, discussing Koestler's *Darkness at Noon* in *Humanism and Terror*, Merleau-Ponty constructs the essential part of his analysis on the fact that "in a period of revolutionary tension or external threat there is no clear-cut boundary between political divergences and objective treason. Humanism is suspended and government is terror" (34). Presupposing that there is no terror without reason, he forgets the imaginary or fantastical, if not paranoid, aspects of the "objectively counterrevolutionary" (9) opposition that he ascribes to the victims. Lacking testimonies more credible than Koestler's novel, he misses what is nevertheless essential, namely, the methodical destruction of the moral, social, and political relations whose genesis and subsequent variations are constitutive not only of all individual singularity but also of collective identity. In his defense, one should probably mention that, written between 1946 and 1947 in a world won over by the logic of the Cold War and gangrened by the survival of colonial systems, the book could still suspect that the testimonies that reached "the West," such as the Victor A. Kravchenko's *I Chose Freedom* (the French translation of which appeared the same year), were an instrument of propaganda in the service of what was then called "the liberal camp [*le camp libéral*]," ignoring or pretending to ignore the violence for which that same camp was itself accountable. It remains no less the case that, when we read these testimonies today, these analyses seem to us not only dated by their historical context and the theoretical debates for which it called but also, in the same stroke, dramatically changed by the perception of the Stalinist era that is possible today, as if terror (this is what interpellates us) remained deliberately *abstract* when reduced to a ruse of history or a political strategy.

The question, then, concerns knowing to what this abstraction pertains and what makes it henceforth untenable; this is where we rediscover literature. For these theoretical analyses of terror miss first and foremost the description of a society grasped, down to its smallest branches, by *the fear of a violent death* in the process engendered by terror: the dreaded and often nocturnal arrival of visitors, the arrest, the confinement, the interrogations (also nocturnal), an expedited trial, the deportation or the execution of the allegedly guilty. Next, these theoretical analyses miss the precise analysis of the way in which this fear affects all the relations of confidence that comprise the tissue of existence: the minimal and in this sense vital credit that we need to place in the relations that link us to our body and make us believe in its right to breathe, to move, and to nourish itself freely; the credit in the relation that attaches us to others, to our loved ones, to our parents, friends, and neighbors; and finally, for society as a whole, the credit in the institutions and in the protection and security that they are supposed to assure without, for all that, reversing into a permanent threat. Which is to say, one could not imagine a more violent and brutal erasure than this abstraction. Inversely, the only way to traverse its density is to understand that, in reality, neither the spirit or future of the revolution nor the absolute of history is at stake in this violence; at stake, rather, is the impossibility for life to remain livable and breathable in a society where fear, as the only common denominator, undoes all relations.

Among the many narratives that could have been evoked to illustrate the way literature introduces the individual and collective dimension of fear, its contagion and madness, into our perception of terror, I will retain *Parania*, a novella by Vladimir Tendriakov (1923–1984). It is the summer of 1937 in a little town in Russia, where a young and simple-minded girl, Parania, is a constant victim of sarcastic remarks. As the radio broadcasts slogans and chants for the glory of Stalin throughout the whole village—"Stalin's name is engraved in our hearts, on all our lips"—the children echo: "Parania! Parania! Who is your fiancé?" (123–24).[4] Until the day when, tired of resisting, Parania ends up threatening her pursuers: "Watch out, you; I'll tell Stalin . . . The great Stalin himself . . . Watch out, he'll get you . . . Enemies of the people" (127). At that moment a child, thinking he was clever, cries out: "Parania's fiancé is Stalin" (127–28). Stupor, consternation. While the radio continues to pour out slogans in the streets, a heavy silence ensues. And Parania, in the days that follow, raises the stakes each time she crosses someone in the street: "He sees everything! . . . He knows everything! . . . Watch out, you! . . . I'm wearing the crown! My fiancé put it on my head. . . . My dear and beloved . . . His goodness is with me. . . Watch out, you!" (130). It is no longer a divine madness [*folle en Dieu*] but, rather, "a Stalin madness [*folle en Staline*]." And no one knows how the authorities will respond. A police officer from the village earnestly tries to lecture her; the chief of police even decides to have her arrested. After some hesitation and suspicion, however, the crowd lashes out against them: how can you arrest someone that ceaselessly exclaims her devotion to and love for Comrade Stalin? In the end, their indignation reaches the ears of the higher authorities that, taking sides with Parania, turn against the commissioner, who in turn, completes the circle by taking it out on the officer at the origin of the pursuit. But the story does not stop there. Released, Parania finds herself invested with an exorbitant power. She regularly targets those she comes across, pointing them out of the crowd with a Pythian exclamation: "I see him! I see him! There! There! It's him! Dissenter! Plotter! Him! I can read it on his face!" (137). And because she is believed to have a veritable power of divination, because everyone is ready to believe her accusations, everyone that she thus apostrophizes and points out with her finger disappears in the night, from one day to the next. Parania, whose name suits her, thus becomes the terror of the village. Anyone that crosses her line of sight is exposed to being immediately suspected of stirring up a conspiracy against the one that the radio, moreover, continues to praise in the village streets. One can imagine what happens next: people no longer dare to go into the streets, to speak to their loved ones or to their neighbors, to show up for work, all paralyzed by the irresistible contagion of fear.

One will easily agree that this novella gives terror a dimension that cannot be grasped by its theoretical justification in the name of the idea, integrity, and survival of the revolution or in the name of history nor the rigorous analysis of its ideology and mechanisms, beginning with the analysis of the repressive apparatuses that implement it. And the first thing that the story recalls is the fact that the efficacy of terror is a farce. Supposing that its objective is the "education of the people" or that it aims at the unification of the people, it produces exactly the inverse. Everywhere that regimes practicing terror through arrests, torture, and executions imagine themselves to be contributing to the formation of a body of citizens, a great people, a great nation disciplined by the idea and by the forces that impose it, terror obtains nothing but a dismembered body, a dislocated society, similar to the villagers fleeing in all directions at the sight of the almost spectral and nevertheless very real apparition of Parania. Terror's inefficiency is that it does not produce any psychic or collective identification, because it destroys any possibility of individual identification. Indeed, this destruction, which Vaclav Havel analyzed so well in his famous "Open Letter to Dr. Husak," is the most immediate consequence of terror, and the contagion of fear is its instrument.

Terror, as literature measures its effects and as Tendriakov's story shows, not without irony at times, thus exemplifies in the extreme the state of a "culture of fear" and its constitutive violence when a government, whatever it may be, makes its *propagation* an element of its action. Like all manipulation of affects and emotions—anger, for example—terror in principle escapes the control of the one attempting to organize it. No one is capable of evaluating in advance the *reactions* that terror produces, least of all the reaction that, after anxiety and terror, constitutes the last concept that must be related to the concept of fear: namely, *panic*. It is thus not by chance that Tendriakov's novella ends with Parania's death. In this precise case, there is only one victim and one murder, but how can one evoke fear in its collective dimension, its fever and contagion, without emphasizing its reversal into murderous madness as the first risk of exploiting in it? This is the paradox of a fear whose common obsession, whether its object is real, imaginary, or fantastical, turns to panic: most often, it finds a way out of its initial paralysis only by unleashing a violence that is either uncontrollable or, on the contrary, too quickly and skillfully controlled. Fear is therefore always threatened-threatening. And there is no shortage of examples in the history of recent centuries to recall the way terror's construction and propagation everywhere in the world—its radio- and tele-diffusion, the rumors on which it feeds, rumors to which new technologies for knowing and informing give today an unprecedented power—have constituted a driving element in the genesis of the murderous consent that still accompanies and nourishes the violence unleashed.

III.

Hence, we are led to the third story that I propose to read in order to illustrate the debt that philosophy has taken on with respect to literature and its perception of and apprehensiveness toward fear. In question is Mandelstam's strange, perhaps hallucinatory, narrative called "The Egyptian Stamp." To believe his biographer, Ralph Dutli, and the wonderful book that he dedicated to the poet, *Mandelstam: Meine Zeit, mein Tier* [*My Time, My Animal*], fear appears as a recurring element in his poems from the 1920s. Fear is inseparable, then, from what signs the poet's political engagement in his era: his refusal to compromise in any way with political violence, which he knew very early to be the truth of the regime that resulted from the revolution, his repeated and often confirmed allergy to capital punishment, if not even his distaste for this taste for murder, this aroma of blood, this murderous contagion that ended up making his era a beast that devoured its children.[5] Despite the torturous meanderings that it takes, the story's plot can be easily summarized: on a day in June, 1917, between the February and the October revolutions, a small, obscure man destined for mediocrity like so many characters in Russian literature, mocked by his colleagues, scared of life, discovers one morning that his morning coat was stolen by Mervis, the tailor that had made it for him. Like a reminiscence of Gogol's *The Overcoat*, an unhappy search ensues in the streets of St. Petersburg. En route, Parnok crosses a raging mob that he tries in vain to prevent from lynching someone, the prospect of which enrages the crowd. Alone against them all, impotent, he manages nothing, neither to waken the State that was "sleeping like a carp" (145) by mobilizing the police forces, which were indifferent or complacent to the crimes being committed, nor to reason with the crowd and calm it—let alone to find his morning coat. He thus incarnates the individual that is weak, isolated, swept away by the contrary winds of history, the individual that is made courageous by his rebellion against murder but that nevertheless always *loses* against violence and its agents, capitulating before the forms of consent that violence incites and, in the end, submitting to the only solution of leaving everything instinctively up to what his fear of dying dictates to him.

But Parnok's story is only one part of "The Egyptian Stamp." Written in the third person singular, it is interspersed with narrative elements written in the first person that, for their part, are presented as the fragments of an anamnesis that history has made practically impossible ever since the traces of the past were dispersed. Furniture, childhood objects, nothing has been conserved:

> I propose to you, my family, a coat of arms: a glass of boiled water. In the rubbery aftertaste of Petersburg's boiled water I drink my unsuccessful domestic immortality. The centrifugal force of time has scattered our Viennese chairs and Dutch plates with little blue flowers. Nothing is left. Thirty years have passed like a slow fire. (133)

Parnok himself seems to be only the double of a figure from this same past, an employee of the narrator's father to whom the child was attached: Nicolas Davidovitch Shapiro. In fact, the parallel is striking between these two characters, both conquered by history. While the first (Parnok) is presented as "a little man with patent leather shoes, who was despised by doormen and women," Mandelstam recalls the second (Shapiro) as "a rough and kindly guest [. . .], big-headed [. . .], eternally rubbing his hands together and smiling guiltily like an errand boy admitted into the house" (137–38). Yet, if Parnok is, during the summer of 1917, "the Kerenski summer" during which the novel is supposed to be situated, a part of Shapiro's memory that lived during the Revolution, his memory—between 1927 and 1928, the time during which Mandelstam is composing his narrative—is haunted by the nightmares of the present. He is the transposition of a mediocre existence, apparently destined for servitude in a furious present that submits everyone to a trial of *courage* that no one expected to find. The story's force thus pertains to their impossible superposition. That force is a witness to the present in the revelation, through the digression of wanderings through the streets of St. Petersburg, of a past that has been lost or damaged and will not return: a whole iconography of childhood, sounds of voices, aromas, forms and colors, Hermitage paintings that all surface and disseminate throughout the narrative in the form of fragmentary lacunae. And this is when, in the very middle of the nightmare and thus at the heart of the anamnesis, what no doubt constitutes the most brutal recollection of the present appears. United and driven by an incomprehensible fear, surrounding the expiatory victim that they are getting ready to lynch, a mob crosses the path of Parnok, who watches the scene from the window at the dentist where he had stopped for treatment:

> Here mutual guarantee was the law: everyone, absolutely everyone, was ready to answer for the preservation and safe delivery of the dandruffy coat hanger to the bank of the Fontanka and the boat with the fish-well. Someone had only to try, with the most modest sort of exclamation, to come to the aid of the owner of the ill-fated collar, which was more highly treasured than sable or marten, and he himself would land in the soup, would be suspect, declared an outlaw and dragged into the empty square. This was the work of that master cooper, fear [*strakh*]. (143, translation modified)[6]

Parnok, however, tries to help the mob's unfortunate prisoner. An obscure character if there ever was one, he cannot bear the sight of this programmatic lynching, just as Mandelstam, the next year, was to address Bukharin so that the lives of five bank employees condemned to death as a means of intimidation could be spared. And one recalls the inscription for the same Bukharin in a copy of his *Poems*, the last collection published during his life (still in 1928): "Every line in this book argues against what you plan to do." Listening only to his heart [*son courage*], as they say, Parnok—who is also, in the same stroke, a double for the poet-witness repulsed by the capital executions—rushes to ask for help. In vain. The old Jewish clockmaker does not have a telephone for him to call the police; the mirror merchant shuts the door on him; the captain, to whom his morning coat was sold, turns his back on him with his mistress. Nothing resists the pressure of the hideous, increasingly threatening crowed: "The innumerable swarm of human locusts . . . blackened the banks of the Fotanka and clung around the fish-well boat. . . . Petersburg had declared itself Nero and was as loathsome as if it were eating a soup of crushed flies" (145). And yet, Parnok, already regarded by the mob with suspicion, persists in his frantic will to help the one that the crowd had already condemned. He knows what he risks, and we do not know what becomes of him at the end of the narrative. Parnok will have disappeared in a St. Petersburg night, vanishing like the deformed figures of a nightmare at dawn. The first-person singular will have then reclaimed its rights. In the meantime, however, like the poet that terror cannot manage to silence as long as it has not devoured him, he pursues his desperate attempts to save the condemned. He telephones everyone and everywhere for help, just as others after him will in vain write dozens and dozens of letters proclaiming their innocence or the innocence of their loved ones, risking their lives in the illusion that a reestablished truth, "the true truth," says Mandelstam, will save their lives:

> Nevertheless, he telephoned from a pharmacy, telephoned the police, telephoned the government, the state, which had vanished, sleeping like a carp.
>
> He might with equal success have telephoned Proserpine or Persephone, who had not yet had a telephone installed. (145)

Parnok will reappear one more time in the last chapter, a few pages before the end of the narrative. Meanwhile, the rights of the narrator are reclaimed. The anamnesis continues as a condensed recapitulation of European culture, itself threatened with disappearance, in the streets of St. Petersburg: music, painting, literature. The one narrating in the first-person singular resurfaces, already worried about escaping Parnok's fate, condemned to the same impotence, devoured in the same solitude, erased in advance from the memory of others, as if the narrative were inhabited by a dark presentiment: "Lord! Do not make me like Parnok! Give me strength to distinguish myself from him" (149). Mandelstam already knew what he was talking about, for "The Egyptian Stamp" was written and published after many years of silence. Like Parnok, he experienced the futility of his calls against violence, beginning with the calls that seemed to him to be the fate of poetry:

> My pen has become insubordinate: it has splintered and squirted its black blood out in all directions, as if it were attached to the desk in the telegraph office, a public pen, ruined by scoundrels in fur coats, having exchanged its swallow flourish, its original stroke, for such phrases as, "Come for God's sake," "Miss you," "kisses," penned by unshaven lechers whispering their little message into their fur collars, warm with their breath. (149)

The pen becomes insubordinate, but only the pen gives rise to the chance, if there is one, of escaping Parnok's fate. Two threads, indeed, tie together in the refusal of violent death in the narrative's final pages, two affects whose indissociable link constitutes the response that Mandelstam's poetry opposes to all the forms of "murderous consent": *the courage for truth* and *the fear of dying*. It is customary, no doubt, to oppose fear to courage, as if fear might always house some form of cowardice. But what would courage be without fear? What would courage be if it were not carried by the overpowering and perhaps even almost hallucinatory ordeal [*épreuve*] of the fear of dying, no doubt like the surge of the decomposed images of the delirious fever suffered by the narrator of "The Egyptian Stamp"? Courage that has not known fear, like a nightmare, can perhaps be only the appearance of courage, an unconscious temerity that does not sufficiently know the price of life. This is, in any case, what could ultimately invert the meaning that is given to fear: not impotence, paralysis, or apathy but the creative impulse, the very first motor of a rebellious upsurge.

Faced with terror, only the one that speaks the truth is the one that knows, as surely as he or she still breathes, the potential cost but does not compromise with this knowledge. The fear of dying guides him or her, as much as the passion for truth. If he or she no longer experiences fear, it is perhaps because he or she has already made a pack with lying and agreed to close his or her eyes and plug his or her ears in order to fear no longer. If there is an homage in "The Egyptian Stamp" to European culture, its monuments and museums, its theaters and concert halls, the homage that it pays to literature in fact carries the memory of this knowledge. It is not in vain that one makes the passion for books—from the moment that it retains the kernel of truth that arms the refusal of violence—a filter through which the course of life flows and is strained. Let us hear what Mandelstam writes some ten years before being carried off in the Kolyma night:

> I hasten to tell the real truth, I am in a hurry. The word, like aspirin powder, leaves a brassy taste in the mouth. [...]
>
> A bird's eye, suffused with blood, also has its own way of seeing the world.
>
> Books melt like chunks of ice brought into a room. Everything grows smaller. Everything seems to me a book. Where is the difference between a book and a thing? I do not know life: they switched it on me as long ago as the time when I recognized the crunch of arsenic between the teeth of the amorous French brunette, the younger sister of our proud Anna.

> Everything grows smaller. Everything melts. Even Goethe melts. Brief is the time allotted to us. As it slips away, the hilt of that bloodless, brittle sword, broken off the drainpipe one freezing day, chills the palm.
> But thought—like the hangman steel of the "Nurmis" skates, which one skimmed along the blue, pimply ice—has not been blunted. [. . .]
> It is more and more difficult to turn the pages of the frozen book, bound in axes by the light of gas lanterns. (156)

The intransigent passion for literature thus constitutes the first of Ariadne's threads, however fragile, on which to cling in the storm when "[r]osy-fingered Dawn has broken her colored pencils" (161). The second thread is fear:

> Fear [*strakh*] takes me by the hand and leads me. A white cotton glove. A woman's glove without fingers. I love fear [*strakh*], I respect it. I almost said "With it, I'm not afraid [*strashno*]!" Mathematicians should have built a tent for fear [*strakh*], for it is the coordinate of time and space: they participate in it like the rolled-up felt in the nomad tent of the Kirgiz. Fear [*strakh*] unharnesses the horses when one has to drive and sends us dreams with unnecessarily low ceilings. (162, translation modified)

Notes

Chapter One

1. TN. Both *rapport* and *relation* would often be translated into English as "relation." Yet, since Crépon uses them to distinguish two sorts of relations, most often (but not always) associating *rapport* with a certain "interior" relation to one's singular self and *relation* with a certain "exterior" relation to the world, we have opted systematically, and somewhat artificially if not arbitrarily, to translate *rapport* as "relation" and *relation* as "relationship." This systematization is limited to this chapter alone.

2. TN. The German phrase *nebensächlichen Konsequenzen* is translated into English as "incidental consequences," as *connaissances secondaires* ("secondary knowledges") into French.

3. The present passage is not included in the German edition of the *Diaries* or its English translation. It is reproduced in "Fragments from Note-Books and Loose Pages" in *Wedding Preparations in the Country and Other Posthumous Prose Writings*. [TN. This passage and others omitted from the German and English are included, however, in the third volume of the more extensive *Œuvres completes*, from which Crépon cites.]

4. TN. The entry dates from 1910: "Finally, after five months of my life during which I could write nothing that would have satisfied me, and for which no power will compensate me, though all were under obligation to do so, it occurs to me to talk to myself again" (Kafka, *Diaries*, 12).

5. December 23, 1911: "One advantage in keeping a diary is that you become aware with reassuring clarity of the changes which you constantly suffer and which in a general way are naturally believed, surmised, and admitted by you, but which you'll unconsciously deny when it comes to the point of gaining hope or peace from such an admission" (*Diaries*, 145).

6. See also Kafka's entry from April 27, 1915: "Incapable of living with people, of speaking. Complete immersion in myself, thinking of myself. Apathetic, witless, fearful. I have nothing to say to anyone—never" (334).

7. "What will be my fate as a writer is very simple. My talent for portraying my dreamlike inner life has thrust all other matters into the background; my life has

dwindled dreadfully, nor will it cease to dwindle. Nothing else will ever satisfy me. But the strength I can muster for that portrayal is not to be counted upon: perhaps it has already vanished forever, perhaps it will come back to me again, although the circumstances of my life don't favour its return." (302)

8. TN. What is here translated into English as "writing" is in Kafka's German *Schreiben*, which is cited by Crépon in French as *littérature*.

9. On this subject, see Kafka's reflections on January 4, 1912, concerning what he reads to his sisters (164–65).

10. See, for instance, the entry from August 27, 1916, on marriage, children, responsibilities, the office, housing, in short, on all the worries of existence:

> Then put a stop to all that. One cannot spare oneself, cannot calculate things in advance. You haven't the faintest idea of what would be better for you. / Tonight, for example, two considerations of equal strength and value battled in you at the expense of your brain and heart, you were equally worried on both their accounts; hence the impossibility of making calculations. What is left? Never again degrade yourself to the point where you become the battleground of a struggle that goes on with no regard as it were for you, and of which you feel nothing but the terrible blows of the warriors. Rise up, then. Mend your ways, escape officialdom, start seeing what you are instead of calculating what you should become. (369)

Chapter Two

1. TN. The title that Crépon cites here and the text out of which he works is, in fact, "Préjugés: Devant la loi" (*La Faculté de juger*, ed. J. Derrida et al. [Paris: Minuit, 1985], 87–139), from which the English translation of Derrida's "Before the Law" is extracted only in part. All the passages cited by Crépon, however, are included in the extract in English translation, which we have therefore retained.

Chapter Three

1. TN. The French title is *Partages de la singularité*. When translating the French *partage*, we largely follow Michael Loriaux's lead in his translation of Crépon's *The Thought of Death and the Memory of War*: "The term *partage* can mean sharing, dividing, or apportioning in French. All three terms will be used in this book in accordance with context" (146, note 1).

2. See Jacques Derrida, *Sovereignties in Question: The Poetics of Paul Celan*, ed. Thomas Dutoit and Outi Pasanen (New York: Fordham UP, 2005). For the question of witnessing, see "Poetics and Politics of Witnessing," 65–97; for the question of mourning, see "Rams: Uninterrupted Dialogue—Between Two Infinities, the Poem," 135–63.

3. For Levinas, see Emanuel Levinas, "Paul Celan: From Being to the Other," in *Proper Names*, trans. Michael B. Smith (Stanford: Stanford UP, 1996), 40–46; for Blanchot, see Maurice Blanchot, "The Last to Speak," in *A Voice from Elsewhere*, trans. Charlotte Mandell (Albany: SUNY UP, 2007), 53–93.

4. Celan continues in these terms (which Derrida does not fail to pick up): "Perhaps what's new in the poems written today is exactly this: theirs is the clearest attempt to remain mindful of such dates? / But don't we all write ourselves from such dates? And toward what dates do we write ourselves?" (30a–b).

5. On this point, see Marc Crépon, *Terreur et poésie* (Paris: Galilée, 2004).

6. TN. The German formulation is *im Geheimnis der Begegnung*. Like Pierre Joris in the now standard translation of Celan's text, Jerry Glenn also gives "mystery of an encounter" in his translation of *The Meridian* (included in *Sovereignties in Question*, 181). The editors of the same volume, Thomas Dutoit and Outi Pasanen, note that Derrida writes Glenn's translation in the margin of his manuscript of *The Beast and the Sovereign* in a discussion of the same passage (*Sovereignties in Question*, 205, note 3). In French, however, Derrida himself ("Shibboleth," 9)—along with Crépon and Jean Launay (*Le Méridien et autres proses* [Paris: Seuil, 2002], 76)—translates the phrase as "le secret de la rencontre," that is, "the secret of the encouter."

7. TN. See *The Beast and the Sovereign*, 228, 231, and 232.

8. On this point, see Marc Crépon, *Terreur et poésie*.

9. See Derrida, *The Beast and the Sovereign*, 259–60.

10. On this point, see Marc Crépon, *Langues sans demeure* (Paris: Galilée, 2005).

Chapter Four

1. One will recall (see chapter 3 above) that, commenting upon Lucile's cry in Büchner's *The Death of Danton*—"Long live the King!" (a cry to which we will return again in the following pages)—Celan exclaims in *The Meridian*: "It is a step" (7b).

2. Republished in 1984 by Fata Morgana, with illustrations from Pierre Tal Coat. One will note that, the same year (1984), Derrida wrote his first text devoted to Celan, "Shibboleth," which was published two years later.

3. TN. The final stanza of the poem to which Crépon is alluding runs as follows (Celan, *No One's Rose*, 49):

> If there came
> if there came a man,
> if there cam a man to the world today, with
> the shining beard of
> patriarchs: if he spoke
> about these
> times, he
> would only go on to
> babble, babble,
> ever-, ever-,
> moremore.
> ("Pallaksch. Pallaksch,")

David Young, Celan's translator, points out that "Pallaksch" is "a nonsense word Hölderlin went around uttering his presumed madness" (49, note).

4. In particular, see both *Proper Names* and *On Maurice Blanchot*, which give a few of the most visible elements of this constellation. [TN. *On Maurice Blanchot* is included in the English translation of *Proper Names*, but the two are published separately in French by Fata Morgana.]

5. TN. These three translations follow the modifications suggested by Michael B. Smith, translator of *Proper Names*, since Levinas's argument, as Smith points out, depends heavily on the wording in French. See Levinas, "Paul Celan," 174 and especially note 4. Similarly, Crépon here substitutes the translation he was previously using (*Le Méridien et autres textes*, trans. Jean Launay [Paris: Seuil, 2002]) with the translation used by Levinas (*Le Méridian*, trans. André du Boucet [Paris: Fata Morgana, 1967]).

6. TN. We have given here David Young's translation, which differs slightly from the translation found in Blanchot's "The Last to Speak":

> A nothing
> we were, are, will
> remain, in flower:
> from nothing the rose,
>   one's rose.
> (quoted in Blanchot, "The Last to Speak," 81)

> In German, the poem reads:
> Ein Nichts
> waren wir, sind wir, werden
> wir bleiben, blühend:
> die Nichts-, die
> Niemandsrose.
> (Celan, *No One's Rose*, 46)

7. TN. What is translated here into English as "bespeaks itself to it" is, in German, *spricht sich ihm zu*, that is, literally "speaks itself to it"; more idiomatically, *zusprechen* ("to speak to") is also "to grant" or "to award." The French translation cited by Crépon, returning to the Launay translation of Celan's text, gives *se promet à lui*, that is, "promises itself to it," which is why Crépon invokes a "promise of language" a few lines below.

8. TN. i.e., *The Beast and Sovereign*.

9. See Derrida, *Monolingualism of the Other*, 68ff. One will recall that, in Derrida's book, Celan is cited by name in the end: "Celan, the poet-translator who, while writing in the language of the other, and about the Holocaust, while inscribing Babel in the very body of each poem, expressly claimed, signed, and sealed the poetic monolingualism of his work just the same" (69).

10. TN. Following Levinas, Crépon returns here to du Boucet's translation of Celan's text. Accordingly, here and in the citation a few lines below, we

once again modify Pierre Joris's translation to match the formulation found in Smith's translation of Levinas's "Paul Celan: From Being to the Other" (*Proper Names*, 43).

11. TN. Celan, *The Meridian*, 25a. While we give here and below references to Joris's translation of Celan's text in *The Meridian: Final Versions—Drafts—Materials*, we recall once again the English translations of Celan in Levinas's citations are regularly modified by Smith in his translation of Levinas's "Paul Celan: From Being to the Other."

12. TN. Celan, *The Meridian*, 32b.

13. TN. Celan, *The Meridian*, 17a.

14. TN. Celan, *The Meridian*, 40b-d.

15. TN. See Levinas, "Humanism and An-archy," in *Humanism of the Other*, 45. Crépon's quotation a few lines later comes from the following (and final) essay in the collection, "Without Identity."

Chapter Five

1. In a text from *Difficult Freedom* entitled "The Struthof Case," Levinas recalls this point in an introductory way:

> The recent trial of Struthof is eight years late. It is just, though, that, mingled with the happy or industrious clamor of the street, amid the murmur of midnight breezes or amorous exchanges, the men of 1954 should once again have heard the indiscreet cries of tortured men. A young Pole cries: "Mummy!" Forgetfulness is the law, happiness and condition of life. But here life is wrong. (149)

2. One will recall, once again, that *Otherwise than Being* is dedicated "[t]o the memory of those who were closest among the six million assassinated by the National Socialists, *next to* the millions on millions of all confessions and all nations, victims of the same hatred of the other man, the same anti-Semitism" (v, my emphasis, translation modified).

Chapter Seven

1. TN. On these words, see chapter 6, "The first three words of the Nazi language" (Klemperer, 41–45).

2. One will recall that, at the moment the Nazis came to power, Klemperer was working on a *History of French Literature in the 18th Century*, which would be published in two volumes in 1954 and 1966.

3. The conclusion of this chapter, entitled "German roots," is irrevocable: "Because all the distinctive features of National Socialism are present in Romanticism in embryonic form: the dethronement of reason, the animalization of man, the glorification of the idea of power, of the predator, of the blond beast..." (140).

188   Notes

4. On this point, see the exchange at the factory that Klemperer recounts in the chapter entitled, "On a single working day," pages 93–94.

5. TN. See *The Language of the Third Reich*, chapter 18, "I Believe in Him."

6. See Marc Crépon, *La Culture de la peur* (Paris: Galilée, 2008).

7. See Marc Crépon, *Le consentement meurtrier* (Paris: Éditions du Cerf, 2012).

8. TN. On this formulation, adopted from Paul Celan, see chapter 4.

9. "In the LTI there is no other appropriation of technical words which could reveal the tendency to mechanize and automate more fully than '*gleichshalten*'" (155).

10. TN. The story is recounted in the chapter, "On a single working day" (see pages 93–94).

11. "For just as it is customary to speak of the face of an age or of a country, so it is also usual to characterize the spirit of a particular epoch as its language" (10).

Chapter Eight

1. This does not, however, prevent the following sentence—written by Sartre in his essay on Memmi's book—from being a jab at Camus, which consummated a break already in effect for some time: "[t]hey [some colonialists] *do* each day, *in deed*, what they condemn *in their dreams*, and each of their acts contributes to maintaining oppression. They will change nothing, be of no use to anyone, and find their moral comfort in their *malaise*, that is all" ("Albert Memmi's *The Colonizer and the Colonized*," 59–60).

2. TN. *La France et des Français*. Because the proper nouns "France" (*la France*) and "the French" (*les français*) are already capitalized in English, the gesture is lost in translation both here and in the English translation of the texts cited by Crépon.

3. These questions were no doubt also unresolved for Sartre, who ultimately returns to this justification of violence in a final text, entitled "The Political Thought of Patrice Lumumba," and grants the principle of nonviolence supported by the Congolese leader its rights.

Chapter Nine

1. TN. Crépon uses the chapter's title, *l'esprit du récit*, as a concept throughout the chapter. The phrase comes from Thomas Mann's novel *The Holy Sinner* and is rendered into English by H. T. Lowe Porter as "the spirit of storytelling [*Geist der Erzählung*]." For continuity, we have chosen to retain this English phrasing. However, when the word *récit* appears in Crépon's chapter independently of reference to Mann's phrase, we have elected to translate it more literally as "story."

2. Here one can turn to the beautiful novel by Catherine Lépront, *Namokel* (Paris: Seuil, 1997), which recounts, through the character Helene and her four friends, the path that had to be taken by the postwar generation to be able to imagine the horror of Jewish persecution and the death camps.

3. TN. Part of Crépon's account of how history "forces its way" into life as a "plurality of stories" plays on the ambiguity of the French word *histoire*, which

means both "history" and "story." Since this ambiguity cannot be replicated easily in English, we have relied on context to render *histoire* either as "history" or "story." Readers in English should thus be aware that references to "history" can never be distinguished absolutely from, and thus always minimally include, an element of "story."

4. And undoubtedly in cinema, too—in which case we should add to this ongoing list *Night and Fog* by Alain Resnais, *The Sorrow and the Pity* by Max Ophüls, *Shoah* by Claude Lanzmann, and *Black Rain* by Shoshei Imamura.

5. TN. The French edition of *The Holocaust as Culture* is a robust "collection of essays," yet the slim English edition is limited to the titular essay and an interview with Kertész. Some of the essays included in the French edition have been translated into English elsewhere. We have cited existing translations whenever possible. "The Enduring Camps" and "Weimar Visible and Invisible" are the only two texts that have no corresponding English translations. English translations of those texts are our own, and we thank Louise Vasvári for clarifying our translations of the French text against the original Hungarian.

6. With an eye toward a future work, I here leave aside the complex question of the relationship among testimony, autobiography, and novels, which Kertész's work poses with exceptional acuity.

7. TN. See chapter 3, where Crépon offers a brief reading of Bonnefoy's *Ce qui alarma Celan*.

8. Recall that the essay previously mentioned, "The Holocaust as Culture," is precisely a text devoted to the person and work of Jean Améry.

9. Imre Kertész himself makes the bitter and cruel conclusion (for which many citizens of Europe today could be responsible, in France, Italy, Denmark, Sweden, Germany, England, Romania, Poland, and always in Hungary, etc.) in *I— Another: Chronicle of a Metamorphosis*: "I see, I live the appalling degradation of this country, its suicidal sinking into paranoia. Each day the national champions of hatred and my own memories distance me from it. How my indifference toward it grows!" [TN. There is no English translation of this text available, so we have rendered it ourselves. We owe a debt of gratitude to Louise Vasvári for her willingness to check our English translation of the French against the original Hungarian. For reference, see *Un autre, chronique d'une métamorphose*, translated by Natalia and Charles Zaremba (Actes Sud, 1999), 34.]

10. On this subject, see Kertész's desperate reflections at the beginning of Fiasco:

> Murder in some degree, over a certain time span and beyond a given number, is after all tiring, systematic, and harrowing work, whose daily continuity is not vouchsafed by the participants' likes or dislikes, bursts of ardor or onsets of disgust, enthusiasm, or antipathy—in short, the momentary mood, or even cast of mind, of single individuals, but by organisation, an assembly-line operation, a self-contained mechanism which does not permit so much as a moment's time to draw breath. In another respect, there can be no doubt about it, that is what put paid to tragic representation. (45)

190   Notes

11. The last two sentences are borrowed from *Fiasco* (46). [TN. The translation of these last two sentences in "Long, Dark Shadow" have been modified to match Tim Wilkinson's translation of *Fiasco*.]

12. See Kertész, *Fiasco* (47):

> [t]hese 340 deaths on the rocks, for instance, might rightly find a place among the symbols of the human imagination, but on one condition: only if they had not occurred. Since they did occur, it is hard even to imagine them. Rather than becoming a plaything, the imagination proves to be a heavy and immovable burden, just like those boulders in Mauthausen: people do not want to be crushed under them.

13. TN. On Celan's image of a bottle thrown to sea, see the end of the Introduction; on Celan's image of a handshake, see chapter 4, "Of a Constellation."

Chapter Ten

1. TN. The quotation with which Crépon opens this chapter is found in *Imre Kertész and Holocaust Literature*, 104. English translations of *Galley Boat-Log* (*Gályanapló*) are currently available only in excerpts. As a result, our citation of this text has remained consistent with the French edition Crépon references (*Journal de galère*). Whenever an English translation of a particular passage is available, we have cited it in an endnote. All other translations are our own. Once again, we thank Louise Vasvári for clarifying our translations of the French text against the original Hungarian.

2. TN. Crépon gives no particular citation here, but see, for instance, *Imre Kertész and Holocaust Literature*, 99.

3. TN. *Imre Kertész and Holocaust Literature*, 97.

4. TN. *Imre Kertész and Holocaust Literature*, 106.

5. TN. On this formulation, adopted from Levinas, see chapter 5 above.

6. "Sartre: there are no characters, only 'freedoms caught in a trap,' and the value of man resides in how he escapes the trap—the typical moralist" (*Journal de galère*, 18).

7. TN. *Imre Kertész and Holocaust Literature*, 104. The formulation "irreplaceability" is translated into French as *singularité*—that is, "singularity."

8. TN. Crépon does not cite any particular passage for this formulation, but see, for instance, page 16 of *Journal de galère*: "True genius is existential genius [*Le véritable génie est le génie existentiel*]." Additionally, it should be noted that the connection between "existential genius [*génie existential*]" in Crépon's paragraph and the "existential greatness [*génialité existentielle*]" in the extended quotation from Kertész is stronger in French than in English. For clarity, we have elected to translate these terms literally into English, which unfortunately sacrifices their etymological proximity. This connection between "genius [*génie*]" and "greatness [*génialité*]" plays a prominent role in section III in this chapter.

9. "If I do not struggle constantly for myself, I renounce myself—every instant

of struggle missed is a day of renunciation; such is the proportion in terms of energy; become what you are!" (*Journal de galère*, 205).

10. TN. *Imre Kertész and Holocaust Literature*, 98.

11. TN. *Imre Kertész and Holocaust Literature*, 102.

12. TN. *Imre Kertész and Holocaust Literature*, 103.

13. "[To] enter into the century's circle of truth, the writer should admit that he can be murdered and that this is nothing extraordinary. Kafka gets himself killed in 'The Metamorphosis' and in *The Trial*, first as a giant bug, then as an honest employee" (*Journal de galère*, 115).

Chapter Eleven

1. TN. In his youth, Isaac Bashevis Singer lived with his family on Krochmalna Street in Warsaw, Poland, which is where Singer sets many of his novels and short stories. The connection Crépon draws between Krochmalna Street and the particular texts listed here is more apparent in the French because the French edition of *Scum* that Crépon cites is titled *Le petit monde de la rue Krochmalna* [*The Small World of Krochmalna Street*]. Later in this paragraph, when Crépon returns to a discussion of Krochmalna Street, we decided to incorporate the title of the French edition in order to emphasize the "world" of prewar Warsaw's Jewish quarter that Singer reconstructs.

Chapter Twelve

1. TN. Although Crépon uses the word *émigrant* throughout this chapter, we have at times chosen to translate this word less literally as "immigrant." Doing so, we are upholding the distinction that *emigrant* refers to the departure *from* a homeland, whereas *immigrant* denotes the position of an arrival *to* a host nation. Therefore, when the perspective of a host is presumed, we have elected to translate *émigrant* as "immigrant." In those moments where the perspective presumes the position of a departure, or at times addresses a generalized status of displacement without reference to any particular arrival, we have translated *émigrant* literally as "emigrant."

2. In "Active Patience," Hannah Arendt writes, "There were always too many naturalized citizens, and no reasonable person could fail to see that the least change in government could suffice to undo naturalizations enacted by a previous government. Naturalized or not naturalized, concentration camps were always standing at the ready. Rich or poor, one belonged to the ever-growing ranks of European pariahs" (*Jewish Writings*, 140).

3. See Hannah Arendt, "Why the Crémieux Decree Was Abrogated," *Jewish Writings*, 244–53.

4. On this point, see Marc Crépon, *La Culture de la peur* (Paris: Galilée, 2008).

5. On this point, see Marc Crépon, *Le Consentement meurtrier* (Paris: Éditions du Cerf, 2012).

6. See Georges Perec, *Ellis Island*, page 54: "[b]ut to every one of those / who marched past the doctors and immigration officers, / what was at stake was vital: / they had given up their past and their history, / they had given up everything for the sake of coming here / to try and live a life they were forbidden to live / in their native land: / and now they were face to face with an inexorable finality."

7. TN. For more on Celan's witness to the human, see chapter 3 above; and for more on Levinas's notion of the spectrality of the "tumor in the memory," see chapter 5 above.

8. TN. The French title of Perec's book is *Récits d'Ellis Island, histoires d'errance et d'espoir*, which can be translated as *Stories of Ellis Island: Histories of Wandering and Hope*. The English edition of Perec's volume, however, truncates the title simply to *Ellis Island*. Since Crépon here uses the subtitle of the French edition as a description of the book, we have decided to render it as a quotation rather than as a title, since the correlation does not exist in English.

9. In "We Refugees," Arendt writes, "As time went on, we got worse—even more optimistic and even more inclined to suicide" (*The Jewish Writings*, 267).

Chapter Thirteen

1. TN. Rather than "spleen," the French translation of Tolstoy cited by Crépon gives *l'angoisse*—that is, "anxiety."

2. TN. The words "horror," "afraid," "frightened," and "terrible" are all translated into French with formulations based on *peur* (fear).

3. TN. The French runs: *histoire, comme on dit, de se faire peur autrement*. The formulation *histoire de* is an idiom meaning "just to," but it literally means "history of." Hence, Crépon's formulation could be translated either as "just to give us something else to fear" or "stories to give us something else to fear."

4. This short story has not yet been translated into English, so we cite the French translation. We thank Tatiana Poddubnykh and Kirsten Lodge for their help with the translations here and below.

5. TN. Dutli's biography is translated into French as *Mandelstam, mon temps, mon fauve*: "Mandelstam, my time, my beast" (more precisely, *fauve* is a large, wild feline). Hence, Crépon's formulation here plays on the French title.

6. TN. Perhaps symptomatically, the Russian word "*strakh*," translated into French as "*la peur*," is translated into English as "terror" both here and in the final citation of the chapter. We have modified the translation accordingly.

Bibliography

Arendt, Hannah. "Franz Kafka: Appreciated Anew." Translated by Martin Klebes. In *Reflections on Literature and Culture,* edited by Susannah Young-Ah Gottlieb, 94–109. Stanford: Stanford University Press, 2012.
———. "The Jewish War That Isn't Happening: Articles from *Aufbau,* October 1941–November 1942." In *The Jewish Writings,* 134–85. New York: Schocken, 2007.
———. "Original Assimilation: An Epilogue to the One Hundredth Anniversary of Rahel Varnhagen's Death." In *The Jewish Writings,* 22–28.
———. "We Refugees." In *The Jewish* Writings, 264–74.
———. "Why the Crémieux Decree was Abrogated." In *The Jewish Writings,* 244–53.
Blanchot, Maurice. "The Last to Speak." In *A Voice from Elsewhere*, translated by Charlotte Mandell, 53–93. Albany: SUNY UP, 2007.
Bonnefoy, Yves. *Ce qui alarma Paul Celan.* Paris: Galilée, 2007.
Celan, Paul. *Glottal Stop: 101 Poems by Paul Celan.* Translated by Nikolai Popov and Heather McHugh. Hanover, NH: Wesleyan University Press, 2000.
———. "Letter to Hans Bender." In *Collected Prose,* edited and translated by Rosemarie Waldrop, 25–27. New York: Routledge, 2003.
———. *The Meridian: Final Version—Drafts—Materials.* Edited by Bernhard Böschenstein and Heino Schmul. Translated by Pierre Joris. Stanford: Stanford University Press, 2011.
———. "The Meridian." Translated by Jerry Glenn. In *Sovereignties in Question: The Poetics of Paul Celan* by Jacques Derrida, edited by Thomas Dutoit and Outi Pasanen, 173–86. New York: Fordham University Press, 2005.
———. "Speech on the Occasion of Receiving the Literature Prize of the Free Hanseatic City of Bremen." In *Paul Celan: Collected Prose,* translated by Rosmarie Waldrop, 33–35. Manchester: Carcanet, 1986.
Crépon, Marc. *Le Consentement meurtrier.* Paris: Éditions du Cerf, 2012.
———. *La Culture de la peur: Démocratie, identité, sécurité.* Paris: Galilée, 2008.
———. *Langues sans demeure.* Paris: Galilée, 2005.
———. *Terreur et poésie.* Paris: Galilée, 2004.
———. *The Thought of Death and the Memory of War.* Translated by Michael Loriaux. Minneapolis: University of Minnesota Press, 2013.

Derrida, Jacques. *The Beast and the Sovereign, vol. 1*. Translated by Geoffrey Bennington. Chicago: University of Chicago Press, 2009.
———. "Before the Law." In *Acts of Literature*, edited by Derek Attridge, 181–220. New York: Routledge, 1992.
———. "Force of Law: The 'Mystical Foundation of Authority.'" In *Acts of Religion*, edited by Gil Anidjar, 228–98. New York: Routledge, 2002.
———. "Language Is Never Owned: An Interview." In *Sovereignties in Question: The Poetics of Paul Celan*, edited by Thomas Dutoit and Outi Pasanen, 97–107. New York: Fordham University Press, 2005.
———. *Monolingualism of the Other, or, The Prosthesis of Origin*. Translated by Patrick Mensah. Stanford: Stanford University Press, 1998.
———. "Rams: Uninterrupted Dialogue—Between Two Infinities, the Poem." In *Sovereignties in Question: The Poetics of Paul Celan*, edited by Thomas Dutoit and Outi Pasanen, 135–63. New York: Fordham University Press, 2005.
———. "Shibboleth: For Paul Celan." In *Sovereignties in Question: The Poetics of Paul Celan*, edited by Thomas Dutoit and Outi Pasanen, 1–64. New York: Fordham University Press, 2005.
Kafka, Franz. "Before the Law." Translated by Willa and Edwin Muir. In *The Complete Stories*, edited by Nahum N. Glatzer, 3–4. New York: Schocken, 1971.
———. *Diaries, 1910–1923*. Translated by Joseph Kresh and Martin Greenberg. New York: Schocken, 1988.
———. "The Eight Octavo Notebooks." In *Wedding Preparations in the Country and Other Posthumous Prose Writings*, translated by Ernst Kaiser and Eithne Wilkins, 54–156. London: Secker and Warburg, 1954.
———. "Fragments from Note-Books and Loose Pages." In *Wedding Preparations in the Country and Other Posthumous Prose Writings*, translated by Ernst Kaiser and Eithne Wilkins, 218–413.
———. "Letter to My Father." In *The Sons*, translated by Arthur Wensinger. New York: Schocken, 1989.
Kertész, Imre. *Dossier K.: A Memoir*. Translated by Tim Wilkinson. New York: Melville House, 2013.
———. "The Enduring Camps." In *Holocaust comme culture: Discours et essais*, translated by Natalia Zaremba-Huzsvai and Charles Zaremba. Paris: Actes Sud, 2010.
———. *Fiasco*. Translated by Tim Wilkinson. New York: Melville House, 2011.
———. "Galley-Boat Log: Excerpts." Translated by Tim Wilkinson. In *Imre Kertész and Holocaust Literature*, edited by Louise O. Vasvári and Steven Tötösy de Zepetnek. West Lafayette, IN: Purdue University Press, 2005.
———. "The Holocaust as Culture." In *The Holocaust as Culture*, translated by Thomas Cooper. London: Seagull, 2011.
———. *Journal de galère*. Translated by Natalia Zaremba-Huzsvai and Charles Zaremba. Paris: Actes Sud, 2010.
———. *Liquidation*. Translated by Tim Wilkinson. New York: Knopf, 2005.
———. "Long, Dark Shadow." In *Contemporary Jewish Writing in Hungary: An*

Anthology, edited by Susan Rubin Suleiman and Éva Forgács, 171–80. Lincoln: University of Nebraska Press, 2003.
———. "Weimar Visible and Invisible." In *Holocaust comme culture: Discours et essais*, translated by Natalia Zaremba-Huzsvai and Charles Zaremba. Paris: Actes Sud, 2010.
———. "Who Owns Auschwitz?" Translated by John MacKay. *Yale Journal of Criticism* 14.1 (2001): 267–72.
Klemperer, Victor. *The Language of the Third Reich*. Translated by Martin Brady. London: Continuum, 2006.
Lépront, Catherine. *Namokel*. Paris: Éditions du Seuil, 1997.
Levinas, Emmanuel. "Contempt for the Torah as Idolatry." In *In the Time of the Nations*, translated by Michael B. Smith, 55–75. Bloomington: Indiana University Press, 1994.
———. *On Escape*. Translated by Bettina Bergo. Stanford: Stanford University Press, 2003.
———. "Nameless." In *Proper Names*, translated by Michael B. Smith, 119–23. Stanford: Stanford University Press, 1996.
———. *Otherwise than Being, or Beyond Essence*. Translated by Alphonso Lingis. Pittsburgh: Duquesne University Press, 1998.
———. "Paul Celan: From Being to the Other." In *Proper Names*, translated by Michael B. Smith, 40–46. Stanford: Stanford University Press, 1996.
———. "Philosophical Determination of the Idea of Culture." In *Entre Nous: On Thinking-of-the-Other*, translated by Michael B. Smith and Barbara Harshav, 179–88. New York: Columbia University Press, 1998.
———. "The Struthof Case." In *Difficult Freedom: Essays on Judaism*, translated by Seán Hand. Baltimore: Johns Hopkins University Press, 1990.
———. *Totality and Infinity: An Essay on Exteriority*. Translated by Alphonso Lingis. Pittsburgh: Duquesne University Press, 1969.
———. "Transcendence and Height." In *Basic Philosophical Writings*, edited by Adriaan T. Peperzak, Simon Critchley, and Robert Bernasconi, 11–32. Bloomington: Indiana University Press, 1996.
Mandelstam, Osip. "About an Interlocutor." In *Osip Mandelstam: Selected Essays*, translated by. Signey Monas, 58–64. Austin: University of Texas Press, 1977.
———. "On the Addressee." In *Critical Prose and Letters*, edited by Jane Gary Harris and translated by Jane Gary Harris and Constance Link, 67–74. Ann Arbor: Ardis, 1979.
———. "The Egyptian Stamp." In *The Noise of Time: The Prose of Osip Mandelstam*, translated by Clarence Brown, 131–64. San Francisco: North Point Press, 1986.
Mann, Thomas. *The Holy Sinner*. Translated by H. T. Lowe-Porter. Berkeley: University of California Press, 1992.
Merleau-Ponty, Maurice. *Humanism and Terror: The Communist Problem*. Translated by John O'Neill. New Brunswick: Transaction Publishers, 1969.
Perec, Georges, and Robert Bober. *Ellis Island*. Translated by Harry Matthews. New York: New Press, 1995.

Sartre, Jean-Paul. "From One China to Another." In *Colonialism and Neocolonialism*, translated by Azzedine Haddour, Steve Brewer, and Terry McWilliams, 22–35. New York: Routledge, 2006.
———. "Colonialism is a System." In *Colonialism and Neocolonialism*, 36–55.
———. "Albert Memmi's *The Colonizer and the Colonized*." In *Colonialism and Neocolonialism*, 56–62.
———. "You are Wonderful." In *Colonialism and Neocolonialism*, 63–71.
———. "A Victory." In *Colonialism and Neocolonialism*, 73–88.
———. "The Wretched of the Earth." In *Colonialism and Neocolonialism*, 153–74.
———. "The Political Thought of Patrice Lumumba." In *Colonialism and Neocolonialism*, 175–223.
Sebald, W. G. *The Emigrants*. Translated by Michael Hulsa. New York: New Directions, 1996.
Singer, Isaac Bashevis. *Conversations with Isaac Bashevis Singer*. New York: Doubleday, 1985.
———. *The Magician of Lublin*. Translated by Elaine Gottlieb and Joseph Singer. New York: Farrar, Straus, and Giroux, 1960.
———. *Nobel Lecture*. London: Jonathan Cape, 1979.
———. *Shosha: A Novel*. New York: Farrar, Straus, and Giroux, 1978.
Tolstoy, Leo. "Memoirs of a Madman." In *Collected Shorter Fiction, volume 1*, translated by Louise Maude, Aylmer Maude, and Nigel J. Cooper. New York: Everyman's Library, 2001.

Index

Alleg, Henri, 120, 121
Alterity, 47
Améry, Jean, 83, 126, 132, 189n8
Anders, Günther, 38, 48
Andreyev, Leonid, 173
Antelme, Robert, 83, 126
Anti-Semitism, 4, 38, 89, 106–112, 132, 160, 165
Arendt, Hannah, 38, 65, 157–168; works by: "Active Patience," 161, 191n2; "Kafka," 162–163; *On Revolution*, 163; "Original Assimilation," 160; "We Refugees," 157, 163, 164–165, 166, 192n9; "What Is Happening in France?," 167–168; "Why the Crémieux Decree Was Abrogated," 162
Arndt, Ernst Moritz, 104
Artaud, Antonin, 49, 65
Assimilation, 117, 159–166. *See also* hospitality, immigration/emigration
Attention, 1, 2, 4, 5, 7, 8, 30, 38, 39, 40, 42, 44, 52, 53, 57, 60, 64, 66, 68, 82, 86, 87, 102, 107, 108, 118, 125, 153, 154, 155, 158, 163, 164, 167, 169, 170

Bachmann, Ingeborg, 58, 64
Benjamin, Walter, 38, 65
Bergman, Ingmar, 11
Blanchot, Maurice, 39, 52, 65–66, 70, 72–74, 79, 186n6

Bober, Robert, 157
Bonnefoy, Yves, 51, 53, 189n7
Borowski, Tadeusz, 126
Bradbury, Ray, 14
Brod, Max, 147
Buber, Martin, 74
Büchner, Georg, 52, 57, 69, 185n1
Burgin, Richard, 150, 152, 154

Camus, Albert, 116, 139, 188n1
Care, 8, 15, 45, 56, 64, 86, 87, 90, 107, 108, 131, 133, 149, 153, 154, 158, 163, 164, 165, 167
Cartier-Bresson, Henri, 113–114
Celan, Paul. 15, 16, 51–79 passim, 89, 128, 130, 136, 166, ; works by: "Alchemical," 62; "Ashglory," 62; *Breathturn*, 73; "Conversation in the Mountains," 66, 98; "Death Fugue," 62; "Letter to Hans Bender," 52, 66–69; *The Meridian*, 52, 53, 54, 55, 56, 57, 59, 61, 63, 66, 68–69, 71–78; *No One's Rose*, 61, 70, 71, 73–74, 185n3; "Speech on the Occasion of Receiving the Literature Prize of the Free Hanseatic City of Bremen," 61–62, 66,
Céline, Louis-Ferdinand, 92
Char, René, 66
Citizenship, 161–162, 176
Colonialism, 113–124, passim

198 Index

Commemoration (of the dead), 81–90, 95, 126, 132–133, 135, 149–155. *See also* memory

Death, 8, 40, 43, 58, 86, 87, 108, 130, 135, 145, 147, 148, 155, 160, 163, 166, 190; going-together-into-death, 69; death of the other, 86, 91; death penalty, 107; death camp, 55, 127, 134, 188n2; fear of death, 169–182, passim, 192n2, 192n6
Delbo, Charlotte, 126
Deleuze, Gilles, 39
Derrida, Jacques, 39, 52–53, 55, 57, 59, 64, 65–66, 69–70, 72, 74, 76; works by: *Beast and the Sovereign*, 52, 54, 56, 59, 60, 68, 75; "Before the Law," 39–43, 47–50; "Force of Law," 42; "Language Is Never Owned," 62; *Monolingualism of the Other*, 44, 45–46, 62, 75, 116–117, 162, 186n9; *Of Grammatology*, 42; "Poetics and Politics of Witnessing," 184n2; "Rams," 53, 184n2; "Shibboleth: For Paul Celan," 52, 54, 56, 63–64, 74, 185n6; *Voice and Phenomenon*, 42; *Writing and Difference*, 42
Dombrovsky, Yury, 126, 170
Dutli, Ralph, 177, 192n5

Ethics, 6, 9, 13, 57, 61, 64, 72, 87–88, 123, 133–136, 140–141, 143, 146–147, 153, 155; hyperbolic demand of, 56, 76
Ellis Island, 157–158, 164, 166, 191n6, 192n8
Europe, 5, 10, 38–39, 55, 66, 81–85, 89, 95, 109, 111, 116, 121–23, 125, 130–33, 139, 144–45, 151, 158, 160–61, 165, 167, 180–81, 189, 191
European Community, 158
Exteriority, 17, 19, 20, 28, 44–45, 53, 159, 183n1; as estrangement 24–25, 27, 78, 138–139, 140, 144, 166–167; as exile, 164–167. *See also* shame

Fanon, Frantz, 115, 121–123

Freud, Sigmund, 37, 38, 65, 94
Friendship, 4–5, 6–7, 8, 70, 99, 105, 107, 164–165. *See also* relation

Gadamer, Hans-Georg, 53
Ginzburg, Eugenia, 126, 170
Goebbels, Joseph, 104, 108, 111
Gogol, Nicolai, 178
Grossman, Vasily, 83, 126, 132
Guattari, Félix, 39

Hatred, 25, 81, 116, 117, 121, 122, 187, 189
Havel, Vaclav, 176
Hegel, G.W.F., 65, 127
Heidegger, Martin, 59, 65, 66, 71, 77, 78, 169
Help, 1, 8, 16, 29, 30, 33, 35, 49, 55, 64, 66, 72, 82, 86, 87, 90, 107, 108, 109, 125, 131, 133, 134, 135, 153, 157, 158, 164, 167, 168, 179, 180
Hitler, Adolph. 82, 104, 108, 110, 155, 165
Hölderlin, Friedrich, 45, 49, 59, 66, 77, 186n3
Holocaust (*Shoah*), 10, 38, 55, 66, 81–90, 95, 125, 127–136, 139–140, 144–145, 147, 151
Hospitality, 52, 54, 60, 75, 158–168. *See also* relation
Human Rights, 115, 121; Universal Declaration of, 117, 163
Husserl, Edmund, 65

Idiom, 15, 29, 46, 50, 58, 61, 62–63, 75, 151
Imagination, 126–127, 134–136, 159, 170, 173
Imamura, Shoshei, 189n4
Immigration/emigration, 157–168 passim, 191n1. *See also* hospitality

Jahn, Friedrich Ludwig, 104
Joyce, James, 154

Kafka, Franz, 11, 19–50 passim, 144–145, 147, 162–163, 170, 191n13; works by: *Amerika*, 19, 21; "Before the Law," 39–44, 46, 47–50; *The Castle*, 19, 23, 38, 48, 144, 147, 162–163; *Diaries*, 17, 19, 21, 23–24, 25–26, 27, 28–33, 34–35, 45, 142, 183n3–7, 184n9–10; *The Trial*, 19, 21, 26, 39, 41, 45, 48, 145, 162, 170, 191n13; "Letter to His Father," 21, 33–34; "The Metamorphosis," 24, 41, 45, 145, 191n13; *Octavo Notebooks*, 33
Kant, Immanuel, 65
Kertész, Imre, 83, 89, 125–148 passim; works by: *Dossier K.*, 127, 131; "Enduring Camps," 127, 128–129, 131–133, 189n5; *Fatelessness*, 126, 127, 129, 130, 134, 139, 143, 145; *Fiasco*, 126, 129, 141, 143, 145, 146, 189n10, 190n12; *Galley-Boat Log (Journal de galère)*, 125, 127, 137–148, 190n1, 190n8–9, 191n13; *I-Another*, 189n9; *Kaddish for an Unborn Child*, 126, 128; *Liquidation*, 146–148; "Long, Dark Shadow," 133–136; *Holocaust as Culture*, 125, 127, 130, 133, 189n5, 189n8; "Weimar Visible and Invisible," 133, 189n5; "Who Owns Auschwitz?," 134
Kierkegaard, Søren, 131, 169
Klemperer, Victor, 11, 101–112
Koestler, Arthur, 170, 174
Kravchenko, Victor A., 174

Lanzmann, Claude, 189n4
Law, 21, 22–23, 29–30, 33–34, 37–50 passim, 54, 94, 127–128, 132, 152–153, 160
Lépront, Catherine, 188n2
Leskov, Nikolai, 173
Levi, Primo, 83, 126, 130, 132
Levinas, Emanuel, 52, 66–71, 74–78, 81–99 passim, 166; works by: "The Case of Struthof," 84, 187n1; "Contempt for the Torah as Idolatry," 97; *Difficult Freedom*, 83, 84; *On Escape*, 91–95; "Freedom and Command," 84; "From the Rise of Nihilism to the Carnal Jew," 95; *Humanism of the Other*, 77, 78; "Nameless," 81–84, 87–89, 166; *Otherwise than Being*, 70, 71–72, 75, 76, 81, 83, 90, 187n2; *Paul Celan: From Being to the Other*, 66–67, 69–71, 74, 76–78; "Philosophical Determination of the Idea of Culture," 85–86; *Proper Names*, 186n4; *Time and the Other*, 74; *Totality and Infinity*, 81, 83, 90, 91, 92, 95, 97–99; "Transcendence and Height," 95–96
Literature, 13–16, 19–21, 25–27, 29, 31–32, 33–35, 37–40, 43–44, 50, 56, 90, 112, 126–134, 143–148, 149, 150, 152, 153, 154–155, 170–171, 173, 174–177, 181–182; relation to law, 37–50, 68; as political engagement, 113, 120–121, 143
Love, 7–9, 18, 106, 108, 122, 147, 153, 154, 176; loved ones, 101, 105, 170, 175, 180
Lyotard, Jean-François, 39

Madness, 45–50, 64, 170, 172, 177
Maimonides, 152
Mallarmé, Stéphane, 65
Mandelstam, Osip, 12, 16, 53–54, 58, 128, 130, 170, 171, 177–182, 192n5
Mann, Thomas, 127–128, 188n1
Memmi, Albert, 115, 117, 188n1
Memory, 4, 16, 23, 29, 34, 40, 45, 48, 52, 53, 54, 55, 62, 64, 65, 66, 70, 72, 81–90, 95, 98, 125–129, 132–135, 140, 145, 147, 150, 151, 155, 165–167, 178, 180, 181, 184, 187, 192, 193; anamnesis, 37–50 passim, 172, 178, 179, 180. *See also* Commemoration
Merleau-Ponty, Maurice, 170–171, 174

200 Index

Montaigne, Michel de, 42
Moscow trials, 111, 170
Murderous consent, 6, 13, 81, 88, 91, 98, 105, 106–107, 109, 110–111, 112, 115, 118–120, 123, 129, 135, 139, 142, 177, 178, 181

Nietzsche, Friedrich, 33, 45, 49, 65, 112, 141

Ophüls, Max, 189n4
Orwell, George, 14, 46

Patočka, Jan, 88
Perec, Georges, 157–158, 164, 166, 191n6, 192n8
Philosophy, 13–16 passim, 17, 37, 42, 52, 72, 81, 90, 103, 126, 127, 130, 139, 149, 169–170, 174, 177
Plato, 65
Poetry, 12, 13, 21, 51–56, 57–61, 62–64, 66–69, 70–73, 74, 76–79, 85, 128, 130, 132, 170, 179– 181, 186n9
Protest, 9, 11, 14–15, 82, 109, 132–133, 149–155
Proust, Marcel, 144, 145, 154
Pushkin, Alexander, 173

Racism, 4, 5, 104, 115–118, 121–122, 132. See also Anti-Semitism
Relation, 8, 11, 20–21, 26–27, 30, 31, 55, 74, 77, 94, 99, 158, 183n1; to being, 91–99; to death, 169–170, 172–173, 175, 181; in colonial situation, 113–115, 117, 120–124, 174; to self, 17–35 passim, 44–45, 51, 59, 76, 78, 92, 142–143, 164, 176. See also, assimilation, exteriority, friendship
Resnais, Alain, 189n4
Responsibility, 6, 8, 9, 11, 13, 14, 26, 31, 34, 52, 54–55, 56, 58–59, 60, 62, 69, 70, 71, 74, 75, 76–77, 82, 86, 87–88, 90, 106–107, 113, 128, 131, 154, 158, 167
Rilke, Rainer Maria, 66
Rosenzweig, Franz, 65, 74

Rousseau, Jean-Jacques, 37
Rwandan genocide, 5

Sachs, Nelly, 55, 58, 64
Sartre, Jean-Paul, 93, 97–98, 113–124, 140, 144, 188n1, 188n3, 190n6; works by: *Being and Nothingness*, 97, 99, 118; "Colonialism Is a System," 116; "Colonizer and the Colonized," 115, 117–118; "From One China to Another," 113–114; *Nausea*, 93; "A Victory," 119–121; "Wretched of the Earth," 121–123; "You Are Wonderful," 119–120
Scheherazade, 50
Schmuëli, Iliana, 64
Sebald, W.G., 159, 165–167
Shalamov, Varlam, 126, 130, 132
Shame, 91–99, 109–110, 119–120, 138, 141
Singer, Isaac Bashevis, 16, 149–155 passim; works by: *Conversations*, 149–150, 152, 153–155; *Family Moskat*, 149; *In My Father's Court*, 149, 152–153, 155; *Magician of Lublin*, 152; *Nobel Lecture* 151; *Scum*, 149; *Shosha*, 150–151, 154, 155
Singularity, 3, 6, 9–10, 11, 14, 15, 16, 17–18, 21, 22, 23–24, 29, 35, 38, 39–41, 42–44, 46–48, 50, 52, 58, 59, 61, 62, 65, 67, 84, 98, 109, 127–129, 130, 135, 143, 146–147, 149, 154, 164, 169; of dates, 52–56, 74. See also Idiom
Sologub, Fyodor, 173
Solzhenitsyn, Aleksandr, 126, 170
Sovereignty, of state 119, 158, 161–162, 163, 167; of self, 3, 7, 33–35, 42, 43, 57, 58–59, 63, 67, 69, 76, 78, 98, 144. See also Singularity
Stalin, Joseph, 111, 170, 174, 175–176

Temporality, 25, 166
Tendriakov, Vladimir, 171, 175–177
Testimony, 54, 58, 71, 84, 118, 121, 126, 127, 150–155, 157, 165, 170, 174, 189n6

Tolstoy, Leo, 171–173
Torture, 95, 97, 115, 118–122
Totalitarianism, 5, 10–11, 13–14, 16, 46, 101, 129, 137–138, 142–144, 169
Trakl, Georg, 66
Translation, 61, 65, 75, 151, 157–158
Trauma, 81–90
Tsvetaeva, Marina, 58, 77

Valéry, Paul, 65
Violence, 1–16 passim, 20, 35, 37, 39, 44, 50, 55, 56, 57, 59, 60, 61, 71–73, 76, 79, 81, 83, 86–90, 93–94, 96, 97–99, 106–108, 123–136, 138, 139, 142–144, 158–161, 164–165, 169–175, 176–178; from parents/family, 1, 3, 7, 11, 23, 33–35, 94–95; of education, 1–2, 4, 11, 94–95; of language, 9, 102–112, 114, 142, 158–159; minimization of, 113–124; resistance to/refusal of, 9, 11, 14–15, 32–33, 35, 51, 59–60, 64, 68, 69, 82, 88, 109, 122–123,142–143, 181, 188n3
Voltaire (François-Marie Arouet), 103

War, 9, 85, 86, 87, 88, 89, 95, 96, 110, 118, 123, 125, 126, 128, 129, 130, 132, 133, 142, 161, 164, 167; Algerian War, 114, 115, 116, 122; Cold War, 174; World War I, 35; World War II, 10, 66, 79, 81; war on terror, 5
Wannsee Conference, 55
Welles, Orson, 28
Wiesel, Elie, 126
Witness/witnessing, 4, 16, 49, 52, 57, 58, 60, 64, 68–69, 71, 81, 82, 109, 128, 166, 179, 184n2, 192n7
Wittgenstein, Ludwig, 65
World, 4, 5, 6, 8, 11, 12, 18, 20, 21, 22, 23, 24, 25, 26, 27, 28, 29, 31, 32, 33, 34, 43, 73, 78, 82, 85, 88, 89, 91, 92, 96, 111, 114, 116, 119, 128, 139, 140, 141, 144, 146, 147, 148, 150, 151, 154, 155, 157, 158, 160, 163, 164, 165, 166, 167, 169, 174, 177, 181, 183n1, 185n3, 191n1; World Spirit, 127

Zamyatin, Yevgeny, 46
Zimmer, Ernst, 45

www.ingramcontent.com/pod-product-compliance
Lightning Source LLC
Chambersburg PA
CBHW020732240426
43665CB00052B/457